Critiquing Sovereign Violence

Critiquing Sovereign Violence
Law, Biopolitics, Bio-Juridicalism

Gavin Rae

Edinburgh University Press is one of the leading university presses in the UK. We publish academic books and journals in our selected subject areas across the humanities and social sciences, combining cutting-edge scholarship with high editorial and production values to produce academic works of lasting importance. For more information visit our website: edinburghuniversitypress.com

© Gavin Rae, 2019, 2021

First published in hardback by Edinburgh University Press 2019

Edinburgh University Press Ltd
The Tun – Holyrood Road, 12(2f) Jackson's Entry, Edinburgh EH8 8PJ

Typeset in 11/13 Bembo by
Servis Filmsetting Ltd, Stockport, Cheshire

A CIP record for this book is available from the British Library

ISBN 978 1 4744 4528 3 (hardback)
ISBN 978 1 4744 4529 0 (paperback)
ISBN 978 1 4744 4530 6 (webready PDF)
ISBN 978 1 4744 4531 3 (epub)

The right of Gavin Rae to be identified as the author of this work has been asserted in accordance with the Copyright, Designs and Patents Act 1988, and the Copyright and Related Rights Regulations 2003 (SI No. 2498).

Contents

Preface   vi

Introduction: The Classic-Juridical Model   1

Part I The Radical-Juridical Critique

1 Critiquing Violence: Benjamin on Law and the Divine   23
2 Divinity within the Law: Schmitt on the Violence of Sovereignty   46
3 Violence and Power: Arendt on the Logic of Totalitarianism   67
4 Disrupting Sovereignty: Deleuze and Guattari on the War Machine   93

Part II The Biopolitical Critique

5 From Law to Life: Foucault, Sovereignty, and Biopolitical Racism   121
6 Life Excluded from Law: Agamben, Biopolitics, and Civil War   147

Part III The Bio-Juridical Critique

7 Life and Law: Derrida on the Bio-Juridicalism of Sovereign
   Violence   173
Conclusion   200

Bibliography   206
Index   215

Preface

This book examines contemporary debates regarding the nature and status of sovereignty, including its use of and relationship to violence. In so doing, it defends three primary arguments: (1) while heterogeneous, one conception of sovereignty, termed here the classic-juridical one, was historically dominant and conceived of sovereignty in terms of indivisibility and the preservation of law. (2) Twentieth-century critical theory, broadly understood to take into consideration debates in biopolitical theory, critical legal theory, deconstruction and post-structuralism, subjected this classic-juridical model to sustained and increasingly radical critiques that not only challenged the notion that sovereignty is indivisible, but also questioned whether it is orientated towards law. These critiques were heterogeneous, but can be grouped under three models: the *radical-juridical* model rejects the notion that sovereignty is indivisible but continues to hold that it is orientated to the creation, preservation or disruption of law. Thinkers within this model offer then a radicalisation of the classic-juridical model rather than a fundamental departure from it. In contrast, the *biopolitical* model rejects both premises of the classic-juridical model to claim that sovereign violence is divisible and orientated around the regulation of life rather than the preservation of law. Finally, there is what I call the *bio-juridical* model that rejects the logic underpinning the other models to claim that the sovereign is a differential, phantasmatic figure existing between law and life, simultaneously existing and influencing one through the other. (3) It is the bio-juridical model that offers the most compelling analysis of the issue, not only because it calls into question the binary logic subtending the other models, but also because its analysis is the most sophisticated and conceptually nuanced. With this, I contribute to our understanding of the individual thinkers discussed, develop three critical analytical models to understand contemporary debates regarding the nature of sovereignty and the role that violence plays in politics, and in introducing the bio-juridical model point to a conceptual paradigm that takes us beyond the dominant juridical and biopolitical frameworks.

These arguments will be more fully worked out in the text, but, at this stage, I am happy to acknowledge that this book forms part of the activities for the Conex Marie Skłodowska-Curie Research Project 'Sovereignty and Law: Between Ethics and Politics' (2013–00415–026), co-funded by the Universidad Carlos III de Madrid, the European Union's Seventh Framework Program for Research, Technological Development and Demonstration under Grant Agreement 600371, The Spanish Ministry of the Economy and Competitivity (COFUND2013–40258), The Spanish Ministry for Education, Culture, and Sport (CEI–15–17), and Banco Santander. Information about the project can be found at https://sovereigntyandlaw.wordpress.com/

Chapter 2 includes (rewritten) material that first appeared in 'The Real Enmity of Carl Schmitt's Concept of the Political', *Journal of International Political Theory*, 12:3, 2016, pp. 258–75; I thank the publishers for permission to include it here. Material from a number of the chapters was presented to audiences at the University of Brighton, the University of Essex, the University of Winchester, and the Universidad Carlos III de Madrid; I am grateful to those in attendance for comments and queries. At Edinburgh University Press, I would like to thank Carol Macdonald for her support for the project and, along with her assistant, Kirsty Woods, help in bringing it to publication; the anonymous reviewers for their very helpful comments on the original text; and Fiona Sewell for her diligent and careful copy-editing. Lastly, but by no means least, *mis gracias más sinceras a* Emma, whose encouragement, help, and support made this book possible.

Introduction:
The Classic-Juridical Model

The question of the meaning and nature of sovereignty and its relationship to violence – or sovereign violence for short – has long had theoretical and practical importance. This is not to say that the answers provided have been homogeneous; it is the almost complete lack of agreement regarding the nature of both concepts, including the relationship between them, that stands out. This is perhaps not surprising given that each concept is a liminal one, transecting disciplines such as ethics, law, ontology, and politics, and topics including agency, instrumental rationality, and normativity. There is a complexity to the notion of 'sovereign violence' that causes significant problems for any attempt to discuss or critically analyse it.

In his celebrated genealogy of the concept, Jens Bartelson[1] traces some of the main epistemological, juridical, and metaphysical alterations that took place from the medieval period (starting from approximately the tenth century) up to the eighteenth century.[2] Engaging with these changes will demonstrate the heterogeneity that has defined the history of the concept, identify the basic co-ordinates informing the classic conception of sovereignty, and so outline the paradigm against which thinkers in the twentieth and twenty-first centuries orientate themselves.

Bartelson notes that sovereignty in high medieval Christian society – roughly equating to the period between the tenth and fourteenth centuries – was marked by the dominance of the Church – the *Ecclesia* – which was held to be 'a mystical body transcending the material existence of its component particulars, which in turn st[oo]d in a relation of functional, organic, and ontological dependence to the overarching whole, without which they could not be imagined to exist'.[3] Three consequences arose: first, the Church not only 'understood itself [to be] an indivisible unity covering every aspect of man's social and political being',[4] but also held that 'the preservation of this essential wholeness was the prime purpose of earthly authority'.[5] That sovereignty was held to be indivisible and orientated around order will be carried through to later conceptions. Second, that the Church assumed centre stage gave society a homogeneous orientation: 'it remained insensitive to all ethnical, regional, and linguistic differences; all social forms were subsumed under the Christian norm'.[6] Finally, its structural unity and uniformity 'were both ontologically associated with the idea of an immutable hierarchical order connecting micro- and macrocosm together in a preordained and harmonious relationship'.[7]

While the Church had a dominant role to play in this cosmological order, it also existed in relation to lay rulers. Indeed, society was 'conditioned by the perennial contest between ecclesiastical and lay power, between the unresolvable claims to exclusive authority by *sacerdotium* and *imperium* respectively'.[8] Things were more complex than this, however, because 'the very demarcation between the temporal and the spiritual was itself a spiritual matter, a question of the proper division of authority within one single body with one single head'.[9] In other words, the Church/lay-ruler distinction was not a division wherein one side assumed absolute power over the other; it was encapsulated by a unifying (spiritual) principle intermixed by both aspects. As a consequence,

> the question of the proper locus of supreme authority involved a continuous exchange of the concepts, symbols, insignia and legal axioms of authority between the church and secular authority, with the effect that theological elements were gradually transposed to a secular setting.[10]

There was, in other words, a gradual transmission of signs, values, and ideas that were originally theologically grounded to the secular realm; a movement that eventually took sovereignty from 'God to King'.[11] Specifically, it led to the development of 'the christomimetic paradigm of rulership',[12] wherein the King was understood to be 'a twinned being, half human, half divine, [who held] his powers by the grace of God'.[13] While the King was understood to express the divine in and through his body, his powers and the recognition of his status were 'bestowed upon him by liturgy and sacramental action before the altar, signifying the duplication of these in Christ, and symbolising this link with God and his distinctive position over and above the community of mortals'.[14] That their sovereignty was recognised and bestowed by the Church made 'lay rulers both *de facto* and *de jure* dependent on papal authority'.[15]

Bartelson explains that 'gradually, however, and as the idiom of Roman law began to penetrate theological discourse on authority during the twelfth and thirteenth centuries, the christological and liturgical paradigm was superseded'.[16] Very simply, 'law was substituted for the dual subjectivity of Christ as the mimetic principle of and mediating link between God and [K]ing'.[17] Whereas the sovereign had previously been bound to the divine – whether through the Church or via the Church-sanctioned King – and, indeed, looked to the divine for guidance, gradually the link between the two was inverted so that the King came to play the role that the divine had previously played. In turn, the opposing principle was no longer God *per se*, but law, with the consequence that the King became associated with 'a hypostasis or an articulation of an immortal, semi-divine idea of law and justice'.[18] With this, mytho-sovereignty – the name that Bartelson uses as shorthand for this notion of sovereignty – achieved two things: first, it started to move authority away from God; and, second, it introduced a relationship between the sovereign and law.

Gradually, these alterations crystallised into another notion of sovereignty, which Bartelson names 'proto-sovereignty'.[19] There are two basic differences between mytho-sovereignty and proto-sovereignty: first, the former 'was largely a *descending* theory of government. All power and authority c[a]me from a transcendental sphere above, and the social body [wa]s a passive recipient of its animating force'.[20] In contrast, 'proto-sovereignty . . . was an *ascending* theory of government, with power and authority flowing from the immanent source of an early community'.[21] This is not, however, to say that sovereignty was based on popular will; it is not the same as the social contract theories that developed in the seventeenth and eighteenth centuries. What proto-sovereignty *was* saying is that authority is increasingly based in this world rather than a transcendent divine one.

Second, there was a fundamental reorientation in the understanding of time. Mytho-sovereignty was based on the distinction between *finite* time and a privileged *eternal* notion of time: the former was linked to man's temporal and temporary weakness; the latter to God, who was also understood to be the aim of the former. This division permitted a transition between two realms defined in terms of movement 'from time to superior eternity'[22] or 'from . . . time to an inferior time'.[23] In the former movement (time to eternity), there was a positive movement towards salvation; in the latter movement (time to inferior time), 'it [wa]s negative and horizontal, involving dissolution, decay, destruction, dissimilitude and discord'.[24] In either case, however, 'sovereignty' was defined by its orientation to eternal time.

This gradually changed with the advent of proto-sovereignty, a transition that was dependent upon the turn to Aristotle in the Middle Ages. According to Bartelson, Aristotle was in agreement with 'a great part of early Greek antiquity'[25] that 'the concept of time was connected to, however not identical with, the movement of physical bodies in space, an argument rejected by Augustine'.[26] Once this was divorced from the transcendence found in Platonic metaphysics, it became possible to hold that the spatio-temporal world did not emanate from a singular point and also that time was infinitely continuous. As a consequence, time – which was previously considered ephemeral – became associated with 'endless duration . . . immortality'.[27] This elicited a response from scholastic philosophy, which tried to split the difference between time and eternity by reintroducing a 'middle term mentioned yet largely ignored by Augustine; the *aveum*, situated between *aeternitas* and *tempus*'.[28] Originally this realm was inhabited by angels and later their subterranean counterparts, but the important points for current purposes are that the *aveum* 'connoted both infiniteness and duration, but also motion and change',[29] and that any entity that existed in the *aveum* was considered to be immutable.

This had dramatic consequences for the notion of sovereignty: First, it 'both presupposed an account of and made it possible to account for the existence of universals other than in purely liturgical and transcendental terms'.[30] Second, it meant that 'things previously understood as discontinuous or transitory now could be understood as continuous'.[31] The combination of both meant that 'the body politic could be accounted for as something ontologically separate from the existence of the ruler within it, yet as something continuous, transcending the life of the ruler in time and space'.[32] As such, 'the body politic stood . . . above the corrosive influence of time',[33] which pointed to a realm or an entity that was divorced from time without this entailing a movement towards the divine. It gave rise, in other words, to 'a theory of inalienability, which implies a set of rights well separated from those of the individual King, and, consequently, the notion of an impersonal Crown protected against alienation through prescription'.[34] It also gave rise to the notion that 'the State never dies'.[35]

Therefore, far from being homogeneous, the State was understood to be complex, composed of a relationship between the body politic, manifested through the eternal State, everyday temporal individuals, and the ruler who occupied a dual status as a finite being and infinite representation of authority. Importantly, 'the immortality of the body politic [wa]s contrasted with the mortality of the individuals within it'.[36] There was, in other words, an entity that transcended the lives of those inhabiting it, one that permitted 'the *regnum* [to] demand their sacrifice for the sake of the *patria*'.[37] This also created a permanent order that needed to be maintained, thereby giving rise to annual taxation, which, in turn, was linked to territory: 'as the concepts, symbols, and insignias of rulership took on sempiternal existence as universals, and as the contest between church and lay authorities gradually were resolved in favour of the latter, they also took on spatial considerations'.[38] Rulers became then synonymous with a permanent territory, one that needed to be established and preserved. This generated a whole discourse, manifested most famously though Machiavelli's *The Prince*, that provided advice to rulers on how to achieve this.[39]

The transition from mytho-sovereignty to proto-sovereignty was then a complex one, but two movements stand out: First,

> the omnipotence of God and the primordial subjectivity of Christ . . . gradually yield[ed] to the twin pressures of cosmological time and political nominalism; the discourse on the locus and scope of authority [wa]s brought down to earth, but so [we]re its teleological and eschatological underpinnings.[40]

Transcendence was not thereby abolished, but, second, re-inscribed from and within the body politic – first in terms of the State, and second in terms of the ruler – to bolster the notion that there exists an entity that transcends everyday individuals. In the sixteenth and seventeenth centuries, these alterations took on new forms, eventually crystallising around a new political figure and concept: 'the general theory of the [S]tate [wa]s replaced by a new theory of sovereignty'.[41]

Bartelson identifies three principles defining this new theory of sovereignty: first, the *principle of individuation*, which describes not an attribute that is given to an already-formed entity, but the fundamental ontological status of sovereignty: 'it is sovereignty which has the power of individuation'.[42] As a consequence, 'sovereignty itself becomes "sovereign" in political discourse',[43] insofar as it is the notion from and around which the political depends and revolves. Importantly, this individuation was held to be a basic unity and so indivisible.

This necessarily leads to the second *principle of identification*, which takes two forms: 'on the one hand, classical sovereignty [necessarily] require[d] the intense divinisation and personalisation of authority in the hands of a sovereign, on the other hand, it necessitates an abstract notion of a naturalised [S]tate as a symbol of depersonalised authority'.[44] The body politic was then understood to be split between two related aspects: the sovereign and the State. Importantly, 'classical theories of sovereignty . . . never arrive[d] at a stable differentiation between these poles and only ma[d]e the locus of sovereignty relative to perspective'.[45] Thus, because the State was necessarily represented by the sovereign, the latter undermined the former's claim to absolute status, while, in turn, the State always transcended its particular manifestation of sovereignty and so undermined any sovereign claim to absoluteness.

The third principle 'is a *principle of order*'.[46] That sovereignty is individuated and identifiable gave rise to a particular epistemology, wherein States were defined by clear-cut dimensions which made 'them accessible to classification, ranking and comparison according to a determined set of variables'.[47]

Jean Bodin was the most famous proponent of this conception of sovereignty. For Bodin, it was not territory that defined a populace, but the union of the people: 'sovereignty is the absolute and perpetual power of a commonwealth'.[48] Sovereignty is perpetual because it does not expire. While it may be passed around to various holders who exercise power in its name, 'they are but trustees and custodians of that power until such time as it pleases the people or the prince to take it back'.[49] Importantly, sovereignty permits others to act in the name of the sovereign without becoming sovereign: 'The person of the sovereign, according to law, is always excepted no matter how much power and authority he grants to someone else; and he never gives so much that he does not hold back even more.'[50] This is because sovereignty cannot be alienated. It defines the very being of the sovereign. This is re-enforced by its indivisibility: 'just as a crown no longer has the name if it is breached, or if its rosettes are torn away, so sovereign majesty loses its greatness if someone makes a breach in it and encroaches a part of its domain'.[51] The primary purpose of the sovereign's inalienable, indivisible, 'absolute power'[52] 'is to give law to all in general and each in particular . . . "without the consent of any other, whether great, equal, or below him"'.[53] This he can do without adhering to 'the laws of his predecessors'[54] or the 'laws and ordinances that he has made himself'.[55] He is, in fact, only limited by God's law. That 'the main point of sovereign majesty and absolute power consists of giving the law to subjects in general without their consent'[56] re-enforces the top-down, hierarchical nature of this conception of sovereignty: the sovereign is, in many respects, an earthly divinity to whom absolute obedience is owed – 'for it is the law of God and of nature that we must obey the edicts and ordinances of him to whom God has given power over us, unless his edicts are directly contrary to the law of God, who is above all princes'.[57]

Quentin Skinner calls this the 'absolutist theory'[58] of sovereignty and explains that it soon influenced wider debates in law and politics through and from two directions. Specifically, 'one arose out of scholastic discussions about *suprema potestas*'.[59] These were complex, but the basic point was to affirm that while the populace *may* have been the original power underpinning sovereignty, any choice of sovereign always requires and entails a quasi-alienation of political rights. There was, in other words, a transfer from the populace to the sovereign. 'The other and more influential way in which the absolutist theory was articulated was as part of the doctrine of the divine right of [K]ings.'[60] This took different forms, but all were united in the common premise that 'Kings are the Lord's anointed, the viceregents of God on earth, and consequently enjoy supreme and unquestionable power over the body of the [S]tate.'[61] There is obviously a tension between these: the first grounds monarchy in the populace, even if that is subsequently abrogated to the sovereign; whereas the latter grounds sovereignty in the divine. This tension quickly came to the fore, giving rise to two different and competing paradigms.

In the seventeenth century, the absolutist theory was initially widely defended, before being subjected to a growing barrage of criticisms. These critiques 'agreed that, when we talk about the State, we are referring to a type of civic union, a body or society of people united under government'.[62] They had this in common with the absolute theory of sovereignty. However, whereas the absolutist theorists tended to hold that society requires an absolute sovereign to lead and direct it, critics claimed that this was not necessary; 'it is equally possible . . . for sovereignty to be possessed by the union of the people themselves'.[63] Thus, sovereignty was understood to refer not to an individual ruler, but 'rather to the body of the people viewed as the owners of sovereignty themselves'.[64] Not surprisingly, Skinner explains that 'no sooner was the populist theory put into circulation than it was vehemently denounced by royalists and absolutists of every stamp'.[65] Initially, this took the form of a simple reversion to the absolutist argument in favour of divine right. Gradually, however, another line of counter-attack developed, manifested most famously in Thomas Hobbes's *Leviathan*, which offered a compatibilist account of the absolutist and popular theories.

To do so, Hobbes rejected the populist notion that the body politic was initially sovereign. The body politic requires, at a minimum, a form of co-operation, which Hobbes famously rejected as being possible in the state of nature, conditioned as it was by a war of all against all in which 'life [is] solitary, poor, nasty, brutish, and short'.[66] Overcoming this to preserve life required the creation of a sovereign to both unite the warring factions and ensure order between them. Importantly, he held that

> the only way to erect such a common power . . . is, to confer all their power and strength upon one man, or upon one assembly of men, to bear their person; and every one to own, and acknowledge himself to be author of whatsoever he that so beareth their person, shall act, or cause to be acted, in those things which concern the common peace and safety; and therein to submit their wills, every one to his will, and their judgements, to his judgement.[67]

The sovereign created by the populace was then singular and 'indivisible'.[68] However, the choice of sovereign did not simply result from the sovereign imposing himself on the populace. The populace externalised itself through the sovereign, saw itself through the sovereign, and so identified with him. For this reason, the popular decision 'is more than consent, or concord; it is a real unity of them all, in one and the same person, made by covenant of every man with every man',[69] a unity that 'is called a COMMONWEALTH, in Latin CIVITAS'.[70] From this, we see that, contrary to the absolutists, sovereignty results not from the divine, but from the populace.

However, while sovereignty is chosen and so legitimated by the populace, the populace's continuing identification with the sovereign does not translate into the exercise of authority; there is no common decision-making; sovereignty is not participatory. Rather, the sovereign 'hath the use of so much power and strength conferred on him, that by terror thereof, he is enabled to conform the wills of them all, to peace at home, and mutual aid against their enemies abroad'.[71] The sovereign is derived and legitimised by popular choice, but, once created, has absolute power over the populace. That the populace unifies itself through the sovereign means that he defines and expresses the populace. For this reason, '[t]he difference of commonwealths, consisteth in the difference of the sovereign, or the person representative of all and every one of the multitude'.[72] The key point, however, is that the sovereign's absolute power is not imposed on the populace; the populace sees itself through the sovereign so that when he acts, they act. For this reason, it is in and through the sovereign that

> consisteth the essence of the commonwealth; which (to define it), is one person, of whose acts a great multitude, by mutual covenants one with another, have made themselves every one the author, to the end he may use the strength and means of them all, as he shall think expedient, for their peace and common effort.[73]

There is obviously much more to Hobbes's theory of sovereignty than I have touched on here,[74] but these very brief comments show that he combines aspects of the absolutist and populist theories: sovereignty emanates from the popular will (rather than the divine) and is indivisible. Once chosen, however, it holds absolute power 'over' the populace. Crucially, the sovereign's actions are not arbitrary; not only does the populace continue to identify with and so see itself expressed through the sovereign, but the sovereign is orientated towards the preservation of law and order.

Hobbes's theory attracted significant attention and stimulated much debate, both within social contract theory and beyond.[75] Gradually, however, a number of epistemic changes led, in the eighteenth century, back to a reconstituted popular version of sovereignty. Bartelson notes three: first, political knowledge started to move away from defining itself in terms of beings to focusing on relations. Rather than emphasise the sovereign figure alone, there was a growing interest in the relations subtending the sovereign figure. Second, 'modern knowledge bestow[ed] subjectivity upon the State'.[76] The State was turned into an autonomous actor, capable of reflexive thought and action. When this was combined with the turn towards relations, we see that the 'internal' dynamics of the State also changed: rather than a homogeneous, static mass dependent on the sovereign figurehead, the State was understood to be a complex of differential relations, with these relations creating sovereignty. As such, third, 'modern knowledge turn[ed] sovereignty into a principle organising our political reality as well as our understanding of it'.[77] Sovereignty was not held to be located at the level of the populace or the sovereign figure, but was understood to be 'simultaneously transcendental and immanent'.[78] It exists through the populace, while, at the same time, being the condition that defines the populace.

Therefore, while modern conceptions of sovereignty remained tied to the absolute notion of sovereignty by virtue of holding sovereignty to be indivisible, they rejected the claim that sovereignty is located in an absolute individuated figure by tying it to the populace instead. This, however, required a rethinking of the nature of the populace. Rather than defining a collection of empirical singularities, the populace was understood to take on a will of its own, one that operated over, above, and through the collective. Sovereignty was located at the level of this collective consciousness and was, as a consequence, both depersonalised and diffused throughout the social body; it was both immanent and transcendent to it.

The most famous example of this is found in Jean-Jacques Rousseau's conception of the general will. Basing sovereignty on a social contract model, Rousseau explains that each individual voluntarily enters into a social pact where 'each ... puts his person and all his power in common under the supreme direction of the general will; and we as a body receive each member as an indivisible part of the whole'.[79] The general will is distinct from the particular will of each individual and the 'will of everyone',[80] which is simply an aggregation of particular wills. It refers to 'a moral and collective body, which is composed of as many members as there are votes in the assembly, and which, by the same act, is endowed with its unity, its common self, its life, and its will'.[81]

With this, Rousseau explains that sovereignty is not located at the level of an individual figure or body; it is a 'collective entity'[82] – something akin to a cultural consciousness – that exists above and beyond the individual wills composing it. This is not, however, to say that the general will simply imposes itself on those composing it. Rather, particular wills continue to spontaneously express themselves through it. As such, 'they are not obeying anyone except their own will'.[83] Rousseau's argument is somewhat more nuanced than this, insofar as it requires the sovereign to act in specific ways, but his overall point is that, structurally speaking, the general will is a collective organic entity that is both transcendent and immanent to the particular wills composing it.

Through the American and French Revolutions, this populist conception of sovereignty quickly became the dominant paradigm, manifested most explicitly through Abraham Lincoln's famous claim that government was made 'of the people, for the people, by the people',[84] and Karl Marx's radical critique of capitalism and affirmation of communism.[85] While obviously quite a departure from Bodin's or Hobbes's absolutist or compatibilist conceptions, Rousseau does agree with them that sovereignty 'can never be transferred',[86] 'cannot be represented except by itself',[87] and is 'indivisible'.[88] While it may be objected that Rousseau claims that the exercise of sovereignty is orientated towards 'the common good',[89] 'public welfare',[90] and 'common interest',[91] these entail some form of order. Indeed, Rousseau makes this point when explaining why individuals come together to make a social pact: they aim to create a political association that will secure their continued existence.[92]

The general will is then always orientated towards the expression of social order. It is this that underpins Rousseau's famous claim that the social pact 'contains an implicit obligation which alone can give force to the others, that if anyone refuses to obey the general will he will be compelled to do so by the whole body; which means nothing else than that he will be forced to be free'.[93] With this, the absolutist, compatibilist, and populist models of sovereignty agree that sovereignty is singular, indivisible, and orientated to the preservation and maintenance of socio-juridical order. For this reason, I will refer to this understanding of sovereignty as the classic-juridical one.

THE ARGUMENT DEFENDED

This brief historical overview is obviously partial and could be expanded in many ways. It does, however, show that, despite substantial differences regarding what exactly sovereignty refers to and where it is located, thinking on the topic, especially from the sixteenth century onwards, has been remarkably consistent in holding that sovereignty is singular, indivisible, and orientated towards the creation and maintenance of legal order.

Violence was held to be tied to this process structurally, insofar as it was understood to be an instrument that can only be legitimately used by the sovereign to restore legal order. Thus, the sovereign could delegate that responsibility to others, but this had to occur through a juridical process whereby the sovereign's authority was explicitly passed to another who acts in his name. For example, the army and police can use violence because they have been given legal authority to use his legitimate sovereign violence in his name. If anyone else uses violence, this violates the law and, by definition, sovereign authority. Such action causes a fissure between legitimate and illegitimate expressions of violence, which requires that the sovereign reassert his authority by either legally penalising the perpetrator in the case of crimes or defeating the alternative in the case of an invading power or internal rebellion.

I have spent some time outlining the basic co-ordinates around which sovereignty has traditionally been thought because this history and specifically the classic-juridical account of sovereignty dominating it form the basis from which the fundamental argument of this book proceeds: namely, that throughout the twentieth century, the classic-juridical conception of sovereign, including the instrumental notion of violence linked to it, was subject to sustained and increasingly radical critique. From this general premise, the book defends two different but ultimately related arguments.

Historically, I argue that the critique of the classic-juridical conception of sovereignty was heterogeneous, cutting across biopolitical theory, critical theory, deconstruction, legal theory, and post-structuralism, and led to the development of three different, but increasingly radical, paradigms. The first, termed the *radical-juridical* model, is outlined through the analyses provided by Hannah Arendt, Walter Benjamin, Gilles Deleuze and Felix Guattari, and Carl Schmitt. I group these thinkers together because their analyses, while heterogeneous, offer a number of radical critiques of the notion of sovereignty – claiming, for example, that it is not singular or indivisible – and the instrumental nature of violence inherent in the classic-juridical model, but continue to be bound to it by virtue of insisting that sovereign violence is orientated around and thought from its relationship to juridical order. For this reason, the radical-juridical model entails a radicalisation of the classic model rather than a fundamental departure from it.

The second, *biopolitical* model, explored through Michel Foucault's and Giorgio Agamben's thinking, goes further in its critique by decisively breaking the connection between sovereign violence and juridical order underpinning the classical and radical-juridical models. Rather than operate through law with the establishment of order as its aim, these critiques insist that sovereign violence is orientated towards the regulation of life, which is often achieved by excluding it from the juridical order.

The third, *bio-juridical* model, manifested through Jacques Derrida's late seminars on the death penalty, acts as a corrective to the logic underpinning the radical-juridical and biopolitical models by claiming that sovereign violence does not simply aim at the creation/maintenance/disruption of the juridical order or the regulation of a juridically excluded life, but is placed between law and life, simultaneously creating and regulating each through the other.

This historical argument lays the foundation for my second, *conceptual* argument that defends and affirms the bio-juridical model over the radical-juridical and biopolitical paradigms. The fundamental problem with the radical-juridical and biopolitical models is that they tend to offer reductionist accounts structured around a binary opposition that sees sovereign violence as being orientated to and defined by its relationship to law (manifested through the preservation or disruption of juridical order) *or* life (established through its exclusion from the juridical order). While these models are bound by their common dependence on the binary opposition between law and life, they differ in terms of the privileged aspect.

In contrast, the bio-juridical model not only offers a more complex and heterogeneous understanding of the complexities involved in the notions of 'law' and 'life', but also develops a notion of sovereign violence that usurps the binary opposition underpinning the two other models. I develop this through Derrida's analysis of the death penalty to argue that it provides a notion of sovereignty that exists *between* law and life, operating on each through the other simultaneously. Sovereignty is not simply a political concept; it is always tied to the juridical order by virtue of making decisions and pronouncements through the creation and regulation of law, both formally, in terms of statutes, and informally, through the development of social norms, that condition, structure, and give meaning to life.

This is different to the relationship between law, life, sovereignty, and violence underpinning biopolitical theory. When, for example, Agamben argues that life is regulated through its exclusion from law, the bio-juridical model holds that this 'exclusion' remains constitutively tied to the juridical order by virtue of being not only premised on the sovereign's juridical status but also enacted through the juridical order. Thus, while Agamben claims that his exclusion always ties *homo sacer* to the juridical order, this tie is an external, exclusive one.

In contrast, the bio-juridical model holds that sovereignty is a juridical-political concept/figure and is, therefore, always 'internally' tied to the political and juridical realms. The exclusion from law that Agamben sees as being constitutive of the state of exception creates, on this understanding, not an exception from law, but an exclusive status *in* law. It reconfigures the meaning and application of law to give those 'excluded' a juridical name and status. The state of exception may entail the suspension of (some aspects of) law, but it does not remove the individual from all law. It reworks the application of law as it relates to that person, thereby subjecting the individual to a different legal relationship to the sovereign; one which, typically, removes any prior legal constraint from sovereign violence regarding that individual. There is not then an exclusion *per se*, but the establishment of a different relationship to the juridical. It is this that the bio-juridical model tries to capture through the insistence that the sovereign regulates life through the exercise of law, which, in turn, depends upon and is structured from that regulation.

This is not, however, to simply insist on a linear movement that passes from sovereign violence through law to life. I argue that Derrida shows that sovereignty is two-faced, simultaneously operating through and on law and life. Life is conditioned and regulated through the creation and management of law (both formal laws and informal norms), while the laws created by sovereign violence are conditioned by life, both the actual one – manifested through norms, values, actions, and so on – and the desired one. Moving from the regulation of the actual life to the creation of the sovereign's desired life depends upon the exercise of law. After all, the sovereign can only operate as a juridical figure and so must act through law. This creates laws that regulate life, but, again, the form and content of law depend upon the social norms and lives that it is orientated to, from, and around. Sovereign violence is then orientated and conditioned by a dual, 'inner' relationship to both law and life and expresses itself through each aspect simultaneously.

Interestingly, recent biopolitical theory itself has started to move in this direction. Miguel Vatter, for example, explains that the development of an affirmative biopolitics – one that recognises that biopolitics can be used for liberatory rather than disciplinary purposes – 'requires overcoming the antinomian opposition between rule of law and politics of life'[94] to affirm 'an internal and affirmative relationship between law and life'.[95]

While this supports my conceptual argument, I disagree with Vatter's claim that such a rethinking remains within the biopolitical paradigm, arguing instead that it entails a fundamental paradigm shift. This is because, despite its heterogeneity, one of the fundamental arguments underpinning the biopolitical paradigm – certainly as outlined by Foucault and Agamben – is that sovereign violence results from a political decision regarding a life excluded from law. Excluding the individual from the juridical order is necessary to create an unmediated relationship between sovereign violence and life, wherein the former can better and more easily regulate the latter. To reintroduce a juridical component into this matrix – as I argue the bio-juridical model does – is to alter this fundamental relationship and so complicate the sovereign's relation to and regulation of life. In itself, complication is not a problem, but my argument is that this fundamental move undermines the unmediated relationship between sovereign violence and life that defines the biopolitical paradigm.

With this, I agree with Vatter's conclusion that we need to develop the biopolitical position by recognising that sovereign violence is simultaneously orientated to both law and life, but claim that (1) this position has already been developed by Derrida's important analyses of the death penalty, (2) this creates not a remodified biopolitical paradigm, but a new paradigm of sovereign violence called the bio-juridical, and (3) the legitimacy and validity of the bio-juridical logic are supported not only by its internal veracity, but also by the fact that biopolitical theory is gradually moving towards it.

CHAPTER STRUCTURE

To develop these arguments, the book is structured around three uneven parts. Part I is composed of four chapters, each of which outlines a different response to the classic-juridical model. Chapter 1 engages with Walter Benjamin's famous critique of violence by engaging with his 1921 essay of the same title. I argue that Benjamin's distinction between divine and legal violence also names two distinct forms of sovereignty, one internal to law and one external to it. With this, he disrupts the classic notion that sovereignty is indivisible. By tracing the relationship between the two forms, I argue that Benjamin develops a sophisticated account of the intimate relationship between law and violence, undermines the classic notion that violence is simply instrumental to (legal) sovereignty, and shows that divine sovereign violence can justifiably usurp legal sovereign violence to offer the possibility of a fresh start. However, I note the ambiguity in Benjamin's account regarding whether divine violence can take on (non-divine) political significance to suggest that his appeal to divine violence is an attempt to develop a just order based on an ethics of responsibility, whereby he allows that we can confront legal sovereignty in the name of a more just legal framework, but insists that we cannot ground that decision on an *a priori* or transcendent principle. Any challenge to legal sovereign violence must then emanate from a pure decision for which we are responsible.

Chapter 2 outlines Carl Schmitt's response to Benjamin. Whereas Benjamin distinguishes between divine sovereign violence and legal sovereign violence and so undermines the classic claim that sovereignty is indivisible, he does so by positing an inside and outside to law. Schmitt claims that sovereignty is not divided between a legal and a divine sovereign; law is distinguished by a division between its explicit, statute form and the subtending power supporting and generating it. Sovereignty is a legal concept and so is always conditioned by this juridical division. At the pre-constitutional level, sovereignty is defined by the populace, who, living in a state of chaos, make a spontaneous and normless decision regarding the constitutional ordering norms. At the constitutional level, Schmitt claims that there must always be an individual who makes the ultimate political decision regarding how to interpret and/or apply those norms. Famously, this requires a decision regarding who is a friend and who is an enemy. Importantly, the constituting-power continues to subtend the constitution, making it always possible that the populace will usurp the constitutional sovereign. Rather than a strict opposition between two forms of violence, wherein juridical sovereignty is deposed by divine violence, Schmitt offers a more complex dual account of sovereignty that, on the one hand, follows Benjamin in describing how another violence deposes juridical sovereignty, but, on the other hand, departs from Benjamin's claim that this power is based in the divine; it is grounded in the constituting-power subtending juridical sovereignty. Sovereignty is divisible, with the consequence that deposing constitutional sovereignty does not rely on divine action; it arises when the constituting-power subtending the constitutional sovereign demands an alternative juridical order.

Schmitt's analysis is based on a (collective) decision regarding how to establish juridical order. Chapter 3 focuses on Hannah Arendt's counter-claim that sovereignty is based not on a collective decision but on *collective agreement*. In so doing, she argues, contrary to Benjamin and Schmitt, that sovereignty is grounded in discussion and a form of rationality while also offering a strong contrast to Derrida's later claim that law is premised on force. To develop this, I first outline her critique of Hobbes's and Rousseau's theories of sovereignty to show how she departs from the classic-juridical model, before setting out to reconstruct her own revised version of sovereignty based on an analysis of violence. First noting an ambiguity in the relationship between her earlier writings – notably a number published during the Second World War that hold violence to be an inherently political action, and the *Human Condition*, which sees violence, in the form of fabrication, as being constitutive of human action – and her later *On Violence*, which maintains that violence is instrumental to rather than constitutive of politics, I subsequently account for it by appealing to her claim that contemporary society has increasingly fetishised the means of fabrication over the end, a logic that sees all things (including humans) as pure means. That everything is perceived to be a pure means permits the legitimate use of violence to achieve political ends. To prevent this politicisation of violence, she advocates that power and violence be radically opposed. In so doing, however, she insists on an undifferentiated, straightforward opposition between power and violence that was undermined by her own empirical examples and much later thought.

Chapter 4 engages with Gilles Deleuze and Felix Guattari's analysis of the war machine to suggest that it contradicts Arendt's analysis and offers the most radical account within the radical-juridical paradigm. Premising their argument on the notion that we must rethink sovereignty from ontological difference rather than identity or unity, I show that Deleuze and Guattari radically undermine the indivisibility that defines the classic-juridical conception. Far from being located in one individual or point, sovereignty is always tied to the State, which is a multiplicity expressing a constantly moving, fluid, and dynamic field of difference. With this, Deleuze and Guattari depart definitively from the classic-juridical conception by showing that sovereignty is not a substance or unity, but a temporary configuration of pre-personal differential flows. These authors do, however, continue to implicitly insist that sovereignty is tied to the maintenance of juridical order, which is, nevertheless, always threatened by or in conflict with the war machine that disrupts it. The point is that the sovereign order is always far more unstable and disordered than it appears to be.

Chapters 5 marks the transition from the first to the second part of the book and the movement from radical-juridical critiques of sovereignty to biopolitical ones. While Deleuze and Guattari offer a post-structuralist account of juridical order, if we follow a different strand of post-structuralist thought, namely that of Michel Foucault, we arrive at a far more radical conception of sovereignty entailing a fundamental rupture with the classic-juridical model. Rather than rethink the ontological structure of sovereignty while continuing to bind it to the question of order, Foucault developed the notion of biopolitics to claim that sovereign violence is not orientated towards the establishment/preservation/disruption of juridical order, but is, first and foremost, orientated towards the regulation of life. This does more than just change the goal of sovereign power while continuing to insist that sovereignty is unified. It calls into question the notion that sovereignty is, in some way, transcendent to that which it rules over. For this reason, biopolitical sovereignty operates immanently to that which it operates on, regulating it through the introduction and management of divisions within the populace. Thus, biological life is both the condition of sovereignty and its political object; that which it violently works on.

Chapter 5 shows that, for Foucault, this operates through a racism dividing those deemed to be biologically acceptable from those deemed to be unacceptable; a logic that arose in the late nineteenth century but which continues to this day. In contrast, Chapter 6 demonstrates that Giorgio Agamben accounts for it by looking to the West's Graeco-Roman heritage, which, he argues, reveals that the Western juridical-political model has not only always excluded some forms of life from law, thereby bifurcating the populace into those included and those excluded, but has also been structured around a fundamental opposition between the *oikos* and *polis*, household and city, private and public. Despite these differences, I argue that biopolitical thought is united in linking sovereignty to biological process and the regulation of life, with this entailing a dramatic departure from previous thinking on the topic.

The fundamental problem with the two paradigms outlined up to this point is that they set up a binary opposition between those thinkers that affirm the relationship between sovereign violence and the juridical order and those that affirm its relationship to life. In part three, I turn (chapter 7) to Jacques Derrida's analysis of the sovereign violence inherent in the death penalty to usurp this binary opposition and show that sovereign violence operates simultaneously through both law and life. To do so, I first outline Derrida's early claim that an originary violence associated with the designation of meaning and signification underpins all subsequent forms of legal and empirical violence, before tying this to his analysis of sovereignty. From this, we see that violence is not distinct from law, but that which underpins it, while justice is that which operates through law, but is always beyond it. Thus, violence subtends law, while law affirms justice without ever fully achieving it.

Having established the relationship between violence and law, I turn to Derrida's late seminars on the death penalty where he deals most forcibly with the question of the relationship between justice, law, sovereignty, and violence. Rather than focus on *homo sacer*, Derrida emphasises the condemned who remains at the mercy of the sovereign decision by virtue of existing within the juridical order. *Pace* Agamben, sovereign violence does not operate on life by excluding it from law; it operates on life through the exercise of law.

However, rather than re-establish the connection between sovereign violence and law found in the juridical models, Derrida develops a compatibilist position of the sovereign's relationship to law and life that shows that sovereign violence is not simply orientated to legal order or the regulation of life through the creation of social norms, but simultaneously expresses itself through two faces – the juridical and biopolitical, or law and life – wherein the one demands and expresses the other: the juridical expression of sovereignty regulates life, whereas the sovereign's regulation of life (and death) always takes a juridical form. Rather than being identified with law *or* life, sovereign violence is always situated *between* the two, working on life through its relationship to and control over law and on law through the regulation of social norms via its symbolic manifestations.

Importantly, Derrida maintains that sovereignty is not located in a unitary figure, but is a phantasmatic spectacle of power and control. Sovereignty results then not from a single locus of decision-making or agreement, but from belief in its power that depends upon spectacular displays of its power; the most explicit manifestations of which occur through the exercise of violence, whether it be through the death penalty or war.

In so doing, Derrida provides a radical critique of the classic-juridical conception of sovereignty, resolves the antimony that exists between the radical-juridical and biopolitical paradigms by showing that the sovereign's phantasmatic power arises and is supported by its spectacular and legally sanctioned displays of violence, and points to a sophisticated and multi-dimensional bio-juridical account of sovereign violence.

The conclusion provides an overview of the project and outlines some of the assumptions underpinning my privileging of the bio-juridical model.

NOTES

1. Jens Bartelson, *A Genealogy of Sovereignty* (Cambridge: Cambridge University Press, 1995), p. 91.
2. This is not to say that this history does not go back further; only that tracing it back to the Middle Ages is sufficient to make the point being developed here. For a discussion of ancient Graeco-Christian conceptions of sovereignty, such as those found in Augustine,

Pericles, Sophocles and Thucydides, see Dimitris Vardoulakis, *Sovereignty and its Other: Toward the Dejustification of Violence* (New York: Fordham University Press, 2013), ch. 2.
3. Bartelson, *A Genealogy of Sovereignty*, p. 91.
4. Ibid. p. 91.
5. Ibid. p. 91.
6. Ibid. p. 91.
7. Ibid. p. 91.
8. Ibid. p. 92.
9. Ibid. p. 92.
10. Ibid. p. 92.
11. Ibid. p. 92.
12. Ibid. p. 92.
13. Ibid. p. 92.
14. Ibid. p. 92.
15. Ibid. p. 92.
16. Ibid. pp. 92–3.
17. Ibid. p. 93.
18. Ibid. p. 93.
19. Ibid. p. 95.
20. Ibid. p. 101.
21. Ibid. p. 101.
22. Ibid. p. 96.
23. Ibid. p. 96.
24. Ibid. p. 97.
25. Ibid. p. 98.
26. Ibid. p. 98.
27. Ibid. p. 97.
28. Ibid. p. 97.
29. Ibid. p. 97.
30. Ibid. p. 97.
31. Ibid. p. 97.
32. Ibid. p. 97.
33. Ibid. p. 97.
34. Ibid. p. 98.
35. Ibid. p. 98.
36. Ibid. p. 98.
37. Ibid. p. 98.
38. Ibid. p. 98.
39. For a discussion of Machiavelli's theory, see Filippo del Luchese, *The Political Philosophy of Niccolò Machiavelli* (Edinburgh: Edinburgh University Press, 2015); Catherine Zuckert, *Machiavelli's Politics* (Chicago: University of Chicago Press, 2017).
40. Bartelson, *A Genealogy of Sovereignty*, p. 107.
41. Ibid. p. 138.
42. Ibid. p. 138.
43. Ibid. p. 138.
44. Ibid. pp. 138–9.
45. Ibid. p. 139.
46. Ibid. p. 139.

47. Ibid. p. 139.
48. Jean Bodin, *On Sovereignty*, ed. and trans. Julian H. Franklin (Cambridge: Cambridge University Press, 1992), p. 1.
49. Ibid. p. 2.
50. Ibid. p. 2
51. Ibid. p. 49.
52. Ibid. p. 7.
53. Ibid. p. 56.
54. Ibid. p. 12.
55. Ibid. p. 12.
56. Ibid. p. 23.
57. Ibid. p. 34. This obviously only scratches the surface of Bodin's theory, a detailed discussion of which is found in Julian H. Franklin, *Jean Bodin and the Rise of Absolutist Theory* (Cambridge: Cambridge University Press, 2009).
58. Quentin Skinner, 'The Sovereign State: A Genealogy', p. 29, in *Sovereignty in Fragments: The Past, Present and Future of a Contested Concept*, ed. Hent Kalmo and Quentin Skinner (Cambridge: Cambridge University Press, 2010), pp. 26–46.
59. Ibid. p. 29.
60. Ibid. p. 29.
61. Ibid. p. 29.
62. Ibid. p. 30.
63. Ibid. p. 30.
64. Ibid. p. 31.
65. Ibid. p. 34.
66. Thomas Hobbes, *Leviathan*, ed. J. C. A. Gaskin (Oxford: Oxford University Press, 1996), part I, chpt. 13, p. 84.
67. Ibid. part 2, chpt. 18, p. 114.
68. Ibid. part 2, chpt. 19, p. 124.
69. Ibid. part 2, chpt. 18, p. 114.
70. Ibid. part 2, chpt. 18, p. 114.
71. Ibid. part 2, chpt. 18, p. 114.
72. Ibid. part 2, chpt. 19, p. 123.
73. Ibid. part 2, chpt. 18, p. 114.
74. More expansive analyses are found in A. P. Martinich, *The Two Gods of Leviathan: Thomas Hobbes on Religion and Politics* (Cambridge: Cambridge University Press, 2003); George Shelton, *Morality and Sovereignty in the Philosophy of Hobbes* (Basingstoke: Palgrave Macmillan, 2014).
75. For an excellent discussion of Hobbes's relationship to later theorists, especially Pufendorf, Locke, Montesquieu and Rousseau, see David W. Bates, *States of War: Enlightenment Origins of the Political* (New York: Columbia University Press, 2012).
76. Bartelson, *A Genealogy of Sovereignty*, p. 188.
77. Ibid. p. 189.
78. Ibid. p. 189.
79. Jean-Jacques Rousseau, *The Social Contract*, trans. Christopher Betts (Oxford: Oxford University Press, 1994), p. 55, italics in original.
80. Ibid, p. 66.
81. Ibid. p. 56.
82. Ibid. p. 63.
83. Ibid. p. 70.

84. Abraham Lincoln, 'The Gettysburg Address', p. 192, in *Political Writings and Speeches*, ed. Terence Ball (Cambridge: Cambridge University Press, 2012), pp. 191–2.
85. For a discussion of the Rousseau–Marx relationship, especially as it is mediated through the notion of the general will, see Andrew Levine, *The General Will: Rousseau, Marx, Communism* (Cambridge: Cambridge University Press, 2008).
86. Rousseau, *The Social Contract*, p. 63.
87. Ibid. p. 63.
88. Ibid. p. 64.
89. Ibid. p. 63.
90. Ibid. p. 66.
91. Ibid. p. 66.
92. Ibid. p. 54.
93. Ibid. p. 58.
94. Miguel Vatter, *The Republic of the Living: Biopolitics and the Critique of Civil Society* (New York: Fordham University Press, 2014), p. 4.
95. Ibid. p. 11.

PART I

The Radical-Juridical Critique

CHAPTER I

Critiquing Violence: Benjamin on Law and the Divine

Walter Benjamin's 1921 essay 'Critique of Violence'[1] has come to play an important, even foundational, role in certain strands of contemporary political theory. It is also the starting point for this inquiry because, in it, Benjamin engages in a sustained analysis of the relationship between violence and law. Largely ignored when first published in the *Archiv für Sozialwissenschaft und Sozialpolitik*, it was Jürgen Habermas's 1972 essay 'Walter Benjamin: Consciousness-Raising or Rescuing Critique'[2] that first resuscitated it, before interest exploded after Jacques Derrida's 1989 lecture 'Force of Law: The "Mystical Foundation of Authority"'.[3] Both of these seminal texts tie Benjamin to the political right: in the case of Habermas, he outlines the conservative nature of Benjamin's appeal to art, history, and myth,[4] while Derrida's admittedly 'risky reading'[5] controversially binds Benjamin's comments on violence to that of the Nazi's 'final solution'.[6] Not surprisingly given Benjamin's tragic experience of the latter, such an assessment has been strongly challenged. Indeed, other thinkers have found a completely different message in Benjamin's essay; specifically, a new form of politics based on the notion of 'a nonviolent violence'.[7] In turn, however, this assessment has been challenged.[8] There is then no agreement regarding the conclusion(s) offered by Benjamin. Indeed, this is probably one of the main reasons why it has generated so much attention.

Uncertainties also surround the purpose(s) of his essay. After all, 'violence' translates the German word *Gewalt*, which can also mean authority, domination, force, and power, all of which have positive and negative connotations in the sense that the violence/force can be legitimate or illegitimate. 'Violence' simply does not have the same number of senses and connotations. Similarly, the notion of 'critique' (*Kritik*) is problematic. Beatrice Hanssen notes, for example, that 'critique' 'derives from the Greek root *Krinein* and related to this term, *diakrisis*, and thus unmistakably refers to the acts of separation and distinction'.[9] Furthermore, 'taken in a historical (not Kantian, universalist) sense of the sort popularised by critical theory, "critique" has come to mean passing judgement on the present, with an eye towards the realisation of a (utopian) future as a way of undoing the errors of the past'.[10] Arguably, however, Benjamin does not use the term in these senses. He undertakes a critique in a quasi-Kantian sense that aims to identify the connection between law and violence to define the role that violence plays 'in' law.[11]

Benjamin argues that legal violence is always closed and mythic. However, this closure points to and even depends upon a limitless form of violence called 'divine violence'.[12] This concept is at the heart of Benjamin's essay. It points not only to a form of violence beyond the closure of legal violence, but also, so I will suggest, to two conceptions of sovereignty, one based in law and the other that transcends law. This undermines the classic-juridical notion that sovereignty is indivisible. It also entails a far deeper engagement with the nature of law and legal violence and the possibility of a legitimate non-legal violence than is found in the classic-juridical conceptions. In so doing, Benjamin radically enhances our understanding of the way(s) in which sovereignty, both legal and otherwise, depends upon and operates through (forms of) violence.

By insisting on a notion of divine violence beyond legal violence, he also points to a conception of politics in which a type of violence, based on a particular theological sentiment, expiates legal violence to permit human being to start afresh. The problem, of course, is that to escape the means/end dichotomy that defines legal sovereign violence, Benjamin cannot provide, and indeed there cannot ever be, a criterion that guides or determines the legitimate appeal to divine violence. This is why, so I argue, divine violence is intimately connected to responsibility. Therefore, on the one hand, Benjamin's appeal to divine violence offers us the possibility of always challenging legal sovereignty to perpetuate radical change. On the other hand, however, he places all responsibility for doing so on us. The power of Benjamin's critique is that it identifies the limits of legal sovereign violence, points to a conception of sovereign violence beyond legal forms, indicates the political consequences of this form of violence, but purposefully leaves open the difficult and dangerous question of how and for what reasons political agents can legitimately appeal to this form of violence.

VIOLENCE AND LAW

Benjamin starts by clarifying that 'the task of a critique of violence can be summarised as that of expounding its relation to law and justice'.[13] To understand 'violence', he will, therefore, turn to the question of its relationship to law, which will eventually bring forth the question of justice. Violence is then understood to be a juridical-moral problem. More specifically, Benjamin claims 'that the most elementary relationship within any legal system is that of ends to means, and, furthermore, that violence can first be sought only in the realm of means, not in the realm of ends'.[14] After all, claiming that violence is a means to an end might be thought to provide its own criterion for assessing the use of violence; namely, whether the violence employed successfully achieved its aim.

Benjamin rejects this, claiming that it is not radically sufficient. At most, this contains 'not a criterion for violence itself as a principle, but, rather, the criterion for cases of its use'.[15] This is problematic because it leaves open the question of 'whether violence, as a principle, could be a moral means . . . to a just ends'.[16] This, however, requires 'a more exact criterion . . . which . . . discriminate[s] within the sphere of means themselves, without regard for the ends they serve'.[17] It requires, in other words, a critique of violence 'itself', regardless of the ends it is employed to serve.

Benjamin notes that this 'more precise critical approach'[18] has been largely ignored by 'the main current[s] of legal philosophy':[19] natural and positive law. Catherine Kellog explains that the former 'regards violence as equivalent to any other means that the law might use in the course of seeking its end. As long as the law is just, then the use of coercion (or anything) is justified.'[20] In contrast, positive law

> recognises that legal authority is performative and in theory contingent, and does not look to objective moral principles like justice to explain legal authority, which it considers instead to be something generated internal to an order of law, which can be evaluated only from an insider's point of view.[21]

Despite their differences, both natural and positive law are understood by Benjamin to agree 'in their common basic dogma: just ends can be attained by justified means, justified means used for just ends'.[22] Natural law 'attempts, by the justness of the ends, to "justify" the means, positive law to "guarantee" the justness of the ends through the justification of the means'.[23] Resolving this antinomy requires a 'mutually independent criterion both of just ends and of justified means'.[24] In other words, natural and positive law can only legitimately claim that their respective privileging of 'ends' and 'means' is justified if a criterion is found that independently verifies whether the notion of 'justice' that both appeal to without discussing is legitimate.

Rather than engage in this exercise, Benjamin side-steps it, claiming that 'the realm of ends, and therefore also the question of a criterion of justness, are excluded for the time being from this study'.[25] Instead, he focuses on 'the question of the justification of certain means that constitute violence'.[26] This does not and cannot be based on natural or positive law, both of which presuppose a value that allows each to determine the validity of different applications of violence. These presuppositions, however, point to the need for a critique to determine the validity of the privileged (implicit) value, which, in turn, requires 'a standpoint outside positive legal philosophy but also outside natural law'.[27] For Benjamin, 'it can be furnished only by a philosophico-historical view of law'.[28]

Benjamin goes on to discuss the distinction between 'legitimate and illegitimate violence'.[29] He rejects the premise of natural law wherein 'a distinction is drawn between violence used for just ends and violence used for unjust ends',[30] to side with the fundamental claim of positive law that 'demands of all violence a proof of its historical origin, which under certain circumstances is declared legal, sanctioned'.[31] Since sanctioned legal violence is most easily determined by its ends, the question arises as to whether the ends used to sanction legal violence are historical or not, with the implication being that '[e]nds that lack such an acknowledgement may be called natural ends; other types may be called legal ends'.[32] The different functions of violence, that is whether 'it serves natural or legal ends',[33] can then be traced against specific legal conditions to determine whether violence is understood to have a natural or historic basis. A critique of violence can, therefore, be undertaken in heterogeneous ways not only based on whether it is grounded naturally or historically, but also depending on the specifics of the legal system in question.

To resolve this issue and '[f]or the sake of simplicity',[34] Benjamin explains that he will devise his critique on the basis of 'contemporary European conditions'.[35] He notes that what is most characteristic about these legal systems is that there 'is the tendency to deny the natural ends of . . . individuals in all those cases in which such ends could, in a given situation, be usefully pursued by violence'.[36] As a consequence, legal systems attempt to deny *individuals* the basis that would permit them to autonomously exercise violence for natural ends. Instead, the 'legal system strives to limit by legal ends, in all areas where individual ends could be usefully pursued by violence, legal ends that can be realised only by legal power'.[37] Benjamin provides the example of corporal punishment in education. Whereas the education authority has relative autonomy to develop its pupils and so achieve the natural end of individual education, any punishment used in this process is strictly controlled by legal ends.[38] There is, then, a division established between legally and non-legally sanctioned ends in which the former usurps the latter.

While the legal system provides autonomy to certain of its spheres and so permits a degree of violence, it continues to impose itself on that sphere to constrain how that violence is deployed. The lesson Benjamin extracts is that 'law sees violence in the hands of individuals as a danger undermining the legal system'[39] and so attempts to remove, as far as possible, all legitimacy from individual expressions of violence. Only a *legal* justification is seen to be adequate, namely because (1) the legal system itself excludes all non- or extra-legal justifications, and (2) it is understood 'that violence, when not in the hands of the law, threatens it not by the ends that it may pursue but by its mere existence outside the law'.[40]

Benjamin provides the example of 'the "great" criminal',[41] who, no matter how repellent his crimes, arouses 'the secret admiration of the public'.[42] Far from being revolted by the criminal's violence, the general public exhibits a strange fascination with his disregard for the law. Jacques Derrida explains that this is because 'the great criminal . . . is the sovereign exception of the one who has been able *either* to defy and contest the monopolisation by law . . . *or else* to reappropriate for himself, as an individual, the violence that the law has taken out of the hands of individuals'.[43] As Benjamin continues, 'the violence that present-day law is seeking in all areas of activity to deny the individual appears really threatening, and arouses even in defeat the sympathy of the masses against the law'.[44] It should not be thought, however, that the legal system only fears those who exist outside its scope. Violence is a danger when it is given permission to operate *within* the legal system.

To show this, Benjamin turns to the question 'of the workers' guaranteed right to strike'.[45] He sees this as a logical move because 'today organised labour is, apart from the [S]tate, probably the only legal subject entitled to exercise violence'.[46] He recognises, however, that it could be objected that a strike does not entail violence, but is simply 'an omission of actions, a nonaction'.[47] While admitting that this is probably one of the arguments that led to strikes being permitted, Benjamin notes that 'its truth is not unconditional'.[48] A strike is not a nonviolent act; it is inherently violent by virtue of the introduction of a 'form of extortion'[49] in which there is 'a conscious readiness to resume the suspended action under certain circumstances that either have nothing whatever to do with this action or only superficially modify it'.[50]

When a strike is understood in this way, labour is opposed to the State, with the former possessing 'the right to use force in attaining certain ends'.[51] By permitting workers the opportunity to strike, the State introduces a 'pressure valve' to release violence *within* the constraints of the legal system. As Tracy McNulty explains, 'the [S]tate authorises the legal violence of means only in order to suppress a violence that might spell the end of its own monopoly of power'.[52]

However, despite intending to keep the workers *within* the legal system, the antagonism created between workers and owners may result in a 'revolutionary general strike'[53] that threatens the existence of the legal system and, by extension, State. Paradoxically, then, the legally permitted violence of the general strike can give rise to a form of violence that not only escapes the means–end economy constitutive of the legal system, but also challenges that system. Benjamin is here pointing to an issue that will become more important when we get to the relationship between mythic(-legal) violence and divine violence: law may wish to portray itself as a closed system, but its closure is always defined by and related to an excess that threatens to annihilate it.

VIOLENCE AS LAW-MAKING AND/OR LAW-PRESERVING

To develop this, Benjamin points to the example of 'military force'.[54] While apparently different to a general strike, he notes that it

> rests on exactly the same objective contradiction in the legal situation as does that of strike law – namely, on the fact that legal subjects sanction violence whose ends remain for the sanctioners natural ends, and can therefore in a crisis come into conflict with their own legal or natural ends.[55]

Military force is, then, employed by the law to maintain its regime. But military force also points beyond the law by virtue of, potentially, overstepping the boundaries of the law that legitimises it. In this way, military force creates a new law. Military force operates then in a double bind: it is that which preserves the legal system, but also that which helps create legal systems. In both instances, military violence makes the law, whether this is through its preservation or through the instantiation of a new law by military force. There is, then, 'a lawmaking character inherent in all such violence'.[56] It is the law-making potential of violence that underpins the previously mentioned 'tendency of modern law to divest the individual, at least as a legal subject, of all violence, even that directed only to natural ends',[57] the public's fascination and horror at the deeds of great criminals, the State's wariness about strikes and the actions of other States.

The latter gives rise to a discussion of militarism, an important topic for Benjamin given the time the essay was written and, indeed, us, for whom the concept has, arguably, only grown in importance. Militarism is defined as 'the compulsory, universal use of violence as a means to the ends of the State'.[58] Militarism does not, then, simply entail the use of violence; it is violence as a means for the ends of the State. It has, therefore, legal importance. Notably, there are two aspects to the relationship between violence and law, insofar as violence has a law-making and a law-preserving function. The former emanates from the way that violence is used to create law. Violence therefore underpins the *creation* of *all* legal systems — whether this is by virtue of the threat of violence or its explicit use — but having been created through violence, the law continues to be tied to violence. It is only through this bond that law can be preserved.

However, no sooner has Benjamin identified the distinction between law-making and law-preserving violence than he calls it into question through the example of capital punishment, which is understood to reveal 'something rotten in the law'.[59] After all, 'if violence . . . is the origin of law, then it may be readily supposed that where the highest violence, that over life and death, occurs in the legal system, the origins of law jut manifestly and fearsomely into existence'.[60] Benjamin's point is that, whereas it is often thought that law and justice are intimately connected to one another to the exclusion of violence, law's recourse to violence, and specifically the ultimate violence that sanctions the death penalty, reveals that law and justice do not exclude violence, but actually depend on it. Indeed, the purpose of the death penalty 'is not to punish the infringement of law but to establish new law. For in the exercise of law over death, more than in any other legal act, the law reaffirms itself.'[61] This reveals that violence does more than preserve law; it actually makes law.

The death penalty is, however, a rather extreme example and, indeed, is not one that is currently carried out in European legal systems. It might, then, appear to be somewhat irrelevant to contemporary discussions. Benjamin notes, however, that the usurpation of the law-making/law-preserving dichotomy is also seen in the far more 'everyday', but fundamental, 'institution of the modern State: the police'.[62]

The police are, of course, charged with maintaining law and order with the consequence that it may appear that their function is to preserve, rather than make, the law. However, while law determines criteria applicable in time and space by virtue of delineating what does and does not count as legal, this alone is insufficient for the preservation of the legal order. Laws cannot be written for every eventuality and so the maintenance of law requires that the police exercise judgement and flexibility to immediately determine whether citizens are committing acts that violate the spirit and content of law. This, of course, means that the police decide on the interpretation of law to be preserved, use that to determine the legality of an individual's actions, and, in so doing, make law. As such, 'the separation of law-making and law-preserving violence is suspended'.[63] Police violence 'is law-making, because its characteristic function is not the promulgation of laws but the assertion of legal claims for any decree, and law-preserving, because it is at the disposal of these ends'.[64]

As a consequence, police violence 'marks the point at which the State, whether from impotence or because of the immanent connections within any legal system, can no longer guarantee through the legal system the empirical ends that it desires at any price to attain'.[65] Instead, the police intervene 'for security reasons' in cases where no clear legal situation exists, when they are not merely, without the slightest relation to legal ends, accompanying the citizen as a brutal encumbrance through a life regulated by ordinances, or simply supervising him.[66]

Law is, then, inherently violent, both at its inception and in its continuation.

Benjamin does, however, wonder 'whether there are no other than violent means for regulating conflicting human interests'.[67] It might be thought that an agreement that results in a contract regulating the activities of both parties might be an option. After all, it entails a nonviolent means (i.e. discussion) that may lead to a nonviolent resolution in the form of the mutually agreed-upon meaning of the articles of the contract.

Benjamin warns, however, that no matter how 'peacefully it may have been entered into by the parties, [a contract] leads finally to possible violence'.[68] Because it is a legal contract, 'it confers on each party the right to violence in some form against the other, should he break the agreement'.[69] The preservation of the agreement, at the very least, implicitly sanctions violence, while 'the origin of every contract also points toward violence'.[70] Violence or even the threat of violence may not be explicitly present at the origins of every agreement, but 'the power that guarantees a legal contract is . . . of violent origin even if violence is not introduced into the contract itself'.[71] Even if the process of negotiation is not *explicitly* violent and the agreement reached does not *explicitly* entail or sanction violence, all agreements are (implicitly) founded on violence and depend upon (the threat of) violence to preserve them.

The failure to recognise this intimate relationship between law and violence lay, so Benjamin thought, at the root of the decay that he witnessed in the German parliament of his time. However, he quickly notes that the problem is a logical not historical one. It is only 'when the consciousness of the latent presence of violence in a legal institution disappears [that] the institution falls into decay'.[72] Rather than recognising that law is grounded in and preserved by violence, Benjamin writes that problems arise if and when parliaments think that they can resolve issues by cultivating and depending upon 'a supposedly nonviolent manner of dealing with political affairs'.[73] Because parliamentarians deal with the law, their affairs are intimately bound to violence: 'what a parliament achieves in vital affairs can be only those legal decrees that in their origin and outcome are attended by violence'.[74] In trying to eschew this, parliaments simply make themselves impotent. This is not to say that violence must be legally affirmed; but, because law is grounded in violence, the latter cannot be ignored or forgotten if the former is to be maintained. Governing depends upon (the possibility of) violence. Only this allows the law to properly function.

This does not mean that Benjamin thinks that nonviolent resolution of conflict is impossible. He does, however, limit this to 'relationships among private persons'[75] who possess 'a civilised outlook [that] allows the use of unalloyed means of agreement'.[76] These are based on principles of 'courtesy, sympathy, peaceableness, trust'.[77] The epitome of nonviolent conflict resolution is, for Benjamin, 'the conference, considered as a technique of civil agreement'.[78] This forum not only permits 'nonviolent agreement . . . but also the exclusion of violence in principle'.[79] Benjamin's conclusion is that 'there is a sphere of human agreement that is nonviolent to the extent that it is wholly inaccessible to violence',[80] but he maintains that this is tied to 'language'[81] not law.

The problem, of course, is that language is governed by a system of laws in the form of the laws of grammar, meaning, and discourse, which dictate how it can be legitimately used. Discussion is not actually then a nonviolent means of settling legal disputes; it depends upon the violence that makes and preserves the laws of language that are, presumably, in dispute. Thus, if discussion is governed by the laws of language and law is tied to violence, is language not intimately and necessarily linked to violence?

To understand why Benjamin thinks not, we have to turn to what he means by 'pure means'.[82] This notion is a crucial one within Benjamin's essay, revealing both the revolutionary political intent of the essay and the conceptual innovation of 'divine violence'.[83] It is, however, a somewhat paradoxical notion and so a quick word is necessary to determine what Benjamin is and is not pointing to with it. The problem with identifying a 'pure means' is that Benjamin's critique of violence is conducted 'against' the means–end schema dominant in legal theory and, we might also say, the classic-juridical conception of sovereignty. To talk of 'means' at all would appear to re-inscribe that logic, insofar as that discussion would entail a 'means' to overcome the 'means–end' schema. However, rather than tie the issue of 'pure means' to the means–end schema, Benjamin divorces it from that restricted economy. His essay is, in many respects, an attempt to discover a non-instrumentalised conception of violence and, by extension, politics. To do so, he develops the notion of 'pure means', a means without an end. Crucially, he identifies two instances of 'pure means' and, by extension, two possible non-instrumentalised versions of violence: language and politics.

To understand why language is a pure means requires that we turn to Benjamin's 1916 essay 'On Language as Such and on the Language of Man' where he identifies an instrumental form of language that aims 'toward the communication of the contents of the mind'[84] but which is dependent on another aspect of language. We might say that, while communication reveals and uses signs, what it reveals and signals is the thing 'itself'.[85] As a consequence, 'it is obvious at once that the mental entity that communicates itself in language is not language itself but something distinguished from it'.[86]

That language communicates a mental image does not, however, mean that the latter is distinct from the former: 'it is fundamental that this mental being communicates itself *in* language and not *through* language'.[87] Mental being is not synonymous with linguistic being, although the former must be communicated in language, which turns it into a linguistic being. When communicating about an idea (mental being), language only ever talks about a mental being *in* language and so only ever talks about a linguistic being. Language reveals and talks about itself. That language communicates itself reveals that 'it is in the purest sense the "medium" of the communication'.[88] Whereas communication is orientated around a means/end dichotomy, its expression depends upon a pure '*language as such*'[89] that 'knows no means, no object, and no addressee of communication'.[90] Indeed, in a move that we will return to, this pure language is linked to the divine.[91]

Politically, the notion of pure means is associated with strike action. Here, Benjamin draws on the distinction that Georg Sorel makes in *Reflections on Violence*[92] between a 'political strike'[93] that uses a form of violence within a means–end economy to extract additional benefits from the owners of the means of production, and a 'proletarian general strike'[94] whose 'use' of violence instantiates a fundamentally new socio-political logic not confined within such an economy. These forms of strike are, then, 'antithetical in their relation to violence'.[95] In the former, violence is used as a means to extract additional resources *within* the existent system. In contrast, the proletarian general strike,

> as a pure means, is nonviolent. For it takes place not in readiness to resume work following external concessions and this or that modification to working conditions, but in the determination to resume only a wholly transformed work, no longer enforced by the [S]tate, an upheaval that this kind of strike not so much causes as consummates.[96]

Whereas the political strike is law-making and so instrumental in orientation, the proletarian general strike is 'anarchistic'.[97] While the former continues to operate through the means/end dichotomy, the latter aims to depose the logic of the former without replacing it with another end.

It might, of course, be objected that the proletarian general strike does have an end, namely, the usurpation of the means–end logic underpinning the general strike, but Benjamin rejects this. The proletarian general strike is an anarchistic one that deposes legal power, but does not have an alternative to replace it, nor is its action defined by a transcendent norm. As Massimiliano Tomba explains, 'it is not the ends that, if realised, must justify the means employed, but, rather, the means themselves that must contain within themselves an intrinsic criterion for their own justness'.[98]

This is why Martin Blumenthal-Barby suggests that it is 'a violence that posits itself without insisting on its moment of foundation'.[99] It is pure means without ends. It is only from the logic of the State, 'which has eyes only for effects',[100] that the proletarian general strike appears to be 'for something' in particular and so can be said to use violence to attain the dissolution of the State.[101] Only by remaining within the means–end economy can the proletarian general strike be understood as a form of instrumental violence. In reality, the proletarian general strike is a violence of 'pure' means without predefined end.

Benjamin's study of legal violence therefore reveals moments within law that point beyond it; namely, in the examples of language and the proletarian general strike. These are permitted and, indeed, needed by the law to preserve its privileged position, but in being permitted point to an alternative logic of violence to the one underpinning legal violence. This, however, generates the question of 'what kinds of violence exist other than all those envisaged by legal theory'.[102]

In response, Benjamin not only identifies the kinds of violence that are pointed to without being analysed when discussing legal violence, but makes the stronger claim that legal violence depends upon these alternative conceptions. The first form examined is mythic violence, which describes the violence that forms legal violence, and which ultimately depends upon divine violence.

MYTHIC VIOLENCE

Mythic violence fulfils, at least, four functions within Benjamin's critique: First, it is the narrative that grounds the foundation of law and, for this reason, is 'identical'[103] to law-making violence. By outlining the myth that describes and justifies the violence that founds law, mythic violence provides the explanation as to why law is so structured. As Brendan Moran notes, mythical violence entails the 'attempted exclusion of exception, [the] attempted elimination of exception, or any other stagnant relation with exception'.[104] It aims to create a closed, hermetically sealed legal system that is its own foundation.[105] Myth is a key component in this process, insofar as it creates a narrative that reveals the absolute status of law.

Second, as that which legitimises law, mythic violence is excluded from law. This, however, reveals that (a part of) mythic violence is beyond the law and so indicates that it is grounded from a 'prior' source: the divine. Specifically, Tracy McNulty explains that 'mythic violence "bastardises" divine violence by rendering visible, and so reducing to a fixed manifestation, what is fundamentally invisible: the expiatory power of divine violence'.[106] This manifestation of divine violence is necessary to render it visible and so instrumental to humanity. As James Martel explains, 'faced with the abyss between the human and divine realms, mythical violence seeks to stand in for God'.[107] By standing in for God, mythic violence, third, permits the divine to appear to humans, albeit in truncated form, which, fourth, reminds humans of the power of the divine.

To demonstrate what this entails, Benjamin appeals to 'the legend of Niobe'.[108] Niobe's fault was to boast to the Goddess Leto that she had fourteen children while the Goddess only had twins. Simon Critchley dismisses this as 'a seemingly mild indiscretion',[109] but, in boasting to the Goddess in this manner, Niobe challenged the Goddess's authority and, by extension, the status of law itself. In revenge, Leto sent her twins, Apollo and Artemis, to kill all of Niobe's children, but leave Niobe alive. This 'br[ought] a cruel death to Niobe's children, [but] it stop[ped] short of claiming the life of their mother, whom it le[ft] behind'.[110] Devastated, Niobe left for Mount Sipylus, where, as the ultimate punishment, she became 'an eternally mute bearer of guilt and . . . a boundary stone on the frontier between men and gods'.[111]

Amir Ahmadi challenges this interpretation, claiming that 'Benjamin's assimilation of law to myth is ambivalent'[112] and 'there is no indication in the story of Niobe that the cause of her metamorphosis is guilt',[113] before rejecting his conclusion because it simply 'does not find support in the myth'.[114] For Ahmadi, Benjamin does not seek to elucidate the myth of Niobe, but interprets it through the lens of his own theo-philosophy. For this reason, it 'can hardly be an acceptable interpretation of this constellation'.[115] While this may be the case, it does not mean that we should reject Benjamin's interpretation out of hand. Rather, we should read Benjamin's account with caution; it is not a scholarly exegesis, but a description of a myth that aims to make a philosophical point; namely, the elucidation of Benjamin's argument regarding the relationship between the human, the mythic, and the divine.

Read in this manner, two issues stand out: first, law-making violence is tied to the question of power and, specifically, who has the power to make laws. It is for this reason that Benjamin explains that 'lawmaking is powermaking, assumption of power, and to that extent an immediate manifestation of violence'.[116] Delineating who has power and who founds law creates the parameters that define the content of law. While Niobe challenges the Goddess, the death of her children re-establishes the authority of the Goddess, confirming that She is the power that makes law. In turn, this confirms that the source of law is divine not human.

Second, Benjamin's interpretation of the myth of Niobe demonstrates the hubris and folly that occur when humans challenge the Gods. The Gods are fate; their word and dominance must prevail. Even when the law is unwritten or the individual unwittingly tramples over it, this is not forgivable; retribution must be sought. This is not a matter of justice *per se*, which is a moral concept and so dependent on law – that which has just been trampled over and so is no longer valid – but is inherent in the nature of fate and hence the divine itself. No matter how supposedly unwitting or unintentional, all human action emanates from and is defined by fate. Fate always wins, which, given that fate is synonymous with the Gods, means that the divine always trumps the human.

With this, Benjamin points to a particularly non-anthropocentrist understanding of the relationship between violence and law. Humans are not central or foundational to this relationship; the divine is. For humans to set themselves up as absolute sovereigns is to challenge this order, a challenge that can only elicit a response from the Gods that humanity will necessarily lose. Only then will the 'correct' order be established in which the divine is foundational.

DIVINE VIOLENCE

Mythic violence depends, then, upon and points to another form of violence called 'divine violence'.[117] Benjamin speculates that, as the ground of mythic violence, divine violence 'might be able to call a halt to mythic violence'.[118] The problem is that Benjamin's comments on the topic are very short and underdeveloped. Outlining precisely what it entails is, therefore, somewhat difficult and has led to numerous interpretations. Indeed, it has been argued that the entire point of Benjamin's essay and, by extension, the way it is interpreted depend upon how divine violence is understood.[119] I will focus on (1) its relationship to mythic violence to show the way in which divine violence deposes the former without replacing it with any ends, and (2) the question of whether divine violence is, as its name suggests, an act of God, or whether it refers to a logic that can be enacted by humans.

That mythic violence founds law leads to the question of what lies 'beyond' law. Benjamin claims that this 'beyond' is the divine; a response that gives rise to the question of the relationship between mythic and divine violence. The former is grounded in the latter, but the latter is only manifested to humans through the former. Mythic violence is a 'contraction' of divine violence in the form of law, which, in emanating from divine violence, continues to point to it.

Importantly, however, while 'mythic violence is confronted by the divine ... the latter constitutes its antithesis in all respects'.[120] For example,

> if mythic violence is lawmaking, divine violence is law-destroying; if the former sets boundaries, the latter boundlessly destroys them; if mythic violence brings at once guilt and retribution, divine violence, only

expiates; if the former threatens, the latter strikes; if the former is bloody, the latter is lethal without spilling blood.[121]

There is, then, a fundamentally different logic at play in divine and mythic violence. Rather than establish and preserve law, divine violence annihilates it from without and, in this act, expiates what previously was.

Crucially, this expiation lacks bloodshed; it is so total that the annihilation is not able to spill blood. It simply wipes its victims out. This is important for, at least, three reasons: first, 'blood is the symbol of mere life'.[122] By this, Benjamin means that blood is the manifestation of a particular instance of life. Divine violence, in contrast, is concerned not with instances of 'mere life',[123] but with 'all life'.[124] It, therefore, acts without blood and without concern for it.

Second, while mythic violence is both bloody and orientated 'for its own sake',[125] meaning that it occurs within the instrumentalism of legal violence, divine violence is a 'pure power'[126] that does not act instrumentally; it simply annihilates.

Third, this pure power is orientated not to the preservation of divine violence, but 'for the sake of the living'.[127] It is, therefore, a pure action (i.e. not an instrumental one) that annihilates the power and closure of mythic violence to permit a space to start anew. Divine violence does not then reveal anything new such as the truth, but only 'deposes'[128] what was, thereby permitting the process of expiation that allows a new beginning.

While mythic violence affirms closure, its attempt must always fail because of its dependence on divine violence and, by extension, the possibility that, at any moment, divine violence may annihilate it. Law is never closed and hermetically sealed. It has an 'outside' and, crucially, this 'outside' is more powerful than law, is always a threat to law, and can, at any moment, annihilate law. Law is fragile, which is not necessarily a negative because it permits renewal and, therefore, the instantiation of a new law.

Divine violence is then a form of violence that lies at the foundation of mythic law, but yet exists outside of law. This outsider status permits it to intercede in law; not to change it *per se*, which would reduce divine violence to the status of law-making and hence mythic violence, but to annihilate it to permit regeneration. The annihilation of mythic violence is guided by the search for 'justice',[129] which is a concept without any form, does not determine in advance divine action, and does not exist within the means/end dichotomy of legal violence. Justice describes the actions of the divine, which, it will be remembered, does not annihilate to re-instantiate anything in particular. It simply abolishes the law to permit a regenerative space for a new mythic and legal violence.

This gives rise to the question of whether divine violence, as the name suggests, is a divine act or whether it points to actions that humans can instantiate. This determines whether Benjamin's notion of 'divine violence' carries political importance or whether it is simply a random act of the divine that humanity must suffer; a question that depends upon a methodological issue regarding whether Benjamin's thought is to be understood with a *theological* emphasis, in which a transcendent divine authority imposes itself on humanity, or a *historical-political* emphasis, in which divine violence refers to an alternative logic (to that of legal-mythic forms) of violence that offers humans the possibility of deposing the law to start again.

The former interpretation is supported by appeal to its name, '*divine* violence', and to the examples Benjamin provides. Richard Bernstein, for example, rejects Butler's and Critchley's claim that divine violence is nonviolent; nonviolence describes 'how *humans* should react to the commandment, not . . . *divine* violence as such'.[130] Instead, Bernstein insists that divine violence describes a particular form of violence that only the divine is capable of perpetrating.

This line of interpretation has, however, been criticised because it contradicts Benjamin's claim that 'this divine power is not only attested by religious tradition but is also found in present-day life in at least one sanctioned manifestation'.[131] From this, Ari Hirvonen, for example, claims 'that Benjamin secularises divine violence . . . There are manifestations of divine violence, which are not defined by miracles directly performed by God but by the moments of bloodless, striking, expiating execution',[132] while Katerina Kolozova explains that 'in spite of the fact that the "pure" and "law-destroying" violence of expiation is defined as divine . . . a human rendition of it is possible and it is one that can bring about true revolutionary change'.[133]

Indeed, to back up this reading, we might point to Benjamin's claim that 'the educative power, which in its perfected form stands outside the law, is one of its manifestations'.[134] Education is a case of divine violence because, when understood in a particular way, namely in terms of enlightenment, it stands outside of mythical law – in that it is not law-preserving or law-making – is not (necessarily) connected to a means–end rationality, and has the power to break laws insofar as laws are that which set the boundaries of rational action. Education has then the ability to go beyond what is currently considered true, and the parameters of the current legal system. It opens up the space for the instantiation of new mythic and legal violence. This alteration is not constituted 'by miracles directly performed by God but by the expiating moment in them that strikes without bloodshed, and, finally, by the absence of all lawmaking'.[135]

But no sooner has Benjamin made this claim than he qualifies it heavily: 'it is justifiable to call this violence, too, annihilating; but it is so only relatively, with regard to goods, right, life, and suchlike, never absolutely, with regard to the soul of the living'.¹³⁶ This appears to point to two forms of divine violence: an *absolute* sense of divine violence that emanates from the divine to annihilate the living, and a *relative* sense that emanates from humans and annihilates a way of life. In turn, this reaffirms the division between a theological and a historical-political reading of 'divine violence'. Slavoj Žižek, for example, points to the latter when he asks us to

> recall, a decade or so ago, the panic in Rio de Janeiro when crowds descended from the favelas into the rich part of the city and started looting and burning supermarkets. This was indeed divine violence . . . They were like biblical locusts, the divine punishment for men's sinful ways.¹³⁷

This action did not destroy the legal system as the absolute sense of divine action would demand, but attacked a way of life and so could appear to entail a relative sense of divine violence.

The problem with this understanding and, indeed, the notion of a relative, human-based conception of divine violence is summarised by Richard Bernstein, who writes that

> frankly, this sounds more like the *manifestation* of anger that Benjamin cites when he introduces the concept of mythic violence (not divine violence). Such outbursts do not destroy [S]tate power and violence; they provoke the demand for more law and order – and are frequently quickly suppressed by [S]tate violence. Consequently they actually increase [S]tate power and violence.¹³⁸

This not only calls into question the legitimacy of the notion of a relative sense of divine violence, which seems to be a version of mythic, not divine, violence, but also reaffirms Bernstein's prior insistence that divine violence can only be based on and come from the divine. As noted, however, this is undermined by Benjamin's claims regarding the revolutionary potential of the proletarian general strike, the divine violence of education, and, of course, his insistence that 'this divine power is not only attested by religious tradition but is also found in present-day life'.¹³⁹

CONCLUDING REMARKS

A problem arises then when we attempt to identify how divine violence is manifested. For Žižek, the actions of Rio's poor were a classic case of it; for Bernstein, such action was mythic, not divine. The danger is that, without being able to identify how divine violence is manifested or what actions can legitimately count as divine violence, any action that annihilates can claim to be divine. It is this insight that lies behind Jacques Derrida's claim that divine violence is linked to the Holocaust because both emphasise pure annihilation. This, for Derrida, reveals the failure of Benjamin's concept of divine violence. It is simply incapable of criticising the Holocaust and, indeed, threatens to provide intellectual cover for it as a divine act.[140]

The obvious problem with such a link is, as Ari Hirvonen points out, that the Holocaust was not a manifestation of divine violence, but 'was realised by a State that used all its legal, administrative, military, economic and technological apparatuses to commit genocide. This was an extreme case of legal violence.'[141] From this perspective, the Nazi State is not a form of divine violence; rather, divine violence would destroy the mythic-legal violence of the Nazi State. Therefore, instead of being reduced to a particular State, divine violence operates 'outside' the mythic-legal violence grounding actual States to always permit the possibility that even the most totalising of political regimes can be overcome.

While my sympathies lie with Hirvonen's assessment, this debate points to a significant difficulty with Benjamin's notion of divine violence: there simply is no criterion that can legitimately justify its use. This is not because of an *aporia* in Benjamin's argument; it is a consequence of the *aporia* at the heart of divine violence. There simply is no law that can determine its legitimate application because if there were, divine violence would be reduced to a law – which, by definition, divine violence exceeds – and so not be divine. Instead, divine violence interrupts legal order, deposing its authority. To appeal to this '"sovereign" violence'[142] is then to place oneself beyond the justification of law; it is to excuse oneself from law for a higher end. However, the problem with this conclusion is, as Derrida pointed out, that it would appear to mean that the appeal to divine violence could be used to justify any action, no matter how atrocious.

Benjamin rejects this, claiming that when the question of releasing divine violence, in the form of '"May I kill?"',[143] arises, it is immediately met by 'the commandment "Thou shalt not kill".'[144] However, this seems to merely reaffirm the problem that arises from any human appeal to divine violence. Not only is there always a divine rule confirming alternative action, but to appeal to the divine to sanction another act is to reduce the divine to a means for an end. But neither can we appeal to law to resolve the issue; after all, law depends upon the divine while the divine is that which expiates law.

Benjamin's conclusion is that the injunction against killing is not a concrete imperative providing a criterion for determining the treatment of others; 'it exists not as a criterion of judgement, but as a guideline for the actions of persons or communities who have to wrestle with it in solitude and, in exceptional cases, to take on themselves the responsibility of ignoring it'.[145] There is simply an unresolvable tension between the two commandments that demands that we make a decision regarding whether to employ divine violence and what form it will take. This must be an individual decision, one in which 'neither the divine judgement nor the grounds for this judgement can be known in advance'.[146]

To guide such a choice, Benjamin considers whether 'the doctrine of the sanctity of life'[147] might be used. The basic premise is that higher than justice or happiness lies the importance of existence itself. As such, it is wrong to kill, not because of some guide, but because the highest goal in life is life itself. Benjamin rejects this because he thinks that it would annihilate divine violence. Placing 'existence', mere life, as the highest value sanctifies mortal life. For Benjamin, however,

> man cannot, at any price, be said to coincide with any other of his conditions and qualities, including even the uniqueness of his bodily person. However sacred man is (or however sacred that life in him which is identically present in earthly life, death, and afterlife), there is no sacredness in his condition, in his bodily life vulnerable to injury by his fellow men.[148]

Benjamin was not able to respond directly to biopolitical theory, but we have here a tentative critique of its affirmation that sovereign violence is orientated to life: to privilege 'life' over all else is to reduce the human to his mortal bodily existence. This ignores the divine that exists beyond the human, linking the latter to the sacred. To ignore the divine is not to elevate human being to a higher status, but to lose the sacred that truly defines the human.

Benjamin is adamant then that the notion of divine violence must stand, but admits that there is no criterion to define it or its legitimate application. Instead, he seeks to drawn out a more fundamental, moral conclusion: any appeal to divine violence can only ever be an immanent, subjective one. As Alison Ross explains, those who purport to commit acts of divine violence 'must have faith that they act under a higher exigency, set apart from merely human motivations'.[149] Such a possibility 'furnishes proof that revolutionary violence, the highest manifestation of unalloyed violence by man, is possible, and shows by what means'.[150] But what legitimately counts as divine violence cannot be predetermined or predefined; it is an anarchic violence that simply deposes all that is. The responsibility for invoking it lies with each individual.

The danger, of course, is that the validity of invoking the notion of divine violence to designate an action as righteous is that the righteousness of that designation cannot be known beforehand. Indeed, it is questionable whether it will ever be known given the 'gap' between the human and the divine.

After all, as Benjamin puts it, in contrast to mythic violence, 'the expiatory power of [divine] violence is invisible to men'.[151] This is the risk of divine violence: it points to an outside-of-law that permits radical change, but the invocation of such violence is a purely individual decision whose justification can only be known, if it can be known at all, after the event. Benjamin's notion of divine violence offers then the possibility of a radically new political beginning, but to invoke it to justify violence subjects oneself to the greatest danger and ethical responsibility.

NOTES

1. Walter Benjamin, 'Critique of Violence', trans. Edmund Jephcott, in *Selected Writings*, vol. 1, 1913–1926, ed. Marcus Bullock and Michael W. Jennings (Cambridge, MA: Harvard University Press, 1996), pp. 236–52.
2. Jürgen Habermas, 'Walter Benjamin: Consciousness–Raising or Rescuing Critique', in *On Walter Benjamin: Critical Essays and Recollections*, ed. Gary Smith (Stanford: Stanford University Press, 1992), pp. 90–128. Originally published as Jürgen Habermas, 'Bechußtmachende oder rettende Kritik: Die Actualität Walter Benjamins', in *Zur Aktualität Walter Benjamins*, ed. Siegfried Unseld (Suhrkamp: Frankfurt-am-Main, 1972), pp. 173–223.
3. Jacques Derrida, 'Force of Law: The "Mystical Foundation of Authority"', trans. Mary Quaintance, in *Acts of Religion*, ed. Gil Andjar (Abingdon: Routledge, 2002), pp. 230–98.
4. Habermas, 'Walter Benjamin: Consciousness-Raising or Rescuing Critique', pp. 98, 99, 112.
5. Derrida, 'Force of Law', p. 258.
6. Ibid. p. 260.
7. Judith Butler, 'Critique, Coercion and Sacred Life in Benjamin's "Critique of Violence"', p. 202, in *Political Theologies: Public Relations in a Post-Secular World*, ed. Hent de Vries and Lawrence E. Sullivan (New York: Fordham University Press, 2006), pp. 201–19; see also Simon Critchley, *The Faith of the Faithless: Experiments in Political Theology* (London: Verso, 2012), p. 219. They do not mention it, but these interpretations linking Benjamin to the radical Left echo Herbert Marcuse's interpretation in his afterword to a slim selection of Benjamin's writing published in 1965. See Herbert Marcuse, 'Nachwort', in Walter Benjamin, *Walter Benjamin, zur Kritik der Gewalt und andere Aufsätze* (Frankfurt-am-Main: Suhrkamp, 1965), pp. 98–107.
8. Richard Bernstein, *Violence: Thinking without Bannisters* (Cambridge: Polity, 2013), p. 61; Alison Ross, 'The Ambiguity of Ambiguity in Benjamin's "Critique of Violence"', p. 40, in *Towards the Critique of Violence: Walter Benjamin and Giorgio Agamben*, ed. Brendan Moran and Carlo Salzani (London: Bloomsbury, 2015), pp. 39–56.
9. Beatrice Hanssen, *Critique of Violence: Between Poststructuralism and Critical Theory* (Abingdon: Routledge, 2000), p. 4.
10. Ibid. p. 4.
11. Support for this interpretation is found in Robert Sinnerbrink, 'Deconstructive Justice and the "Critique of Violence": On Derrida and Benjamin', *Social Semiotics*, 11:3, 2006, pp. 485–97; and Ari Hirvonen, 'The Politics of Revolt: On Benjamin and Critique of Law', *Law Critique*, 22:2, 2011, pp. 101–18.

12. Benjamin, 'Critique of Violence', p. 248.
13. Ibid. p. 236.
14. Ibid. p. 236.
15. Ibid. p. 236.
16. Ibid. p. 236.
17. Ibid. p. 236.
18. Ibid. p. 236.
19. Ibid. p. 236.
20. Catherine Kellog, 'Walter Benjamin and the Ethics of Violence', *Law, Culture, and the Humanities*, 9:1, 2011, pp. 71–90 (p. 75).
21. Ibid. p. 75.
22. Benjamin, 'Critique of Violence', p. 237.
23. Ibid. p. 237.
24. Ibid. p. 237.
25. Ibid. p. 237.
26. Ibid. p. 237.
27. Ibid. p. 238.
28. Ibid. p. 238.
29. Ibid. p. 238.
30. Ibid. p. 238
31. Ibid. p. 238.
32. Ibid. p. 238.
33. Ibid. p. 238.
34. Ibid. p. 238.
35. Ibid. p. 238.
36. Ibid. p. 238.
37. Ibid. p. 238.
38. Ibid. p. 238.
39. Ibid. p. 238
40. Ibid. p. 239.
41. Ibid. p. 239.
42. Ibid. p. 239.
43. Jacques Derrida, *The Death Penalty, vol. 2*, ed. Geoffrey Bennington and Marc Crépon, trans. Elizabeth Rottenburg (Chicago: University of Chicago Press, 2017), p. 45.
44. Benjamin, 'Critique of Violence', p. 239.
45. Ibid. p. 239.
46. Ibid. p. 239.
47. Ibid. p. 239.
48. Ibid. p. 239.
49. Ibid. p. 239
50. Ibid. p. 239.
51. Ibid. p. 239.
52. Tracy McNulty, 'The Commandment against the Law: Writing and Divine Justice in Walter Benjamin's "Critique of Violence"', *Diacritics*, 37:2–3, 2007, pp. 34–60 (p. 39).
53. Benjamin, 'Critique of Violence', p. 239.
54. Ibid. p. 239.
55. Ibid. p. 240.
56. Ibid. p. 240.
57. Ibid. p. 241.

58. Ibid. p. 241.
59. Ibid. p. 242. The topic of capital punishment and, by extension, the relationship between law, sovereignty, and violence will be taken up in a later chapter through an engagement with Jacques Derrida's comments on the death penalty. Benjamin connects the question of capital punishment to sovereignty, law, and violence and, indeed, sees in this relationship a critical moment that anticipates Derrida's argument. This reaffirms my claim that, whether explicitly mentioned or not, Benjamin's essay is foundational for much subsequent thought on violence.
60. Ibid. p. 242.
61. Ibid. p. 242.
62. Ibid. p. 242.
63. Ibid. p. 243
64. Ibid. p. 243.
65. Ibid. p. 243.
66. Ibid. p. 243.
67. Ibid. p. 243.
68. Ibid. p. 243.
69. Ibid. p. 243.
70. Ibid. p. 243.
71. Ibid. pp. 243–4.
72. Ibid. p. 244.
73. Ibid. p. 244.
74. Ibid. p. 244.
75. Ibid. p. 244.
76. Ibid. p. 244.
77. Ibid. p. 244.
78. Ibid. p. 244.
79. Ibid. p. 244.
80. Ibid. p. 245.
81. Ibid. p. 245.
82. Ibid. p. 245.
83. Ibid. p. 248.
84. Walter Benjamin, 'On Language as Such and on the Language of Man', p. 62, trans. Edmund Jephcott, in *Selected Writings, vol. 1, 1913–1926*, ed. Marcus Bullock and Michael W. Jennings (Cambridge, MA: Harvard University Press, 1996), pp. 62–74.
85. Ibid. p. 63.
86. Ibid. p. 63.
87. Ibid. p. 63.
88. Ibid. p. 64.
89. Ibid. p. 65.
90. Ibid. p. 65.
91. Ibid. p. 65.
92. Georg Sorel, *Reflections on Violence*, ed. Jeremy Jennings (Cambridge: Cambridge University Press, 1999), pp. 109–74.
93. Benjamin, 'Critique of Violence', p. 245.
94. Ibid. p. 245.
95. Ibid. p. 245.
96. Ibid. p. 246.
97. Ibid. p. 246. For a good discussion of Benjamin's anarchism, see James Martel, 'Walter

Benjamin and the General Strike: Non-Violence and the Archeon', in *The Meanings of Violence: From Critical Theory to Biopolitics*, ed. Gavin Rae and Emma Ingala (Abingdon: Routledge, 2019), pp. 13–30.
98. Massimiliano Tomba, 'Another Kind of *Gewalt*: Beyond Law Re-Reading Walter Benjamin', *Historical Materialism*, 17:1, 2009, pp. 126–44 (p. 134).
99. Martin Blumenthal-Barby, 'Pernicious Bastardisation: Benjamin's Ethics of Pure Violence', *Modern Language Notes*, 124:3, 2009, pp. 728–51 (p. 729).
100. Benjamin, 'Critique of Violence', p. 246.
101. On this point, see Duy Lap Nguyen, 'On the Suspension of Law and the Total Transformation of Labour: Reflections on the Philosophy of History in Walter Benjamin's "Critique of Violence"', *Thesis Eleven*, 130:1, 2015, pp. 96–116.
102. Benjamin, 'Critique of Violence', p. 247.
103. Ibid. p. 248.
104. Brendan Moran, 'Exception, Division and Philosophical Politics: Benjamin and the Extreme', *Philosophy and Social Criticism*, 40:2, 2014, pp. 145–70 (p. 149).
105. Ibid. p. 147.
106. McNulty, 'The Commandment against the Law', p. 43.
107. James R. Martel, *Divine Violence: Walter Benjamin and the Eschatology of Sovereignty* (Abingdon: Routledge, 2012), p. 51.
108. Benjamin, 'Critique of Violence', p. 248.
109. Critchley, *The Faith of the Faithless*, p. 215.
110. Benjamin, 'Critique of Violence', p. 248.
111. Ibid. p. 248.
112. Amir Ahmadi, 'Benjamin's Niobe', p. 62, in *Towards the Critique of Violence: Walter Benjamin and Giorgio Agamben*, ed. Brendan Moran and Carlo Salzani (London: Bloomsbury, 2015), pp. 57–71.
113. Ibid. p. 63.
114. Ibid. p. 64.
115. Ibid. p. 66.
116. Benjamin, 'Critique of Violence', p. 248.
117. Ibid. p. 248.
118. Ibid. p. 249.
119. Bernstein, *Violence*, p. 4.
120. Benjamin, 'Critique of Violence', p. 249.
121. Ibid. pp. 249–50.
122. Ibid. p. 250.
123. Ibid. p. 250.
124. Ibid. p. 250.
125. Ibid. p. 250.
126. Ibid. p. 250.
127. Ibid. p. 250.
128. Werner Hamacher, 'Afformative, Strike: Benjamin's "Critique of Violence"', trans. Dana Hollander, p. 115, in *Walter Benjamin's Philosophy: Destruction and Experience*, ed. Andrew Benjamin and Peter Osborne (Abingdon: Routledge, 2000), pp. 110–38.
129. Benjamin, 'Critique of Violence', p. 248.
130. Bernstein, *Violence*, p. 61.
131. Benjamin, 'Critique of Violence', p. 250.
132. Ari Hirvonen, 'Marx and God with Anarchism: On Walter Benjamin's Concepts of History and Violence', *Continental Philosophy Review*, 45:5, 2012, pp. 519–43 (p. 535).

133. Katerina Kolozova, 'Violence: The Indispensable Condition of Law (and the Political)', *Angelaki: Journal of the Theoretical Humanities*, 19:2, 2014, pp. 99–111 (p. 101).
134. Benjamin, 'Critique of Violence', p. 250.
135. Ibid. p. 250.
136. Ibid. p. 250.
137. Slavoj Žižek, *Violence* (London: Profile Books, 2009), p. 171.
138. Bernstein, *Violence*, p. 65.
139. Benjamin, 'Critique of Violence', p. 250.
140. Derrida, 'Force of Law', p. 298.
141. Hirvonen, 'The Politics of Revol', p. 109.
142. Benjamin, 'Critique of Violence', p. 252.
143. Ibid. p. 250.
144. Ibid. p. 250.
145. Ibid. p. 250.
146. Ibid. p. 250.
147. Ibid. p. 250.
148. Ibid. p. 251.
149. Alison Ross, 'The Distinction between Mythic and Divine Violence: Walter Benjamin's "Critique of Violence" from the Perspective of "Goethe's Elective Affinities"', *New German Critique*, 41:1, 2014, pp. 93–128 (p. 97).
150. Benjamin, 'Critique of Violence', p. 252.
151. Ibid. p. 252.

CHAPTER 2

Divinity within the Law: Schmitt on the Violence of Sovereignty

For all its revolutionary potential in promising a fundamental rupture with past legal systems, one aspect of Benjamin's essay was almost immediately challenged: the division between divine and legal violence. Whereas Benjamin claimed that only this allows divine violence to expiate mythic-legal violence and so permit revolutionary alteration, it was, for many, problematic insofar as it not only prevented any analysis of divine violence, but, perhaps worse, also permitted any position to claim that its violence was actually divine, leaving it up to fate – based on its success in expiating legal violence – to determine whether it was or not.

The necessity of divine violence emanated from Benjamin's conception of law as a closed system. If law is a closed system, its interruption cannot be an internal event, but must come from 'without', which, in Benjamin's terms, means the divine. For Carl Schmitt, however, law is not a closed system, but one that always contains lacunae that need to be resolved through decisions. Whereas Benjamin argued that the divine was outside of all law, Sigrid Weigel explains that 'Schmitt . . . defines the concepts of constitutional law as seculari[s]ed theological concepts, theology is sublated in constitutional law'.[1] This gives rise to a fundamentally different understanding of the relationship between law, politics, theology, and violence.

We should not, however, think of the Benjamin–Schmitt relationship in strict oppositional terms; it is a highly nuanced and subtle relationship orientated from and around an investigation into similar questions and topic. Indeed, their intellectual interests were sufficiently similar to overcome their not insubstantial biographical differences – Benjamin was, after all, a Jewish, Marxist, literary theorist, whereas Schmitt was a Catholic, conservative, legal scholar who held rabid anti-Semitic views and joined the Nazi party; the very party that Benjamin tragically died trying to escape from – and stimulate contact between them. Benjamin, for example, wrote a letter to Schmitt on 9 December 1930 with a copy of *The Origins of German Tragic Drama*, in which he acknowledged his intellectual debt to Schmitt:

> You will quickly notice how much this book in its presentation of the seventeenth-century doctrine of sovereignty owes to you. Perhaps I could say in passing that I have also inferred from your later work, above all *Die Diktatur*, a confirmation of the research approach of my philosophy of art through your philosophy of [S]tate.[2]

Interestingly, and while it's highly contestable whether this fragment, which as far as we know was not responded to, constitutes, as Jacques Derrida insists, 'a correspondence',[3] it was considered so damning that

> when Gershom Scholem and Theodor Adorno first published an extensive selection of Benjamin's correspondence in 1966, they left out the letter to Schmitt. Apparently, they did not want the memory of Benjamin, who had taken his life while fleeing National Socialism, to be associated with the conservative lawyer, who had actively supported Hitler's Third Reich.[4]

Whatever violence their act of exclusion may have entailed and resulted in, Scholem's and Adorno's reaction was perhaps an understandable one. After all, to this day, there are those who describe the association as, in the assessment of Giorgio Agamben, 'scandalous',[5] while Horst Bredekamp condemns it as 'one of the most irritating incidents in the intellectual history of the Weimar Republic'.[6]

From Schmitt's side, we know that he was influenced by Benjamin's work, or, at least claimed to be after the Second World War. Whether this was due to genuine interest or was part of his attempt to rebuild his shattered image is unclear, but there are references to Benjamin's work in *Hamlet or Hecuba*[7] (published in 1956), while, in 1973, Schmitt wrote to Hansjörg Viesel claiming that his 1938 book *The Leviathan in the State Theory of Thomas Hobbes* was 'a response to Benjamin [that has] remained unnoticed'.[8]

The purpose of this chapter is not to engage in this biographical relationship further,[9] but to argue that, while they were orientated to similar questions, Benjamin and Schmitt differ in the responses given to the question of the relationship between the divine, law, and violence. Rather than making a distinction between divine violence and legal violence, wherein the former lies outside of law to depose the latter through an act of absolute annihilation, Schmitt argues that the divine moment, under the title of sovereignty, is always found 'within' the law. Law is not a closed whole that needs to be violently expiated from without; it always contains *aporias* that require sovereign decisions to resolve them.[10]

Importantly, law is not grounded in an exterior foundation, but is conditioned by, emanates from, and codifies the normless decision of the constituting-power (*pouvoir constituent*) subtending each constitution. As a consequence, Schmitt insists that the constituting-power plays something akin to the role that divine and mythic violence plays in Benjamin's schema. The difference is that the constituting-power is intimately connected to law, rather than being external to it. This alters the nature and meaning of sovereign violence, which is no longer caught between two opposing realms – the divine and legal – but is divided across the two aspects – the constituting-power and the constitution – that constitute law.

Furthermore, the moment of law-making – that is, the moment in which the constituting-power makes the normless decision regarding the constitutional norms that will define it – is not a violent one, but is based on the spontaneous acclamation of the populace. Violence may be part of the pre-juridical exceptional state in which the normless decision about the constitutional order is made, but such an exceptional state is not capable of founding juridical order because it does not permit agreement about the foundational norms that will ground order. It is only once the constituting-power is unified, meaning in sufficient agreement to make an acclamative statement, that law can be founded. Schmitt's point is that violence is not law-making; violence must be absent for law to be founded.

However, while violence is not part of the law-making process, once constitutional law has been created, violence re-enters the scene. As a political entity defined through the friend/enemy distinction, the constitutional sovereign/State finds that he/it must, potentially at least, defend himself/itself against other States that disagree about the fundamental norm to be followed. As a consequence, the existence of the constitutional State is intimately tied to (the possibility of) violence.

To demonstrate this, I first, briefly, outline the relationship between the constituting-power and the constitution, before moving to the question of the role that violence plays in the relationship between the political and juridical by examining Schmitt's distinction between classical, real (= relative), and absolute forms of warfare; a discussion that will show that, for him, the sovereign decision, in both its constituting-power and constitutional forms, is always intimately linked, albeit in different ways, to the violence of war. This means not that Schmitt glorifies war, but that he insists on a delicate balancing act that, on the one hand, recognises the inevitability of war and, indeed, the necessary role it plays in the political decision, but which, on the other hand, claims that the political decision cannot entail the glorification of war or the annihilation of the enemy. It necessarily requires a bracketed *real* war that defeats, rather than aims to annihilate, the enemy.

VIOLENCE AND THE LAW-MAKING PROCESS

Schmitt's *Constitutional Theory*,[11] originally published in 1928, is a wide-ranging work whose main purpose is to offer a theory of the nature and ontogenesis of constitutions. It not only argues that order is created from disorder but also shows how this order is legitimised. Prior to juridical order is a chaotic, exceptional, and violent existence. The decision taken within this state creates order by determining the nature of the legal system. As Paul Kahn explains, 'the sovereign decision . . . exists for the sake of the entire system [meaning that] the sovereign decides outside of law for the sake of law'.[12]

Importantly, Schmitt does not simply equate sovereignty with a particular actor or institution, but shows that this formal (juridical) sense of sovereignty is located in and emanates from a prior source: the sovereignty of the pre-juridical constituting-power. The aim then is not to glorify the exception *per se*, but to account for it and show how order (manifested through the establishment of norms) is created through the sovereign decision in disorder (= normlessness). The creation of order out of chaos is the miraculous moment of political sovereignty whereby, without any solid foundation or norm to help it, the populace pulls itself up by its 'hair' to create a society from the disorder of the exceptional situation.

To explain how this is possible, Schmitt distinguishes between two aspects of each constitution: the constituting-power and the constitution. First introduced in *Dictatorship*, published in 1921, the former accounts for the genesis of constitutions by showing that they are rooted in and gain legitimacy from the popular will. As Schmitt explains

> all constituted powers are opposed to a constituting-power, which lays down the foundations of the constitution. This constituting-power is in principle unlimited and can do everything, because it is not subject to the constitution: it provides the foundation for the constitution itself.[13]

'The constitution-making power is',[14] as Schmitt explains, 'the political will, whose power or authority is capable of making the concrete, comprehensive decision over the type and form of its own political existence'.[15] This decision involves the choice of the foundational norm that underpins the State's political existence: 'every legal order is based on a decision, and also the concept of the legal order, which is applied as something self-evident, contains within it the contrast of the two distinct elements of the juristic – norm and decision'.[16]

Order is not then prior to the decision; order emanates from a decision regarding the norm(s) (= order) of society. This decision is not violently imposed on the populace, but emanates from the popular will.

For this reason, Seyla Benhabib is mistaken in claiming that 'Schmitt's legacy ... disempowers citizens by giving the [S]tate the monopoly of interpretation over its own strategic interests of survival in the *multiversum* of States'.[17] The aim of Schmitt's constitutional theory is to show that each State, as manifested in its constitution, is based on and comes from the decision of the people regarding its own fundamental organisation and values. This is what is most troubling about his analysis. The State does not impose itself on the people; such action would risk producing a fundamental cleavage between the constituting-power and the constitutional State emanating from it. While there is a difference, the constituting-power is always expressed 'in' and through the constitution it creates. As such, the people choose the fundamental values that are expressed through its constitution (= State). It is this that gives the State legitimacy.

This also means that each State, even the most barbarous, is, for Schmitt, a manifestation of the political decision of its people. Responsibility for the actions, norms, values, and structure of the community is shared by all members; there are no scapegoats or factions that impose themselves on the rest. If such fundamental disagreement exists, the State will be riven by internal conflict; a situation that would render the State normless. As such, if factions exist, they survive with the consent of the rest of the populace, meaning that they are an expression of the popular will.

This reaffirms Schmitt's claim that a strong constitutional State needs to be based on agreement over its fundamental values.[18] As David Dyzenhaus puts it, 'Schmitt's view is that a strong State must be based on some set of values which can found the substantive homogeneity of the people, and only once such a basis is in place can space be opened up for either pluralism or values like freedom or autonomy.'[19] Minimal agreement regarding the ends of the society, is, therefore, a precondition for the existence of a political community; it is only once a populace agrees on its fundamental founding social values that social order, based on the creation of norms, can be created and maintained.

There is, then, violent chaos prior to the decision of the constituting-power, but the decision of the constituting-power is not itself violent. As David Pan notes, the constituting-power is not 'a violent and chaotic act that negates order, but the constituting *form* of law that establishes the first set of distinctions and value judgements upon which the law itself is based'.[20] This decision is made because of a violent chaotic state, but is itself nonviolent, being possible only when violence has abated and/because there is sufficient agreement in the population regarding the foundational norms that will establish order.

This is not to say that every legitimating decision of the constituting-power is explicitly made or even made explicit. As George Schwab explains,

> the people, to Schmitt, c[an] make the decision of decisions, namely under what kind of constitution they would like to live ... But once [this] decision ha[s] been made, the people ... recede to the background until again called upon to decide on basic constitutional norms, laws, or just political acts.[21]

This is because 'the people as bearer of the constitution-making power are not a stable, organised organ',[22] and so cannot always implement its vision of society.

It is also why the people, in the form of the constituting-power, delegate administrative duties to constitutional bodies that do implement the political decision regarding the norms of society made by the people, and do so with the blessing of the populace. This is possible because, even if the formless mass of the people cannot formulate detailed policy proposals, they are always 'able to say yes or no to the fundamental questions of their political existence'.[23] Whether a constitutional decision expresses the popular will or not is revealed through the acclamation of the people; that is, whether 'the people ... consent [to] or reject'[24] it. This acclamation is not always explicit – Schmitt mentions that it may be absent in times of peace because there is no need to make a decision regarding the established order – but when expressed, it is always expressed through a simple yes or no.[25]

Contrary to absolutist theories that hold that the constitutional sovereign dominates the populace that chose it, Schmitt holds that the constituting-power founds, conditions, and subtends each constitution, meaning that the latter must continue to express the former. One consequence of this is that constitutional change depends upon the constituting-power subtending each constitution. If a constitution is abolished but the underlying constituting-power remains and reactivates itself in another constitution which 'rests on the same principles as the previous one',[26] the constitution is said to be *eliminated*. In contrast, constitutional *annihilation* entails the annihilation of the entire constitution and the constituting-power that underpins it. With this, a new political decision regarding the values of society is made, one different from the first constituting-power, which means a different constituting-power has arisen, which leads to a change in constitution.

Violence plays a somewhat complicated role in this process. Strictly speaking, *pace* Benjamin, violence is not part of the law-making process; it is part of the state of affairs prior and successive to this process. Schmitt does not explicitly put it in these terms, but the chaos of the exceptional state is violent. Battle commences to determine which way of life and which norm will become dominant over others. This is not an ordered battle, but a chaotic one. Crucially, this chaotic violence must stop to permit order and law, in the form of a constitution, to be made because legal order can only be instantiated when there is sufficient agreement in the constituting-power regarding the norms that do and should dominate and define it. If there is still contention about this, chaos reigns and the conditions – namely, sufficient social unity – necessary to create juridical order will not exist. But, crucially, having established the legal order, violence returns: the constitutional State is a political entity defined by dominant norms that privilege a particular way of life. It will, therefore, come into contact with other States that may not necessarily share its norms and way of life; a situation that may lead to violent conflict. This brings forth an analysis of the relationship between warfare and the juridical-political State, which first requires a few words on the political decision.

THE PROBLEM OF THE POLITICAL

The problem that motivates Schmitt's analysis of the political is the problem of depoliticisation. Schmitt's most explicit comments on this occur in the 1929 lecture 'The Age of Neutralisations and Depoliticisations',[27] a lecture that has, somewhat hyperbolically, been called 'the most disturbing counter-revolutionary manifesto ever written'.[28] Within this lecture, Schmitt charts the historical process through which the political has become downgraded and, increasingly, neutralised.

More specifically, Schmitt mentions a four-stage movement whereby the political was first replaced by the theological so that it was collapsed into and so defined by the theological, which then morphed into the metaphysical view where questions of metaphysics pre-determined or gave inspiration to the political.[29] In turn, the metaphysical view morphed into the humanitarian one, meaning that humanistic concerns orientated the political, which was subsequently overcome by the rise of economics so that the question of the political became associated with 'unbiased economic management'.[30] By subordinating the political to the economic, Schmitt claims that not only has the question of the political been forgotten, but politics itself has become nothing but a dry, sterile discourse based on techno-calculative considerations of economic worth.[31] To correct this, he aims to (1) reveal the essence of the political and so secure a place for the political among other disciplines, and (2) identify how the political, and politics, must be thought and structured to reverse the depoliticisation process.

Rather than define the political negatively, Schmitt looks to provide a 'positive'[32] definition of it. We are therefore told that the political is defined by the friend/enemy distinction, which emanates from a sovereign decision regarding the existential threat posed by a concrete other. The friend/enemy distinction is, for Schmitt, unique to the political and distinguishes it from other spheres such as the moral, defined by the good/bad oppositions, and the aesthetic, defined by the beautiful/ugly opposition. While this secures a unique domain for the political, Schmitt quickly goes beyond this by suggesting that the political distinction is the fundamental one upon which all others depend.[33] To determine why this is the case, he depends upon the notion of 'intensity'.[34]

For Schmitt, each association is defined in terms of the 'intensity of an association or dissociation of human beings',[35] meaning the strength of the bonds that bind the various members of an association. The political is the most intense association, in the sense both of its state of being and of the actions involved, because it is intimately connected to the threat of being physically killed.[36] As Schmitt explains, 'the friend, enemy, and combat concepts receive their real meaning precisely because they refer to the real possibility of physical killing',[37] thereby ensuring that it is 'only in real combat [that] the most extreme consequence of the political grouping of friend and enemy [is revealed]. From this most extreme possibility human life derives its specifically political tension.'[38] The immediate possibility of being physically annihilated not only binds the members together but does so in a state of the highest tension; that is, the most intense state of being.

However, Schmitt also seems to admit that a political association can entail a slightly less intense form of association if it encounters a *potential* violence that threatens the life of the community. In turn, the notion of 'life of the community' seems to entail two options, insofar as it can refer to the physical life of the community or the spiritual values and ideas that define it. Regarding the latter, David Pan explains that the political association is not simply concerned with killing the other or defending itself from the threat of the other; it does so to conserve a way of life. The political decision regarding the other is then always 'expressed in terms of cultural assumptions about the final goals of a society'.[39] As such, the friend/enemy distinction exists on a continuum ranging from (1) a perceived immediate threat of physical annihilation, via (2) a perceived possible threat of physical annihilation and (3) a perceived immediate threat to a way of life or cultural identity, to (4) a perceived possible threat to a way of life or cultural identity.

Crucially, determining whether the other poses a threat requires that its actions be *perceived* as such. Only then will the various members intensify their bonds to form a political association. As Schmitt puts it, 'the political does not reside in the battle itself . . . but in the mode of behaviour which is determined by . . . clearly evaluating the concrete situation and . . . being able to distinguish correctly the real friend and the real enemy'.[40] This is underpinned by the community's pre-reflective conception of how the world is and should be. It is this schema that allows 'the actual participants [to] correctly recognise, understand, and judge the concrete situation and settle the extreme case of conflict'.[41]

While Schmitt warns that the specifics must be worked out by the individuals involved, he is clear that a political association requires, as a minimum condition, that the other is a 'stranger . . . [who is] in a[n] [e]specially intense way, existentially something different and alien'.[42] Far from being an 'objective' determination, the status of the other depends upon a number of 'subjective' interpretations regarding the nature of selfhood and otherness, including the other's actions and intentions, and prescriptions as to how social relations with the other should take place. These, in turn, are dependent on the perception of the political community, which is defined by the values it has chosen to define itself by. For this reason, the political is linked to the chosen spiritual values of the community.

Because the political is defined through the friend/enemy distinction, which is based on the (perceived) threat the other poses to the life of the community, Schmitt explains that it is constituted by an intimate relationship to violence, which, because the political is located at the level of the collective, aims at another social collective.[43] For this reason, the political is intimately connected to war. This relationship is unique to the political and re-enforces Schmitt's attempt to identify a privileged place for the political. Indeed, he claims that 'a world in which the possibility of war is utterly eliminated, a completely pacified globe, would be a world without the distinction of friend and enemy and hence a world without politics'.[44]

However, as Ernst Wolfgang Böckenförde[45] points out, linking the political to war does not mean that Schmitt holds that the political aims at war. Confirming this, Schmitt explains that

> the definition of the political suggested here neither favours war nor militarism, neither imperialism nor pacifism. Nor is it an attempt to idealise the victorious war or the successful revolution as a 'social ideal', since neither war nor revolution is something social or something ideal.[46]

War does not define the political because war always presupposes 'that the political decision has already been made as to who the enemy is'.[47] Furthermore, as noted, the political decision is not synonymous with actual war, but arises from its possibility.[48]

Schmitt's description of war is, therefore, rather agnostic. He does not mourn its loss, nor does he advocate it, but recognises that the antagonism inherent in the political requires an enemy and, thus, the possibility of war. Even pacifism, a doctrine that supposedly advocates the abolition of war, is, for Schmitt, thoroughly political because it has identified its enemy: war.[49] Indeed, in clearly and explicitly identifying its enemy, pacifism meets Schmitt's definition of the 'high point' of politics and so is political in the most intense sense.[50]

We have seen then that, for Schmitt, war results from disagreement over the fundamental values of the State and is ultimately, therefore, a confrontation between different social values and ideas. As he insists: 'there exists no rational purpose, no norm no matter how true, no program no matter how exemplary, no social ideal no matter how beautiful, no legitimacy nor legality which could justify men in killing each other'.[51] While this may be thought to call into question my assessment that Schmitt's thinking on the relationship between war and the political entails a battle over values and ideas, Schmitt is here referring to the justification of war. When read in this manner, the above refers to the rejection of *a priori* standards that can determine whether and at what point the other becomes an enemy and so must be fought against. The enemy becomes an enemy when recognised as such, with this recognition coming when the other is perceived to be an existential threat to the community's existence. No prior rule or norm can identify this, and for this reason, it is not possible to determine, in advance, when it is necessary to identify the other as the enemy or when it is necessary to go to war.[52]

This does, however, depend upon an understanding of what constitutes war, which is a problem because, as Schmitt points out, we have become accustomed to thinking that the meaning of warfare is singular, simply pitting one State against other.[53] This, however, ignores the history of warfare, which reveals, at least, three forms of war, based on different types of enmity. Schmitt therefore outlines these, as a precursor to identifying which form of warfare/enmity the political decision should be orientated towards.

VIOLENCE AND CONSTITUTIONAL SOVEREIGNTY

Schmitt starts his analysis with the traditional notion of war, which is rooted in what he calls classical enmity and which is intimately connected to the *jus publicum Europaeum* that arose from the religious wars of the sixteenth and seventeenth centuries.[54] The *jus publicum Europaeum* tried to temper these religious wars by limiting conflict through a number of heavily prescribed norms, including a number of static, immutable oppositions that clearly distinguished 'between war and peace, combatants and non-combatants, enemy and criminal',[55] created an international legal framework that re-enforced these 'rules', and depended upon a particular configuration of political entities whereby each State's spatial limits were clearly demarcated. As a consequence, for the first time, the notion of a State, as opposed to a mere sovereign individual, arose, both in the public consciousness and in international law.[56] This enabled war to move from a private battle between two sovereigns or one conducted against the populace, as had occurred in the religious wars, to battles between States represented by clearly defined armies.

Accompanying this move was the acceptance that States can wage war and that this is not a criminal act. Rather, as Schmitt puts it, 'war became somewhat analogous to a duel'[57] where each combatant recognised the worth of the other and treated him with respect. Importantly,

> compared to the brutality of the religious and factional wars, which by nature are wars of annihilation wherein the enemy is treated as a criminal and a pirate, and compared to colonial wars, which are pursued against 'wild' peoples, European 'war in form' signified the strongest possible rationali[s]ation and humani[s]ation of war.[58]

This form of war was rational and human because it recognised the enemy was a personalised King and so considered it to be a *justus hostis*. Two armies going to war were, in reality, two Kings going to war, meaning it entailed a battle between equals, who recognised themselves as equals.[59] While the enemy was to be defeated, they were not to be annihilated, nor were they to be criminalised.

Furthermore, while a private duel was based on a number of pre-reflective norms that shaped its content and form and distinguished it from pure aggression or crime, it was also subject to witnesses who ensured the 'rules' were followed and, subsequently, recognised the victor. Similarly, in the *jus publicum Europaeum*, there were rules to warfare that distinguished it from pure military aggression, private hatred, or simple crime, with these rules being, to a degree, enforced by the other European States that witnessed the war and recognised the victor. These other States had an interest in upholding conventional warfare because any infraction would potentially establish a new norm of warfare and a return to the barbarity of the religious wars that preceded the *jus publicum Europaeum*. There was, in other words, self-censorship, insofar as each State purposefully and voluntarily limited its actions towards the enemy by recognising the enemy as a *justus hostis*, which was accompanied and re-enforced by external censorship from the other European States.[60]

The capacity to bracket hatred and confront the existential threat in a clear, ordered, and disciplined manner was, as Schmitt puts it, 'real progress'[61] that gave war 'its justice, honour, and worth'.[62] Indeed, in a later text, Schmitt goes further and claims that

> with the bracketing of war, European humanity had achieved something extraordinary: renunciation of the criminali[s]ation of the opponent,

i.e., the relativi[s]ation of enmity, the negation of absolute enmity. That really was extraordinary, even an incredibly human accomplishment, that men disclaimed a discrimination and denigration of the enemy.[63]

The religious wars that preceded the *jus publicum Europaeum* were, in contrast, wars of attrition where the enemy was moralised and/or criminalised, meaning that he had to be annihilated to re-establish right. In many respects, Schmitt sees the *jus publicum Europaeum* as the high point of warfare which has subsequently been undone as warfare has moved back to the moralisation of absolute enmity inherent in religious wars. This feeds into his critique of the depoliticisation process which, far from making war more humane and unnecessary, moralises/criminalises the enemy so that 'he' is perceived to be a dangerous monster to be annihilated.[64]

Importantly, the movement away from the regularity of the *jus publicum Europaeum* came, paradoxically enough, from an incursion by a regular army into another State that simply could not match the strength of the invader. Schmitt locates the movement in the Spanish guerrilla war of 1808.[65] Rather than simply accept defeat, Schmitt claims that the defeated Spanish changed tactics, became irregular, and so gave rise to the notion of the partisan. The partisan is a modern figure of warfare defined by a particular relationship to war and enmity,[66] insofar as it describes any non-State actor who resorts to violence or terror to pursue their stated political aims.

However, while the partisan is a non-State actor, each partisan is always dependent on what Schmitt calls 'an interested third',[67] who is a State actor. For this reason, the partisan operates outside of the State in the service of the State. Whereas the *jus publicum Europaeum* was constituted around strict rules of engagement, the partisan, while still being a member of a political union, does not conform to these strict rules. Schmitt identifies four aspects that distinguish the partisan from the regular soldier: (1) irregularity, (2) increased mobility, (3) political intensity, and (4) a telluric nature.[68]

The partisan's irregularity emanates from his dress and from his place in relation to the enemy. Whereas the armies of classic war/enmity wore their insignia in open view, displayed their allegiance and engaged one another openly, the partisan hides or disguises himself.[69] This allows him to be highly mobile, utilising his speed and surprise to ambush the enemy; a tactic helped by the fact that the partisan operates in small groups that can move far more easily than the great armies of classical war. This is linked to the partisan's intensity of engagement which is much greater than that of the regular soldier.[70] The partisan is not simply a paid soldier following orders, but is, to a degree, autonomous and innovative. The fight against the enemy can take place any time anywhere, meaning that the partisan is always ready for it.

The final criterion that Schmitt identifies is the telluric nature of the partisan, meaning that he is concerned with a particular political territory.[71] It is this telluric link that ensures the partisan is distinguished from both the pirate and the thief. While all three are irregular, the partisan is orientated towards a public notion of territory that he aims to defend, whereas the pirate and thief are orientated solely towards private gain and, in the instance of the former, located at sea.

Schmitt's point in describing the partisan is not only to show how different forms of war arose, but also to highlight that the arena of war has become much more heterogeneous. Despite this additional complexity, however, he claims that the enemy of the partisan was treated as a political opponent, with the consequence that the partisan engages in an intense yet limited, or bracketed, engagement with the enemy-other and so 'has a real . . . not an absolute enemy'.[72]

Furthermore, it must be remembered that the partisan fights for a particular political territory, meaning that his actions, while irregular, are conducted within and for specific spatio-temporal boundaries. Gabriella Slomp takes this to mean that the fundamental feature of (limited) real enmity is not that it contains a different level of intensity to other forms of enmity but that it is spatio-temporally limited: 'Schmitt's concept of limited enmity does not mean that enmity is limited in intensity but rather that it is limited to specific targets that are circumscribed in space and time.'[73]

However, while there is no doubt that the telluric nature of the partisan means that spatial constraints are an aspect of the factors that define his comportment towards the enemy and distinguish it from classical enmity,[74] Slomp's attempt to remove all intensive features seems a step too far. It not only contradicts Schmitt's claim that the partisan is far more intensively engaged than the State soldiers of the *jus publicum Europaeum*, but also seems to ignore the fact that the partisan's limitations are not necessarily quantitative; that is, he is not simply limited because he attempts to overcome a particular target that exists within spatio-temporal co-ordinates, but is also limited because he has a real enemy not an absolute one. *Contra* Slomp, therefore, the distinction between classical, real, and absolute enmity cannot be reduced to differences in spatio-temporal reach, but is *also* determined by the intensity of the political community, which, it will be remembered, is premised on the strength of the ties that bind the political community together, the values it has chosen to define itself from and through, and the actions of others.

Importantly, however, we also need to recognise that Schmitt differentiates between the (1) autochthonous partisan and (2) global revolutionary partisan.[75] So far, the focus has been on the former type of partisan who is tied to a particular spatio-temporal configuration and is linked to a real enemy. The global revolutionary partisan, however, abstracts from this spatio-temporal configuration and fights a war over abstract principles that have global significance. Furthermore, whereas the autochthonous partisan is telluric, limited, and concrete, the global revolutionary is globally orientated, expansive, and focused on the abstract. As a consequence, the autochthonous partisan wages a war against a real enemy, whereas a global revolutionary wages one against an absolute enemy who must be *annihilated* rather than simply defeated. There is, in other words, a '*justa causa* without recognition of a *justus hostis*'.[76] For this reason, the global revolutionary partisan is intimately connected to absolute enmity.

Absolute enmity is the most intense form of enmity because it takes its cue from morality. Rather than accept an alternative way of doing things and/or the right of the State to conduct war, as the classical enmity of the *jus publicum Europaeum* and, to a lesser degree, real enmity accept, absolute enmity passes judgement on the actions of the enemy. This moralisation leads to a war that is

> unusually intense and inhuman because, by transcending the limits of the political framework, it simultaneously degrades the enemy into moral and other categories and is forced to make of him a monster that must not only be defeated but also utterly destroyed.[77]

By taking its cue from morality rather than politics, absolute enmity not only contributes to the depoliticisation process that Schmitt laments, but also cultivates a far more savage and brutal form of warfare. This feeds into Schmitt's attempt to show that morality is and must be grounded in a political decision because if it is not, only brutality follows. This goes against many commonly held assumptions that see the moral realm as being in some way superior to the political one because it entails a closer affinity to justice. In contrast, Schmitt sees it as an attempt to affirm universality, which can only lead to dogmatism, moralising judgement, criminalisation, and the attempt to annihilate the other.

Schmitt bases this assessment on the implicit claim that morality is structured around a same/other dichotomy wherein the other is held to be wholly other; a position that makes it easier to hold that the other must be destroyed. For this reason, absolute enmity is the most intense form of engagement, the most 'free', and the most global. It is not constrained by 'respect' for the enemy, spatio-temporal concerns, or (inter)national law. The absolute enemy is understood to be so dangerous that anything and everything must be done to annihilate it.

The point in highlighting the unbracketed intensity of absolute enmity is not only to outline as fully as possible Schmitt's understanding of the different forms of political enmity, but also to re-enforce my argument that reducing Schmitt's analysis of enmity to distinctions between the spatial ambitions of the enemy fails to take into account the crucial role that intensity plays in Schmitt's analysis of the political. We can only distinguish between the *jus publicum Europaeum*, autochthonous partisan, and global revolutionary partisan, and remain true to Schmitt's claim regarding the increased intensity inherent in the partisan and absolute enmity, if we recognise that all are distinguished by their spatial orientations *and* degree of political intensity.

This leads to a hierarchy in which the classical enmity of the *jus publicum Europaeum* has the least intensive political relationship to the enemy in that it respects the enemy and aims to defeat rather than annihilate it; real enmity has a more intense relationship, but continues to recognise some form of equality with the enemy and so brackets the conflict to defeat it, not annihilate it; while the most intense relationship is found in the absolute enmity of the global revolutionary partisan, who not only abstracts from a particular spatio-temporal territory but also moralises and obsesses over the abstract immoral enemy to the point that the only possible response is for the enemy to be annihilated.

Slomp rejects this hierarchy because she claims that all war entails killing and, because 'nothing can be more intense than killing and dying'.[78] As a consequence, she concludes that all war is equally intense. Intensity, in other words, cannot be used to distinguish between different forms of war. What can distinguish between the forms of enmity is the size of the territory towards which the enmity is directed. However, it is not clear how Slomp can reconcile Schmitt's differentiated understanding of the partisan (i.e. the partisan can be autochthonous or global) with his analysis of the different types of enmity/war and insistence that intensity distinguishes the political from the non-political. If Slomp is correct and the distinguishing feature of the different forms of enmity is their quantitative geographical scope, how does this fit into Schmitt's insistence that the political – which is defined by the relationship to the enemy (and friend) – is defined from intensity? Surely, if the enemy is defined *quantitatively*, the political, which is defined by perception of the enemy, should also be *quantitatively* defined; yet Schmitt insists it is *qualitatively* defined by virtue of entailing the greatest degree of antagonistic intensity.

Therefore, what actually distinguishes the different types of enmity is not simply the act of killing or the breadth of territory upon which the enemy exists, but *also* the way in which the enemy is perceived and, from this, the way the combatants comport themselves towards each other. Slomp's reduction of enmity to quantifiable spatio-temporal distinctions remains purely externally focused and is unable to account for how the perception of the enemy shapes the actions and understanding of each political community. As Schmitt reminds us, it is the understanding of the enemy that gives rise to the type of enmity that defines the political.[79] The defining difference is not simply that the enemy of the conventional army is more geographically localised than the autochthonous real enemy, which is a more geographically focused enemy than the globalised enemy of the revolutionary partisan, but that the enmity of classical war is also less intense than the real enmity of the autochthonous partisan, which is less intense than the absolute enmity of the revolutionary partisan. This intensity results from the actions of the other which are interpreted through the spiritual values that the community has chosen to define itself by. It is only by placing intensity at the heart of the distinction that Schmitt's understanding of the partisan can be made consistent with his differentiated understanding of war and analysis of the relationship between the political and non-political, which, it will be remembered, claims that it is the intensity of the antagonism that distinguishes the political from the non-political.[80]

Slomp rejects this because she claims that, if intensity is taken to be the distinguishing feature of the different types of enmity, 'we would be bound to claim that the political for Schmitt assumes absolute enmity'.[81] This argument is repeatedly found in the secondary literature, but is one that fails to properly understand the relationship between enmity, intensity, and the political. To unravel this confusion, the concluding section turns to discuss the type of enmity that Schmitt associates with the political.

CONCLUSION: THE POLITICAL AND REAL ENMITY

Schmitt's overall point regarding the three forms of enmity is that the development of the depoliticisation process has resulted not in the disappearance of war, but rather its opposite: the intensification of war. This thesis is part of Schmitt's attempt to combat the 'myth' that the abolition of the political will lead to a peaceful existence. The depoliticisation process has led to and will lead to the *intensification* of war as the bracketing of war synonymous with the political is overtaken by the moralisation of the enemy.

Schmitt is highly critical of this move, seeing it as an occurrence that can only lead to 'enmity becoming so frightening that perhaps one no longer should speak of the enemy or enmity, and both should be outlawed and damned in all their forms before the work of destruction can begin'.[82] For Schmitt, the political enemy is always a real enemy, one who is fought against in relative terms, in accordance with a sense of soldierly respect which has the definite aim of defending defined territories. Only real enmity can stop the blood-letting that accompanies absolute enmity. As a consequence, he maintains that the political is tied to a bracketed war based on real enmity.[83]

However, a number of commentators have expressed concern about the relationship between Schmitt's use of intensity as the criterion that distinguishes the political from the non-political, his insistence that the political is the most intense antagonism, and his subsequent affirmation of real enmity.

Giovanni Sartori argues that because Schmitt privileges the political, based on the conflictually determined friend/enemy division, over other non-political antagonisms and maintains that intensity is the criterion that differentiates the political from the non-political, Schmitt should conclude that (1) the political friend–enemy antagonism takes precedence over other non-political antagonisms, and (2) 'within' the political antagonism, there are degrees of intensity, with absolute intensity being the 'purest' form of the political. If coherently adhered to, Schmitt's arguments should, therefore, lead to '(i) "hot politics", to conceiving politics as all the more authentic the more it was passionate, emotionally loaded and ideologically heated, and all the way to (ii) the absolute enemy, all the way to the foe'.[84] Because he does not follow this path, Sartori charges that Schmitt's argument is logically inconsistent. For Sartori, Schmitt's conception of the political should lead to a politics of absolute destruction, with this revealing his lack of 'moral scruples'[85] and presumably his political affiliations.

Richard Bernstein[86] agrees with this assessment, stating that that there is nothing in Schmitt's conceptual categories that allows him to distinguish between real and absolute enmity in a way that permits the privileging of the former, while Kam Shapiro approves of the general orientation of these criticisms, to conclude that it demonstrates that Schmitt's justification for real enmity is simply arbitrary.[87] Bernstein and Shapiro do, however, disagree on the reasons behind Schmitt's unjustified preference for real enmity, with Bernstein claiming that it is not simply arbitrary, but demonstrates that Schmitt's thinking emanates from an implicit normative-moral stance, which, by making the political dependent on the moral, undermines the privileged place Schmitt gives to the political.

While, on first acquaintance, these criticisms may appear to reveal a logical inconsistency in Schmitt's argument, insofar as he rejects the moralisation of the enemy that his intensity criterion seems to require, if we remember that Schmitt (1) is fighting against the depoliticisation process to identify an autonomous, privileged sphere for the political, and (2) claims that the political friend/enemy distinction emanates from the possibility of an existential conflict from the other, we see that this is not the case.

Given that Schmitt wants to maintain the political, he must find a way to preserve conflict and, through this, the friend/enemy distinction. The problem with moralising the enemy is that it leads to the desire to annihilate the enemy, an action that would kill him and, in doing so, lead to the annihilation of the political. As Schmitt explains, 'as long as a people exists in the political sphere, this people must ... determine by itself the distinction of friend and enemy ... When it no longer possesses the capacity or will to make this distinction, it ceases to exist politically.'[88] If the populace is incapable of distinguishing between its friends and enemies because, for example, it has killed all its enemies then it can no longer exist politically. What remains is not 'politics or State, but civili[s]ation, economics, morality, law, art, entertainment etc.'.[89] Rather than a positive event, a world without the white heat of political conflict is, on Schmitt's telling, a world empty of meaning and conditioned by absolute enmity and the barbarity this entails.

For this reason, Mathias Lievens is correct to note that Schmitt's analysis calls not for blood-letting in the name of the State, but for 'a metapolitical struggle against depolitici[s]ing types of spirit or ways of thinking and for the particular spiritual form that makes conflicts political in the first place'.[90] If the political decision gives existence ultimate meaning, any attempt to abolish the conflict of the political in the name of peace would annihilate the fundamentally important aspect of our existence. If the enemy were annihilated, as absolute enmity demands, the distinction that conditions the political would also disappear and with it the political. To secure the existence of the political and fight the depoliticisation process, the political distinction must exist, which requires that the enemy continues to exist. Absolute enmity prevents this, while real enmity permits it. As such, the continued existence of the political requires the latter.

Schmitt's analysis of sovereign violence is, then, complicated. Prior to the advent of a constitutional order, violence is inherent in the chaotic exceptional state. But, for law to be created, such violence must stop to allow the populace to spontaneously agree – through an acclamative act – on its foundational values. Only this permits the advent of law and (constitutional) politics. However, having created a constitutional political system, violence returns to play a fundamental, if not always explicit, role in the juridical-political system as the constitutional State comes into contact with others who may not necessarily share its fundamental values.

From here, Schmitt advocates a difficult balancing act that, on the one hand, recognises the inevitability of war and, indeed, the necessary role it plays in the juridical-political system; while, on the other hand, claiming that if the constitutional sovereign is not to dissolve its political status or find itself in the chaotic, normless situation of absolute warfare, it must bracket its enmity and engage in real warfare against its designated others. This is a subtle and differentiated understanding of the tangled bond between violence and the juridical-political sphere, but it is one that was subsequently challenged by, amongst others, Hannah Arendt, who emphasised the role that discussion rather than decision plays in maintaining and preserving juridical order. It is to her thought that we now turn.

NOTES

1. Sigrid Weigel, *Walter Benjamin: Images, the Creaturely, and the Holy*, trans. Chadwick Truscott Smith (Stanford: Stanford University Press, 2013), p. 62.
2. Walter Benjamin, *Gesammelte Briefe* (Frankfurt-am-Main: Suhrkamp, 1997), vol. 3, p. 558.
3. Jacques Derrida, 'Force of Law: The "Mystical Foundation of Authority"', trans. Mary Quaintance, p. 281, in *Acts of Religion*, ed. Gil Andjar (Abingdon: Routledge, 2002), pp. 230–98.
4. Marc de Wilde, 'Meeting Opposites: The Political Theologies of Walter Benjamin and Carl Schmitt', *Philosophy and Rhetoric*, 44:4, 2011, pp. 363–81 (p. 364). De Wilde quotes Jacob Taubes's description of his exchange with Adorno when he (Taubes), having discovered the letter, confronted Adorno over its existence to ask why it had not been included in Benjamin's correspondence: "'A letter like that doesn't exist, was the answer. I say, Teddy, I know the handwriting, I know the typewriter Benjamin wrote with, don't tell me stories, I've got it right here! Can't be. Typically German answer. So I made a copy and sent it to him.' This description is found in Jacob Taubes, *The Political Theology of Paul*, trans. Dana Hollander (Stanford: Stanford University Press, 2004), p. 98.
5. Giorgio Agamben, *State of Exception*, trans. Kevin Attell (Chicago: University of Chicago Press, 2005), p. 53.
6. Horst Bredekamp, 'Walter Benjamin to Carl Schmitt, via Thomas Hobbes', trans. Melissa Thorson Hause and Jackson Bond, *Critical Inquiry*, 25:2, 1999, pp. 247–66 (p. 247).
7. Carl Schmitt, *Hamlet or Hecuba: The Interruption of Time in the Play*, trans. Simona Draghici (Oregon: Plutarch Press, 2006), pp. 8, 51–6.
8. Hansjörg Viesel, *Jawohl, der Schmitt: Zehn Briefe aus Plettenberg* (Berlin Support, 1988), p. 14.
9. There are very few book-length studies of the relationship between the two thinkers. One that provides a good overview is Susanne Heil, *Gefährliche Beziehungen: Walter Benjamin und Carl Schmitt* (Stuttgart: J. B. Metzler, 1996).
10. For a more detailed discussion of the normless nature of the Schmittian sovereign decision, see Gavin Rae, *The Problem of Political Foundations in Carl Schmitt and Emmanuel Levinas* (Basingstoke: Palgrave Macmillan, 2016), ch. 4.
11. Carl Schmitt, *Constitutional Theory*, trans. Jeffrey Seitzer (Durham: Duke University Press, 2008).
12. Paul Kahn, *Political Theology: Four New Chapters on the Concept of Sovereignty* (New York: Columbia University Press, 2012), p. 50.
13. Carl Schmitt, *Dictatorship*, trans. Michael Hoelzl and Graham Ward (Cambridge: Polity Press, 2014), p. 121.
14. Schmitt, *Constitutional Theory*, p. 125.
15. Ibid. p. 125, italics removed from the original.
16. Carl Schmitt, *Political Theology: Four Chapters on the Concept of Sovereignty*, trans. George Schwab (Chicago: University of Chicago Press, 2005), p. 10.
17. Seyla Benhabib, 'Carl Schmitt's Critique of Kant: Sovereignty and International Law', *Political Theory*, 40:6, 2012, pp. 688–713 (p. 706).
18. Carl Schmitt, *The Crisis of Parliamentary Democracy*, trans. Ellen Kennedy (Cambridge, MA: MIT Press, 1988), p. 9; Schmitt, *Constitutional Theory*, p. 258; Carl Schmitt, *Legality and Legitimacy*, trans. Jeffrey Seitzer (Durham: Duke University Press, 2004), p. 28.

19. David Dyzenhaus, 'Putting the State Back in Credit', p. 80, in *The Challenge of Carl Schmitt*, ed. Chantel Mouffe (London: Verso, 1999), pp. 75–91.
20. David Pan, 'Carl Schmitt on Culture and Violence in the Political Decision', *Telos*, 142, Spring, 2008, pp. 49–72 (p. 67).
21. George Schwab, *The Challenge of the Exception: An Introduction to the Political Ideas of Carl Schmitt between 1921 and 1936* (Berlin: Duncker and Humblot, 1970), p. 114.
22. Schmitt, *Constitutional Theory*, p. 131.
23. Ibid. p. 131.
24. Ibid. p. 131.
25. Ibid. p. 132.
26. Ibid. p. 141.
27. Carl Schmitt, 'The Age of Neutralisations and Depoliticisations', trans. Mathias Konzeit and John P. McCormick, in *The Concept of the Political*, trans. Georg Schwab (Chicago: University of Chicago Press, 1996), pp. 80–96.
28. Gopal Balakrishnan, *The Enemy: An Intellectual Portrait of Carl Schmitt* (London: Verso, 2000), p. 125.
29. Schmitt, 'The Age of Neutralisations and Depoliticisations', p. 82.
30. Schmitt, *Political Theology*, p. 65.
31. Schmitt, 'The Age of Neutralisations and Depoliticisations', p. 82.
32. Carl Schmitt, *The Concept of the Political*, trans. Georg Schwab (Chicago: University of Chicago Press, 1996), p. 26.
33. Ibid. pp. 29, 37, 38.
34. Ibid. p. 26.
35. Ibid. p. 36.
36. Ibid. p. 37.
37. Ibid. p. 33.
38. Ibid. p. 35.
39. Pan, 'Carl Schmitt on Culture and Violence', p. 50.
40. Schmitt, *The Concept of the Political*, p. 37.
41. Ibid. p. 27.
42. Ibid. p. 27.
43. Ibid. p. 35.
44. Ibid. p. 35.
45. Ernst W. Böckenförde, 'The Concept of the Political: A Key to Understanding Carl Schmitt's Constitutional Theory', *Canadian Journal of Law and Jurisprudence*, 10:1, 1997, pp. 5–19 (p. 6).
46. Schmitt, *The Concept of the Political*, p. 33.
47. Ibid. p. 34.
48. Ibid. pp. 34–5.
49. Ibid. p. 36.
50. Ibid. p. 67.
51. Ibid. p. 49.
52. Ibid. p. 27.
53. Carl Schmitt, 'The Turn to the Discriminating Concept of War', p. 37, in *Writings on War*, ed. and trans. Timothy Nunan (Cambridge: Polity, 2011), pp. 30–74.
54. Carl Schmitt, *The Nomos of the Earth in the International Law of the Jus Publicum Europaeum*, trans. G. L. Ulmen (New York: Telos, 2006), p. 140.
55. Carl Schmitt, *Theory of the Partisan: Intermediate Commentary on the Concept of the Political*, trans. G. L. Ulmen (New York: Telos, 2007), p. 9.

56. Schmitt, *The Nomos of the Earth*, p. 145.
57. Ibid. p. 141.
58. Ibid. p. 142.
59. Ibid. pp. 143–4.
60. Ibid. p. 143.
61. Ibid. p. 14.
62. Schmitt, 'The Turn to the Discriminating Concept of War', p. 71.
63. Schmitt, *Theory of the Partisan*, p. 90.
64. Schmitt, *The Concept of the Political*, p. 36.
65. Schmitt, *Theory of the Partisan*, p. 4.
66. Ibid. p. 10.
67. Ibid. p. 75.
68. Ibid. p. 22.
69. Ibid. p. 14.
70. Ibid. p. 14.
71. Ibid. p. 92.
72. Ibid. p. 92.
73. Gabriella Slomp, *Carl Schmitt and the Politics of Hostility, Violence and Terror* (Basingstoke: Palgrave Macmillan, 2009), p. 11.
74. See, for example, Schmitt, *Theory of the Partisan*, p. 92.
75. Ibid. p. 30.
76. Ibid. p. 30.
77. Schmitt, *The Concept of the Political*, p. 36.
78. Slomp, *Carl Schmitt and the Politics of Hostility, Violence and Terror*, p. 91.
79. Schmitt, *The Concept of the Political*, pp. 34–5.
80. Ibid. pp. 36–7.
81. Slomp, *Carl Schmitt and the Politics of Hostility, Violence and Terror*, p. 94.
82. Schmitt, *Theory of the Partisan*, p. 94.
83. Ibid. p. 92.
84. Giovanni Sartori, 'The Essence of the Political in Carl Schmitt', *Journal of Theoretical Politics*, 1:1, 1989, pp. 63–75 (pp. 71–2).
85. Ibid. p. 67.
86. Richard Bernstein, 'The Aporias of Carl Schmitt', *Constellations*, 18:3, 2011, pp. 403–30 (pp. 418, 423).
87. Kam Shapiro, *Carl Schmitt and the Intensification of the Political* (New York: Rowman & Littlefield, 2008), p. 71.
88. Schmitt, *The Concept of the Political*, p. 49.
89. Ibid. p. 53.
90. Mathias Lievens, 'Carl Schmitt's Metapolitics', *Constellations*, 20:1, 2013, pp. 121–37 (p. 121).

CHAPTER 3

Violence and Power: Arendt on the Logic of Totalitarianism

Hannah Arendt's thinking is intimately, if not always explicitly, tied to the question of sovereign violence. By holding that inquiries should take off from experience, she contended with issues – concentration camps, the Holocaust, the rise of totalitarianism, and so on – that she witnessed in her life. Her conclusion was that these events were underpinned by a Hobbesian conception of sovereignty whose 'basis and ultimate end is accumulation of power'.[1]

For Arendt, Hobbes is a key figure in the development of totalitarianism because his conception of sovereignty is implicitly premised on a certain configuration of society, itself dependent on particular norms and values that privilege war and discrimination. By making the sovereign absolute, she claims that Hobbes removed public participation from politics, thereby confining the ordinary citizen to private activities: 'excluded from participation in the management of public affairs that involves all citizens, the individual loses his rightful place in society and his natural connection with his fellow man'.[2]

Furthermore, consigning citizens to the private sphere in this manner fails to recognise that this arena continues to depend on the public sphere. That citizens cannot participate in public life means that they are excluded from the law-making process that their private life depends upon. As such, their 'private' success or failure – which is contingent on (public) law – is dependent on actions and content beyond their control.

This is problematic because bourgeois morality (mistakenly) holds that those who fail do so because of some personal imperfection on their part. Their failure is then their own, rather than due to circumstances beyond their control. Based on this premise, such failure cannot be 'rewarded' through welfare programmes or subsidies, with the consequence that the poor are cast out of society. This, however, creates a division between those included and those excluded from law, a division that can only lead to conflict and the need for a strong sovereign to reimpose juridical and social order. As a result, Hobbes's conception of sovereignty has as a pre-condition the exclusion of some, since it is only if some are excluded from society and subsequently forced to compete with those included that the chaos needed to justify absolute sovereignty can be generated.

Furthermore, by claiming that sovereignty is orientated towards the accumulation of power, Arendt also claims that Hobbes's sovereign must continually find new forms of instability to stabilise: 'only by acquiring more power can it guarantee the status quo; only by constantly extending its authority and only through the process of power accumulation can it remain stable'.[3] This reveals the paradox underpinning Hobbes's theory of sovereignty: it justifies itself with the aim of securing order, but doing so requires the ever-present possibility of war; only this 'guarantees the Commonwealth a prospect of permanence because it makes it possible for the State to increase its power at the expense of other [S]tates'.[4] Thus, in order to secure stable peace, Hobbes's sovereign must perpetually wage war:

> By 'Victory or Death', the Leviathan can indeed overcome all political limitations that go with the existence of other peoples and can envelop the whole earth in its tyranny. But when the last war has come and every man has been provided for, no ultimate peace is established on earth ... If the last victorious Commonwealth cannot proceed to 'annex the planets', it can only proceed to destroy itself in order to begin anew the never-ending process of power generation.[5]

Arendt's reading of Hobbes has been criticised, namely because it is based on the notion that sovereignty is orientated towards the accumulation of power,[6] but her critique is important for our purposes because it demonstrates her rejection of the classic-juridical notion of sovereignty. By locating sovereignty in a single absolute figure orientated around juridical order, she maintains that Hobbes laid the foundations for totalitarianism, which is based on exactly that premise.

According to Arendt, the same applies to Rousseau's notion of the sovereignty of the general will. While Arendt recognises that this locates sovereignty in a collective, rather than in the singular 'figure' that Hobbes did, she argues that it depends upon the populace being homogeneous and so prefigures and justifies the emphasis that totalitarian regimes place on such homogeneity.[7] Her conclusion is that 'if men wish to be free, it is precisely sovereignty they must renounce'.[8] While this seems to indicate that she rejects the notion of 'sovereignty' in its entirety, I will argue that her comment only applies to the classic-juridical form of sovereignty; she actually points to another form of sovereignty that is explicitly opposed to the logic underpinning the (Hobbesian-Rousseauian inspired) classic-juridical model.

While her 1929 doctoral dissertation on love in Augustine has little to say on the question of violence, her focus seemed to change after the Nazis' ascension to power in 1933, with the topic pervading, if only implicitly, her famous analyses of totalitarianism and revolution.[9] One of her first explicit discussions of the issue is found in an essay published on 14 November 1941, called 'The Jewish Army: The Beginning of Jewish Politics?', in which she calls for the establishment of a Jewish army to 'battle against Hitler as Jews, in Jewish battle formations under a Jewish flag'.[10] Specifically, she warns that this would not come about through divine intervention or the actions of 'leaders', but from the Jewish people themselves:

> We will never get that army if the Jewish people do not demand it and are not prepared by the hundreds of thousands with weapons in hand to fight for their freedom and the right to live as a people. Only the people themselves, young and old, poor and rich, men and women, can reshape public opinion, which today is against us. *For only the people themselves are strong enough for a true alliance.*[11]

With this, Arendt recognises that violence, as a communal activity, can take political form and, indeed, must do so to combat Nazism.

The notion that politics is based on communal action continues to find expression in her later *On Violence*, first published in 1970, where power and, therefore, politics are associated with 'the human ability not just to act but to act in concert'.[12] However, there is also a fundamental distinction between the Arendt of 'The Jewish Army' and the Arendt of *On Violence*, wherein the former accepts that violence can be *constitutive* of political action, insofar as the creation of a Jewish army to combat Nazism is a communal action based on popular will; while, in the later 1970 text, she rejects this: power and violence are and must be diametrically opposed, with violence relegated to being a short-term *instrument* of politics. Furthermore, in 'The Jewish Army', Arendt argues that violence has a positive role to play in politics, while this is rejected in *On Violence*, where violence has a negative function, insofar as it clears a space from and in which the discussion necessary for politics and the establishment of the State can take place.

To account for this alteration, I argue that we have to turn to her account of fabrication in *The Human Condition* (from 1958).[13] Here, she maintains that all acts of fabrication involve violence and that this violence is necessary to permit the creation of a communal and hence political world. The final stage is to recognise that the political is a diachronic activity and so must be continuously (re)made. As such, she repeats the position pointed to in 'The Jewish Army' that violence is necessary and *constitutive* of the juridical-political.

Towards the end of *The Human Condition*, however, Arendt becomes more critical of this connection and, in particular, the influence that the instrumental logic inherent in 'fabrication' has had on the political in the modern age.[14] Specifically, she maintains that, rather than value the end of action over the means, the modern age has come to privilege the means over the end, with the consequence that the political has gone from being concerned with communal action based on discourse to being defined by continuous individual (means-based) action. The privileging of instrumental logic and the attempt to remove value from things themselves so that they can be considered 'pure means' lies, for Arendt, at the heart of totalitarianism. As such, she rejects Benjamin's and, as we will see, Agamben's affirmation of a politics of pure means. These simply continue to affirm the fetishisation of the modern form of fabrication that lies at the root of totalitarianism.

In *On Violence*, Arendt's solution is to reaffirm that politics must be created, which ties her analysis to her comments on fabrication, all the while insisting that this creation has to be based on a form of discussion that is structured differently to the means–end logic inherent in fabrication. Politics must be created (through discussion) not fabricated (according to a prior plan). For this reason, the violence of fabrication will not be part of the genesis or constitution of the political. Instead, violence can only be an instrument of politics, albeit one of short-term application and last resort. With this, she departs from the classic-juridical model by pluralising the ground of sovereignty, but remains bound to it by holding that violence is an instrument through which sovereignty re-establishes and maintains order.

VIOLENCE AND THE HUMAN CONDITION

The Human Condition is, perhaps, Arendt's best-known purely *philosophical* work. In it, she sets out to offer a 'reconsideration of the human condition from the vantage point of our newest experiences and our most recent fears'.[15] By this, she means the new political realities that were created and experienced in the first half of the twentieth century: communism, fascism, the Gulags, mass exterminations, totalitarianism, and so on. These experiences could not be adequately explained within and from the confines of previous theories and so required a new analysis. To achieve this, she proposes to do 'nothing more than to think what we are doing'.[16]

The question of doing is broken into three components – labour, work, and action – because these are 'the basic conditions under which life on earth has been given to man'.[17] Labour 'is the activity which corresponds to the biological process of the human body, whose spontaneous growth, metabolism, and eventual decay are bound to the vital necessities produced and fed into the life process by labour'.[18] It is then intimately bound up with the self-perpetuation of life itself.

Work 'is the activity which corresponds to the unnaturalness of human existence, which is not imbedded in, and whose mortality is not compensated by, the species' ever-recurring life-cycle'.[19] It is tied to the '"artificial" world of things, distinctly different from all natural surroundings'.[20] Through work, the individual creates the artificial things that populate, define, and create a world for himself. As such, work is tied to the production of goods.

Action is 'the only activity that goes on directly between men without the intermediary of things or matter'.[21] It therefore 'corresponds to the human condition of plurality, to the fact that men, not Man, live on the earth and inhabit the world'.[22] It is, in other words, through action that individuals interact with one another. It is *'the* condition – not only the *conditio sine qua non*, but the *conditio per quam* – of all political life'.[23] Politics is not then defined by an abstract essence, but, as Steve Buckler explains, 'is constituted by speech and action undertaken by plural beings in public view, interacting on the basis of autonomous viewpoints and freely-formed opinions'.[24]

Work, labour, and action are distinct, but intimately related to one another. While each aspect is key to the human condition, each has its place. As Paul Voice explains, for Arendt,

> we are most fully ourselves when we speak with our equals in the agora, engaged in the political realm, sharing a common world (that is, a common reality) created through work, and this is possible because the labour required to reproduce us as individuals (enabling our capacities for work and action) has been accomplished by someone.[25]

Work, labour, and action are also intimately tied to 'birth and death, natality and mortality'.[26] Labour, for example, 'assures not only individual survival, but the life of the species. Work and its product, the human artefact, bestow a measure of permanence and durability upon the futility of mortal life and the fleeting character of human time.'[27] In turn, action founds and preserves political bodies and so 'creates the condition for remembrance, that is, for history'.[28]

Arendt explains that work, labour, and action are 'rooted in natality in so far as they have the task to provide the world for, to foresee and reckon with, the constant influx of newcomers who are born into the world as strangers'.[29] The human world is not static, but is always being refreshed through individual actions and the introduction into the world of new children. This requires additional labour and work to provide the resources and structures to deal with these.[30] There is then no fixed, ahistoric political world for Arendt; it is continuously shaken up and refreshed through individual actions and the introduction of new children. This is an ongoing process, meaning that the political world needs to be continually updated, which always permits the possibility of starting afresh. For this reason, Arendt concludes that 'natality, not mortality . . . may be the central category of political . . . thought'.[31]

Individuals therefore find themselves living in a world that they condition and which, in turn, conditions them. Thus,

> the objectivity of the world – its object- or thing-character – and the human condition supplement each other; because human existence is conditional existence, it would be impossible without things, and things would be a heap of unrelated articles, a non-world, if they were not the conditioners of human existence.[32]

Individual life, 'in so far as it is actively engaged in doing something, is always rooted in a world of men and of manmade things which it never leaves or altogether transcends'.[33] Both aspects, sociality and fabrication, are crucial to human life and, indeed, are intertwined: 'the activity of labour does not need the presence of others, though a being labouring in complete solitude would not be human but an *animal laborans* in the word's most literal significance'.[34] Similarly, 'man working and fabricating and building a world inhabited only by himself would still be a fabricator, though not *homo faber*'.[35] Only action, which entails both social being and the creation of a world, 'is the exclusive prerogative of man'.[36]

VIOLENCE AND FABRICATION

That the human world is rooted in labour – and, more specifically, the sociality inherent in action constitutive of it – and in the fabrication of work links the human world intimately to violence. We see this if we turn to Arendt's comments on the way in which the ancient Greeks understood the relationship between freedom and necessity. For them, freedom was understood to be 'exclusively located in the political realm',[37] whereas necessity was understood to be 'a prepolitical phenomenon'.[38] The freedom of politics was to solve the pre-political problem of necessity. Crucially, violence was a key moment in the transition from the pre-political realm of necessity to the political realm: 'because all human beings are subject to necessity, they are entitled to violence toward others; violence is the pre-political act of liberating oneself from the necessity of life for the freedom of the world'.[39] This prefigures Arendt's later comments on the violence–political relationship, where she accepts that violence may be required to create a political sphere that satisfies individual necessity. This can take different political forms, but her basic point is that action is, at least, initially inherently violent.

However, if a politics is to be created, this violence must abate so that discussion regarding the structures and norms of society can take place. This is somewhat similar to Schmitt's understanding of the violence–politics relationship: violence may define the pre-political sphere, but it must stop for politics to occur. As Andreas Kalyvas points out, the fundamental difference between Arendt and Schmitt is that, for the latter, the violence of the exceptional, pre-constitutional state must abate for the *decision* about the norm that will found the political, constitutional State to be made. For Arendt, the violence of the pre-political must subside to establish a space that allows for the *discussion* that permits the creation of a *polis*.[40]

If violence is the condition that permits the creation of the political realm, Arendt argues, in *The Human Condition*, that a form of violence is also found *within* the political realm through the work necessary to fabricate the objects that create and populate the human world. With this, Arendt introduces a conceptual innovation to the discussions of violence we have so far examined: violence does not simply entail a physical act that one individual does to the other; it also results from the individual's relationship to the things it needs to create a human world. To live, each individual must shape its world, with this shaping entailing a violent act.

To understand this, we need to recognise that 'fabrication, the work of *homo faber*, consists in reification'.[41] The apparent solidity and permanence of the surrounding world are not, contrary to all appearances, 'given and there, like the fruits of field and trees which we may gather or leave alone without changing the household of nature'.[42] Rather, the material of the world

> is already a product of human hands which have removed it from its natural location, either killing a life process, as in the case of the tree which must be destroyed in order to provide wood, or interrupting one of nature's slower processes, as in the case of iron, stone, or marble torn out of the womb of the earth.[43]

Crucially, Arendt notes that the violence at play here is not contingent or a local phenomenon; rather, 'this element of violation and violence is present in all fabrication, and *homo faber*, the creator of the human artifice, has always been a destroyer of nature'.[44]

At least three issues stand out from this: first, the act of fabrication – work – is inherently violent. Because work is essential to the survival of the individual, he, and by extension humanity, must necessarily violate the earth to create a world. Second, Arendt extends the scope of our understanding of what violence can refer to. Rather than being limited to human–human relations, or even human–animal ones, she notes that humanity's relations to its world are inherently violent. Third, Arendt points out that violence is not necessarily simply an addition to human being; violence is integral to human existence. We need to act on the earth to not only extract its resources, but also refashion it to make a world for us. This is an inherently violent process.

Significantly, Arendt notes that humans can experience satisfaction through this violence:

> The experience of this violence is the most elemental experience of human strength and, therefore, the very opposite of the painful, exhausting effort experienced in sheer labour. It can provide self-assurance and satisfaction, and can even become a source of self-confidence throughout life.[45]

The solidity of the human world, its apparent immovable permanence, is a consequence not of the sheer repetition of labour, but of the 'strength'[46] that permits the violence of work. Only this violence, bound up as it is with strength, permits the raw material of the earth to be fashioned into a world. Arendt's point is that, rather than simply finding itself within a hospitable environment, a human world has to be made through a violent refashioning of the earth that the human is thrown into. The human world 'is not simply borrowed or plucked as a free gift from nature's own eternal presence, although it would be impossible without the material torn out of nature; it is already a product of man's hands'.[47]

Arendt goes on to suggest that the act of fabrication 'is performed under the guidance of a model'.[48] Work does not just occur, but is done in a particular way for a particular purpose. The model 'can be an image beheld by the eye of the mind or a blueprint in which the image has already found a tentative materialisation through work'.[49] In either case, however, 'what guides the work of fabrication is outside the fabricator and precedes the actual work process'.[50]

Crucially, 'the image or model whose shape guides the fabrication process not only precedes it, but does not disappear with the finished product'.[51] Rather, the blueprint 'survives intact, as it were, to lend itself to an infinite continuation of fabrication'.[52] Through this, the same activity can be reproduced; an action that permits the efficient reproduction of a component that contributes to a way of life. This is very different from the production governing labour, which 'is urged upon and remains subject to the biological cycle; the needs and wants of the human body come and go, and though they may appear again and again at regular intervals, they never remain for any length of time'.[53] Labour does not then permit replication, whereas fabrication does because it is always conducted from and against a plan that determines its parameters and scope.

For this reason, fabrication is always governed by an instrumental, means–end rationality: 'the fabricated thing is an end product in the twofold sense that the production process comes to an end in it . . . and that it is only a means to produce this end'.[54] Importantly, the difference between the means–end production of labour and that of fabrication is that, in the former, the object produced

> lacks the worldly permanence of a piece of work, the end of the process is not determined by the end product but rather by the exhaustion of labour power, while the products themselves . . . immediately become means again, means of subsistence and reproduction of labour power.[55]

On the contrary, in fabrication 'the end is beyond doubt: it has come when an entirely new thing with enough durability to remain in the world as an independent entity has been added to the human artifice'.[56] Further, while the end product need not be repeated, if it is, it emanates 'from the craftsman's need to earn his means of subsistence, in which case his working coincides with his labouring; or it comes from a demand for multiplication in the market'.[57] Arendt's point is that 'the process [of fabrication] is repeated for reasons outside itself and is unlike the compulsory repetition inherent in labouring, where one must eat in order to labour and must labour in order to eat'.[58]

Fabrication is, then, motivated by an external (politically defined) source that aims to bring about a thing that is situated externally to the act of fabrication itself. Indeed, only fabrication has a definitive beginning and end: labour is governed by the movement of the body's life cycle and so has neither a definitive beginning nor end, while action may have a definitive beginning, but never has a predictable end.[59] That fabrication has a definitive beginning and end means that it is wholly artificial. As a consequence, 'everything produced by human hands can be destroyed by them, and no use object is so urgently needed in the life process that its maker cannot survive and afford its destruction'.[60]

That the maker remains in control of the object created ensures that he maintains a particular relationship towards the object: '*Homo faber* is indeed a lord and master, not only because he is the master or has set himself up as the master of all nature but because he is master of himself and his doings.'[61] The fabricator is then the lord and master of his creations, a position that cultivates a certain self-conception of his powerfulness: 'alone with his image of the future product, *homo faber* is free to produce, and again facing alone the work of his hands, he is free to destroy'.[62]

Gradually, however, Arendt notes that the image and place of *homo faber* changed, so that, rather than being an activity distinct from but supportive of the political, the logic of fabrication came to define the political. In the modern age, there was, in other words, a reversal in the relationship between fabrication and the political, work and action, wherein the former came to dominate and define the latter. It is for this reason that we identify with the characteristics of *homo faber*:

> [The] instrumentalisation of the world, his confidence in tools and in the productivity of the maker of artificial objects; his trust in the all-comprehensive range of the means–end category, his conviction that every issue can be solved and every human motivation reduced to the principle of utility; his sovereignty, which regards everything given as material and thinks of the whole of nature as 'an immense fabric from which we can cut out whatever we want to resew it however we like'; his equation of intelligence with ingenuity . . . ; finally, his matter-of-course identification of fabrication with action.[63]

On becoming the dominant cultural norm, the logic of *homo faber* transcended its initially limited situatedness to rule over all facets of life. It became an explicitly political concept rather than an apolitical concept that had political consequences. Arendt is, however, aware that this alteration did not simply transplant the mentality of *homo faber* into the political realm. There were 'certain deviations and variations from the traditional mentality of *homo faber*',[64] namely regarding the meaning and significance of 'process'.

Traditionally, *homo faber* focused on *what* to make, but its newfound dominance resulted in a shift 'from the "what" to the "how", from the thing itself to its fabrication process'.[65] This shift had significant political consequences: by focusing on the process alone, 'it deprived man as maker and builder of those fixed and permanent standards and measurements which, prior to the modern age, have always served him as guides for his doing and criteria for judgment'.[66] In so doing, it made the builder, the one creating the object, the sole determiner of the object: it 'elevated *homo faber*, the maker and fabricator, rather than man the actor or man as *animal laborans*, to the highest range of human possibilities'.[67] This not only decoupled the human maker from a prior world, but also brought forth the domination of the instrumental rationality defining *homo faber*. Now all 'things' in the world were objects to be used for an end defined by the maker. All it took was one last movement to see the explosive and violent implications that this could have politically.

This occurred when the violence inherent in the instrumental rationality of *homo faber* became orientated not only to the world of inanimate objects as it had always been, but to the world of action; that is, the world of intersubjective human exchange. Once human individuals began to be thought of as instruments for the attainment of a subjectively determined end, the violence that the earth suffers at the hands of the fabrication process crossed into the realm of political action.[68] As Arendt explains in *On Revolution*, when politics becomes defined by the instrumental logic underpinning *homo faber*, violence enters and defines politics, and 'where violence rules absolutely, as for instance in the concentration camps of totalitarian regimes, not only the laws – *les lois se taisent*, as the French Revolution phrased it – but everything and everybody must fall silent'.[69]

That individuals came to be thought of in terms of means for a subjectively determined end was politically dangerous enough, but it was also accompanied by the threat of a greater danger: the possibility that the end would become valued absolutely over individuals. If this occurred, individuals would be understood not merely as instruments to the attainment of the end, but as *superfluous* instruments; ones that could be easily interchanged or dispensed with for the attainment of the end. This would only end in totalitarianism and evil.[70]

After all, as Arendt explains, totalitarian terror does not necessarily aim to eradicate individuals, but 'simply and mercilessly presses men, such as they are, against each other so that the very space of free action – and this is the reality of freedom – disappears'.[71] This remorseless pressure, achieved through 'the arbitrary selection of various groups for concentration camps, by constant purges of the ruling apparatus, by mass liquidations',[72] gradually breaks individuals down so that they become 'superfluous'.[73] Indeed, in a famous letter to Karl Jasper, she defines radical evil as action that makes 'human beings as human beings superfluous (not using them as a means to the end, which leaves their essence as humans untouched and impinges only on their human dignity: rather, making them superfluous as human beings)'.[74] If the modern age has introduced the instrumental logic and necessary violence of *homo faber* into politics and this has led to the horrors and violence of totalitarianism and radical evil, the question arises as to what can be done to alter this. Arendt provides a provocative and innovative response in her 1970 essay *On Violence*.

VIOLENCE AS A POLITICAL WEAPON

On Violence grew out of the heated discussion that took place on the panel 'The Legitimacy of Violence' that was held in 1967 at the famous Theatre for Ideas; a gathering place for intellectuals in New York. It was chaired by Robert Silvers of the *New York Review of Books* and included Noam Chomsky, Conor Cruise O'Brien, and Robert Lowell. Arendt wrote and expanded the piece over the next three years, an undertaking that benefitted not only from the panel discussion, but also, no doubt, from the tremendous social upheavals that were taking place in the United States, which brought the violence–power relationship to the forefront of social-political analysis.[75]

To this end, Arendt starts by examining the state of the world at the time of writing; that is, at the height of the Cold War. She sets out the violence that conditions international relations, showing that it mediates the relationship between countries in ways not previously seen, before moving to theoretical debates. Sorel's analysis is rejected for synthesising aspects of Marx and Bergson, albeit 'on a much lower level of sophistication'.[76] Sartre's is rejected because while he tries to amalgamate his existentialism with Marxism, he ends up making statements that reveal the extent to which he 'is unaware of his basic disagreement with Marx on the question of violence'.[77] Finally, Frantz Fanon's analysis is criticised, although she concedes that it 'manages to stay closer to reality than most'.[78]

Arendt's most strident criticisms are reserved for the New Left's use of violence to effect the revolutionary struggle and those groups – such as the Black Power Movement – who sought to use violence *within* the State to effect social change. These two groups came together in the student protests of 1968, where she explains that

> serious violence entered the scene only with the appearance of the Black Power movement on the campuses. Negro students, the majority of them admitted without academic qualifications, regarded and organised themselves as an interest group, the representatives of the black community. Their interest was to lower academic standards.[79]

The point behind this highly problematic portrayal of the student movement is that violence had come to be seen as a viable and, indeed, important method for effecting social change within those groups advocating it. The problem was that these groups had only a tenuous grip on what violence entailed; while they were 'clearly inspired by Fanon, their theoretical arguments contain usually nothing but a hodgepodge of all kinds of Marxist leftovers'.[80] There was, in other words, no intellectual veracity subtending their practical actions, with the consequence that their actions lacked justification.

This ignorance was reflected in and the effect of a larger historical problem: while there was a large literature on war and warfare, Arendt found it 'rather surprising that violence has been singled out so seldom for special consideration'.[81] It is against this background that she 'propose[d] to raise the question of violence in the political realm',[82] an endeavour that would not only identify what 'violence' entails, but also show how it is distinguished from and related to power.

CONCEPTUAL DISTINCTIONS

Arendt distinguishes between three contemporary conclusions regarding the violence–power relationship. First, she notes that the most common understanding is to conflate the two so that violence is understood to be 'nothing more than the most flagrant manifestation of power'.[83] She finds this formulation 'very strange'[84] because it rests on the assumption that the State is 'an instrument of oppression in the hands of the ruling class'.[85] As such, power is manifested through the State apparatus and, indeed, is secured by the use of violence. Second, Arendt engages with whether violence defines the essence of the State.[86] She rejects this because it would mean that the 'end of warfare . . . would mean the end of States'.[87] The third understanding holds that 'power . . . is an instrument of rule',[88] which is based on an instinct to dominate. This, however, reduces power to the expression of violence and the latter to force, which makes it 'difficult to say in "which way the order given by a policeman is different from that given by a gunman"'.[89]

While critical of these definitions, she does accept that aspects of them are important. After all, they not only 'derive from the old notion of absolute power that accompanied the rise of the sovereign European nation-[S]tate',[90] but also 'coincide with the terms used since Greek antiquity to define the forms of government as the rule over man – of one or the few in monarchy and oligarchy, of the best or the many in aristocracy and democracy'.[91] Her main problem with them, however, is that they depend upon 'the Hebrew-Christian tradition and its "imperative conception of law"',[92] in which power is orientated from and located in a strict, straightforward, command–obedience economy. Lest we think that they belong to a bygone age, Arendt notes that they continue to find more ominous expression in contemporary bureaucracies, before she explains that 'modern scientific and philosophical convictions concerning man's nature have further strengthened these legal and political traditions'.[93]

Arendt points out, however, that 'there exists another tradition and another vocabulary no less old and time-honoured';[94] namely, the insistence found in the Athenian city-states that the constitution is defined by 'isonomy'[95] and the Roman conception of '*civitas*',[96] both of which indicate 'a concept of power and law whose essence d[oes] not rely on the command–obedience relationship and which d[oes] not identify power and rule or law and command'.[97] She claims that this understanding of the relationship between power and law motivated the French revolutionaries to institute 'a republic, where the rule of law, resting on the power of the people, would put an end to the rule of man over man'.[98] With this, they, of course, accepted that obedience to the law was necessary, but by 'obedience' meant 'support of the law to which the citizenry had given its consent'.[99] Law did not, then, entail an imposition on the citizenry, but expressed the will of the populace.

This points to a populist theory of sovereignty, although it is important to note that Arendt rejects Rousseau's account of the general will, which is understood to depend upon homogeneity that undermines the plurality upon which a vibrant political union depends. She does, however, note that by shifting the source of legitimacy from God to the populace, Rousseau was able to emphasise the instability inherent in law. While the populace obeys the laws (it legitimises) because it sees itself manifested through them, Arendt points out that 'such support is never unquestioning, and as far as reliability is concerned it cannot match the indeed "unquestioning obedience" that an act of violence can exact'.[100] The populace voluntarily *consents* to the law, rather than being forced to *obey* it, but that consent can be removed at any moment. For this reason, 'it is the people's support that lends power to the institutions of a country, and this support is but the continuation of the consent that brought the laws into existence to begin with'.[101] Political institutions 'petrify and decay as soon as the living power of the people ceases to uphold them'.[102]

Schmitt makes a similar point with regards to the relationship between the constituting-power and the constitution: the latter emanates from the former, while the former always subtends the latter. The moment that constitutions lose the support of the populace, the exceptional situation occurs that calls out for the populace to decide on its foundational value. As we have seen, Arendt agrees, but claims that the founding of the constitution is based on discussion, not on decision. Whereas Schmitt maintains that the political decision is based on the intensity of 'feeling' that binds the populace, Arendt initially holds that 'the strength of opinion, that is, the power of the government, depends on numbers',[103] before recognising that numbers alone are insufficient; for a group to take power requires and depends upon a tacit understanding of 'we-ness' in the plurality that defines it. This is not fixed and stable, but is constantly made. As Maurizio Passerin d'Entrèves explains,

> by engaging in this or that course of action we are, in fact, entering a claim on behalf of a 'we', that is, we are creating a specific form of collective activity. Political action and discourse are, in this respect, essential to the constitution of collective identities.[104]

Thus, while the political is defined by a plurality of voices competing for dominance, the one that becomes dominant depends upon and instantiates a collective sense of we-ness.

Following on from this, Christian Volk suggests that Arendt's conception of power is two-fold, insofar as it refers to the concerted action that people engage in when they 'come together as a political group or organisation'[105] *and* a second aspect 'that refers to the degree to which people living under a political and constitutional order agree to abide by the rules and regulations set therein'.[106] It is because people have agreed to those rules and regulations and, indeed, can sort out any disagreements regarding them through discussion and persuasion that violence does not define the political. Power is achieved through persuasion and consensus and so is willingly and voluntarily respected; it does not normally have to impose itself on others to ensure their obedience.

In a sense this confirms Schmitt's claim that the creation of law requires and in turn re-enforces a certain homogeneity, or agreement, in the populace regarding the understanding of itself and its ends. The difference is that Arendt accepts and accommodates plurality to a far greater degree than Schmitt, for whom plurality always risks dissension about the dominant norms of society, which, on his telling, risks falling back into the exceptional state of violence. For Arendt, the plurality of voices and positions that compete discursively in the space between violence and the founding of the *polis* is not wiped out in this founding, but must continue to exist to ensure a vibrant public realm.

The group that takes power is the one that not only has the greatest support, but also is able to bind itself together by creating a collective sense of identity. This reveals, so Arendt claims, a fundamental distinction between power and violence: 'power always stands in need of numbers, whereas violence up to a point can manage without them because it relies on implements'.[107] Power is based on consent and emanates from support and agreement; the greater the number of supporters throughout a populace, the greater and more secure that power. Violence, in contrast, is, for Arendt, a means. It is an action that interrupts power, can always be committed by one individual and so does not depend on numbers, and, as an interrupting action, never establishes anything semi-permanent. For this reason, 'the extreme form of power is All against One, the extreme form of violence is One against All'.[108]

The problem is that power and violence are frequently conflated. This is, for her, a consequence of the dominance of the command–obedience conception of law, wherein 'the most crucial political issue is, and always has been, the question of Who rules Whom?'[109] Arendt rejects this model of law to affirm the participatory model found in Athens and Rome. This points to a fundamental difference with Benjamin.

Whereas Benjamin holds that the divine is a means to expiate legal-mythical violence, with the consequence that the divine acts as a saviour, Christopher Finlay points out that 'for Arendt, it was the Judeo-Christian conception of the Divine that engendered the problem'.[110] Specifically, the appeal to 'a transcendent moment external to the world ... guaranteed the perseverance of attempts at violent political making'.[111] Rather than appeal to the divine to depose power and law, Arendt undertakes a conceptual examination that distinguishes between the concepts – authority, force, power, strength, violence – that the command–obedience model typically conflates.

Thus, we find that '[p]*ower* corresponds to the human ability not just to act but to act in concert. Power is never the property of an individual; it belongs to a group and remains in existence only so long as the group keeps together.'[112] For this reason, Arendt warns that 'when we say of somebody that he is "in power" we actually refer to his being empowered by a certain number of people to act in their name'.[113] Political sovereignty is a consequence of the action of groups. The group discusses and decides on its leader, who, assuming the group has the greatest power, adopts a position of sovereignty. But Arendt warns that 'the moment the group, from which the power originated to begin with (*potestas in populo*, without a people or group there is no power) disappears, "his power" also vanishes'.[114] Sovereignty is dependent on the will of the group that the sovereign belongs to. If that group is overcome or loses faith in the sovereign, his source of power disappears. Power is then a consequence of collective participation that can disappear at any moment if the collective underpinning power dissolves, alters, or is overcome.

'*Strength* unequivocally designates something in the singular, an individual entity; it is the property inherent in an object or person and belongs to its character, which may prove itself in relation to other things or persons, but is essentially independent of them.'[115] Whereas power is collectively located, strength is individually based. Crucially, Arendt claims that, regardless of the strength of an entity, it 'can always be overpowered by the many'[116] – that is, power – 'who often will combine for no other purpose than to ruin strength precisely because of its peculiar independence'.[117] Indeed, she notes that there is an inbuilt antipathy between power and strength: 'it is in the nature of a group and its power to turn against independence, the property of individual strength'.[118]

While Arendt notes that 'force' is often used as a synonym for violence, she recommends that it 'should be reserved, in terminological language, for the "forces of nature" or the "forces of circumstances" (*la force des choses*), that is, to indicate the energy released by physical or social movements'.[119] Force is not then a human act, but the effect of natural or social movements.

'Authority' is the most elusive term because it 'can be vested in persons',[120] such as 'in the relation between parent and child, between teacher and pupil',[121] or 'offices, as, for instance, in the Roman senate (*auctoritas in senatu*) or in the hierarchical offices of the Church'.[122] Authority is based on the command–obedience economy and consists in 'unquestioning recognition of those who are asked to obey; neither coercion nor persuasion is needed'.[123] Crucially, authority is based on respect for the office or person. It is, therefore, grounded not in a formal or transcendent principle, but in popular perception. It is only if the populace respects the person/office that he/it will be sufficiently respected to maintain his/its authority. For this reason, Arendt notes that 'the greatest enemy of authority . . . is contempt, and the surest way to undermine it is laughter'.[124] But, of course, this undermining will only occur if the authority has lost power, meaning the support of the largest number.

In contrast to power, strength, force, and authority,

> *violence* . . . is distinguished by its instrumental character. Phenomenologically, it is close to strength, since the implements of violence, like all other tools, are designed and used for the purpose of multiplying strength until, in the last stage of their development, they can substitute for it.[125]

Two consequences of this description stand out: first, violence is an instrumental act and so defined by the means/ends dichotomy. Second, it is, as such, always an individual act that disrupts power. Thus, while Benjamin insists that an act of divine violence interjects to depose law and legal violence, Arendt insists that *all* violence disrupts and deposes power and, by extension, law and politics. In contrast to Benjamin's subtle account of the ways in which different forms of violence correspond to law and politics, and to Schmitt's differentiated analysis of the ways in which violence adheres to law and politics, Arendt insists on a dichotomy between violence and politics/law.

Having established this dichotomy, however, she notes that it is *logical*, not *experiential*: 'these distinctions, though by no means arbitrary, hardly ever correspond to watertight compartments in the real world, from which nevertheless they are drawn'.[126] To explain what she means, Arendt points to the example of a breakdown on the New York subway in which the governmental power dissipated because the passengers would not leave. There was, in other words, a power struggle between the two groups in which the legitimate authoritative power of the governmental agency was undermined by the power of the passengers. The actions of the passengers did not overthrow the government, but, by undermining its authority, the passengers prevented the governmental authority from exercising its power. Her conclusion is that in the *practical* sphere, power and authority are, more often than not, entwined. This extends to the violence–power relationship: 'nothing . . . is more common than the combination of violence and power, nothing less frequent than to find them in their pure and therefore extreme form'.[127] While this would appear to indicate that violence and power 'are interwoven phenomena',[128] Arendt disagrees, ignores the conclusion that her empirical analysis seems to point towards, and instead affirms the logical separation of the two. Despite admitting that, in practice, violence, power, and authority are entwined, she concludes that 'it does not follow that authority, power, and violence are all the same'.[129]

To support this, she turns to 'the phenomenon of revolution'.[130] Contrary to the notion that the possibility of successful revolution has decreased as the destructive capability of weapons has increased, Arendt argues that there is no correspondence between the two. While, in relation to violence, 'the superiority of the government has always been absolute . . . this superiority lasts only as long as the power structure of the government is intact'.[131] In other words, it lasts only as long as its 'commands are obeyed and the army or police are prepared to use their weapons'.[132] If the government loses its support, its power diminishes rapidly.

Arendt's conclusion is that it is not violence that secures power; power secures power; that is, the capacity to be followed and supported defines power. It is only once power has diminished sufficiently that an alternative is possible. 'When commands are no longer obeyed, the means of violence are of no use; and the question of this obedience is not decided by the command–obedience relation but by opinion, and, of course, by the number of those who share it.'[133] Violence is not key to the success of revolution; 'the sudden dramatic breakdown of power'[134] is. This is not to say that the breakdown of power necessarily leads to revolution, only that revolution, as an expression of power, is nothing but 'the outward manifestation of support and consent'.[135]

VIOLENCE AND POWER

Arendt's point is that power and violence are two distinct phenomena. While power may resort to violence, it does so only for short period of times and for a specific task. 'No government exclusively based on the means of violence has ever existed. Even the totalitarian ruler, whose chief instrument of rule is torture, needs a power base – the secret police and its net of informers.'[136]

She supports this by appealing to regimes of slavery, wherein the masters were always outnumbered by their slaves, but continued to rule because their power 'did not rest on superior means of coercion as such, but on a superior organisation of power – that is, on the organised solidarity of the masters'.[137] Without support, violence is merely an isolated act that can be overcome by the violence of those in power. So, in domestic affairs, power may resort to violence to contain criminals or rebels; that is, single individuals who have resorted to violence but who do not enjoy widespread support to turn it into power. Alternatively, as in the case of the Vietnam war, overwhelming superiority in terms of the capacity for violence 'can become helpless if confronted with an ill-equipped but well-organised opponent who is much more powerful'.[138]

The conclusion drawn is that 'power is indeed of the essence of all government, but violence is not. Violence is by nature instrumental; like all means, it always stands in need of guidance and justification through the end it pursues.'[139] While violence is instrumental, power is '"an end in itself"'.[140] Arendt is aware that the government pursues policies and goals via the exercise of violence, but claims that 'the power structure itself precedes and outlasts all aims, so that power, far from being the means to an end, is actually the very condition enabling a group of people to think and act in terms of the means–end category'.[141] The instrumentality of violence is, then, an effect of power, power always subtends the use of violence, and power uses violence to obtain power.

Because power defines the political community it 'needs no justification',[142] only legitimacy. Legitimacy does not result from God or an external source, but 'from the initial getting together rather than from any action that then may follow'.[143] The source of power is therefore the populace who acts in concert and, for this reason, the *legitimacy* of power is always referred back to its source: the consensual moment of agreement to act in a particular way. This is distinct from 'justification', which 'relates to an end that lies in the future'.[144] It therefore lends itself to the means/end dichotomy, which is why 'violence can be justifiable, but it never will be legitimate'.[145]

Violence can be justified because it may be necessary to secure a future end. For this reason, violence 'is rational to the extent that it is effective in reaching the end that must justify it'.[146] But since the final outcome of actions cannot be known for certain, its rationality can only be secured if it limits itself to short-term goals. Crucially, while it can be justified and rational, violence can never be legitimate because legitimacy is based on consensual agreement to act in a particular way. If violence was grounded in consensual agreement, there would be no need for it; the group would simply agree on a course of action. For this reason, Arendt notes that while power and violence 'usually appear together',[147] when they are combined 'power . . . is the primary and predominant factor'.[148]

This is not, however, to say that violence cannot impact on power. Arendt points out that 'if a foreign conqueror is confronted by an impotent government and by a nation unused to the exercise of political power, it is easy for him to achieve such domination'.[149] This is because 'violence . . . does not depend on numbers or opinions, but on implements, and the implements of violence . . . like all other tools, increase and multiply human strength'.[150] If violence is simply opposed by mere power, the latter 'will soon find that [it is] confronted not by men but by men's artefacts, whose inhumanity and destructive effectiveness increase in proportion to the distance separating the opponents'.[151] Violence can only ever destroy power; it has a negative function in relation to power.

Arendt recognises, however, that while power can never grow out of violence, violence may be necessary to depose power. Here, its negative role actually has positive significance in that 'under certain circumstances violence ... is the only way to set the scales of justice right again'.[152] Arendt does warn, however, that this is a risky endeavour: 'the practice of violence, like all action, changes the world, but the most probable change is to a more violent world'.[153]

For this reason, Elizabeth Frazer and Kimberly Hutchings are mistaken in claiming that 'there seems to be no particular reason ... why political actions should reject non-political [i.e. violent] (strictly speaking) actions if they bring about desired political effects'.[154] Arendt admits that there is a rationality to the use of violence in that it can be used for political ends, but warns that this carries significant risks because it reveals the frailty of its power and justifies the future use of violence. After all, power only resorts to 'sheer violence ... where power is being lost'.[155] This can bring victory, 'but the price is very high: for it is not only paid by the vanquished, it is also paid by the victor in terms of his own power'.[156] In having to resort to unbridled violence, power reveals that it no longer enjoys the consensus that provided it with legitimacy. It must therefore try to command obedience through imposition; an action that it presumably would not have to take if it continued to be legitimate. As such, recourse to violence to secure power actually ends up demolishing the power it was to safeguard.

For Arendt, this is nowhere 'more evident than in the use of terror to maintain domination'.[157] Terror is not the same as violence; it is one step beyond violence and describes 'the form of government that comes into being when violence, having destroyed all power, does not abdicate but, on the contrary, remains in full control'.[158] In other words, terror arises when violence deposes power, but the vacuum created is not filled by another power. When this occurs, violence acts unabated, both against others and against itself. This gives rise to the decisive difference between 'totalitarian domination, based on terror, and tyrannies and dictatorships, established by violence'.[159] The former 'turns not only against its enemies but against its friends and supporters as well, being afraid of all power, even the power of its friends'.[160]

The danger of violence as a political tool is then that its negative function may come to dominate so completely that it annihilates its opponents and itself: 'the climax of terror is reached when the police [S]tate begins to devour its own children, when yesterday's executioner becomes today's victim. And this is also the moment when power disappears entirely.'[161] To avoid this fate, practical politics should adhere to and affirm the *conceptual* division between violence and politics. While violence has a place in politics, its role should be severely limited to that of a last resort to achieve specific, short-term goals. Rather than affirm violence, politics should privilege the concerted action through discussion that defines and generates power.

CONCLUDING REMARKS

By basing sovereignty on the popular will, Arendt continues the populist theory of sovereignty that became dominant in the eighteenth century. She does, however, offer a far more subtle understanding of the ways in which the populace creates and supports juridical sovereignty. This feeds through to her analysis of violence. She agrees with Benjamin that violence can depose juridical sovereignty in search of justice, but, whereas he limits this function to divine violence, she claims that *all* forms of violence can achieve this. In this respect, Arendt affirms a straightforward absolute division between violence and power that removes the divine component to posit violence in opposition to law.

With regard to Schmitt, Arendt agrees that, for law to be created, violence must cease, but insists that the creation of law results from discussion and hence plurality, rather than decision and homogeneity. She also introduces a conceptual innovation, insofar as she does not limit her analysis to the relationship between violence and law, but, through her discussion of the violence inherent in fabrication, recognises that violence is both necessary for our daily activities and, by extension, constitutive of what it is to be human.

The fundamental problem with her position relates to the coherence of her strict division between violence and power. While she wants to maintain a strict *conceptual* distinction, she admits that, *practically*, the two are entwined. While this might be thought to call into question her conceptual distinction, her solution is to affirm the conceptual distinction over the conclusion generated from her phenomenological or historical descriptions; namely, that violence and power are interwoven. This, however, means that she affirms abstract categories over concrete experience. Not only does this contradict the concrete historical analysis she undertakes in her studies of totalitarianism, revolution, and evil, but it risks de-legitimising her conclusions.

Arguably, Arendt falls into this problem because her conceptions of 'violence' and 'power' are simply too static and homogeneous. Having been defined independently from one another, it appears that they are two fully formed 'blocks' facing one another. This makes violence an external instrument of power, rather than 'something' that can enter into power or that subtends power. Arendt's theoretical binary opposition simply cannot analyse the fluidity of the relationship or its component pieces to show how violence can be both external and internal, creative and disruptive of power.

To outline what such a conception of the violence–power relationship might look like, the next chapter turns to Gilles Deleuze and Felix Guattari's attempt to ground sovereign violence in a differential ontology, before showing how the State apparatus is always threatened from the outside by the war machine. With this, they agree with Arendt that violence is always external to power, but go beyond her analysis by conceptualising each aspect in terms of fluid relations that better capture the differential, but entwined, relationship between them.

NOTES

1. Hannah Arendt, *The Origins of Totalitarianism* (New York: Harcourt, 1951), p. 139.
2. Ibid. p. 141.
3. Ibid. p. 142.
4. Ibid. p. 142.
5. Ibid. pp. 146–7.
6. Annelies Degryse, 'The Sovereign and the Social: Arendt's Understanding of Hobbes', *Ethical Perspectives*, 15:2, 2008, pp. 239–58 (pp. 248–9).
7. For a detailed discussion of Arendt's critique of Rousseau, see Margaret Canovan, 'Arendt, Rousseau, and Human Plurality in Politics', *Journal of Politics*, 45:2, 1983, pp. 286–302.
8. Hannah Arendt, *Between Past and Future* (London: Penguin, 2006), p. 163.
9. Hannah Arendt, *Love and Saint Augustine*, ed. Joanna Vecchairelli Scott and Judith Chelius Stark (Chicago: University of Chicago Press, 1996); Arendt, *The Origins of Totalitarianism*; Hannah Arendt, *On Revolution* (London: Penguin, 1963).
10. Hannah Arendt, 'The Jewish Army: The Beginning of Jewish Politics?', p. 137, in *The Jewish Writings*, ed. Jerome Kohn and Ron H. Feldman (New York: Schocken Books, 2007), pp. 136–8.
11. Ibid. pp. 138–9.
12. Hannah Arendt, *On Violence* (New York: Harcourt, 1970), p. 44.
13. Hannah Arendt, *The Human Condition*, 2nd edn (Chicago: University of Chicago Press, 1998), pp. 139–44.
14. Ibid. pp. 305–13.
15. Ibid. p. 5.
16. Ibid. p. 5.
17. Ibid. p. 7.
18. Ibid. p. 7.
19. Ibid. p. 7.
20. Ibid. p. 7.
21. Ibid. p. 7.
22. Ibid. p. 7. The earth/world distinction is a key one within Arendt's thinking and has been influential in contemporary debates in environmentalism. For a discussion of it, see Paul Ott, 'World and Earth: Hannah Arendt and the Human Relationship to Nature', *Ethics, Place and Environment: A Journal of Philosophy and Geography*, 12:1, 2009, pp. 1–16.
23. Arendt, *The Human Condition*, p. 7.
24. Steve Buckler, *Hannah Arendt and Political Theory: Challenging the Tradition* (Edinburgh: Edinburgh University Press, 2011), p. 7. For a critical discussion of the relationship between communication and power, see Jürgen Habermas, 'Hannah Arendt's Communications Concept of Power', trans. Thomas McCarthy, *Social Research*, 44:1, 1977, pp. 3–24.

25. Paul Voice, 'Consuming the World: Hannah Arendt on Politics and the Environment', *Journal of International Political Theory*, 9:2, 2013, pp. 178–93 (p. 181).
26. Arendt, *The Human Condition*, p. 8.
27. Ibid. p. 8.
28. Ibid. p. 9.
29. Ibid. p. 9.
30. For a more detailed discussion of natality in Arendt, see Jeffrey Champlin, 'Born Again: Arendt's "Natality" as Figure and Concept', *The Germanic Review*, 88:2, 2013, pp. 150–64.
31. Arendt, *The Human Condition*, p. 9.
32. Ibid. p. 9.
33. Ibid. p. 22.
34. Ibid. p. 22.
35. Ibid. p. 22.
36. Ibid. p. 22.
37. Ibid. p. 31.
38. Ibid. p. 32.
39. Ibid. p. 31.
40. Andreas Kalyvas, *Democracy and the Politics of the Extraordinary: Max Weber, Carl Schmitt, and Hannah Arendt* (Cambridge: Cambridge University Press, 2008), p. 233.
41. Arendt, *The Human Condition*, p. 139.
42. Ibid. p. 139.
43. Ibid. p. 139.
44. Ibid. p. 139.
45. Ibid. p. 140.
46. Ibid. p. 140.
47. Ibid. p. 140.
48. Ibid. p. 140.
49. Ibid. p. 140.
50. Ibid. pp. 140–1.
51. Ibid. p. 141.
52. Ibid. p. 141.
53. Ibid. p. 142.
54. Ibid. p. 143.
55. Ibid. p. 143.
56. Ibid. p. 143.
57. Ibid. p. 143.
58. Ibid. p. 143.
59. Ibid. p. 144.
60. Ibid. p. 144.
61. Ibid. p. 144.
62. Ibid. p. 144.
63. Ibid. pp. 305–6.
64. Ibid. p. 306.
65. Ibid. p. 307.
66. Ibid. p. 307.
67. Ibid. p. 305.
68. Arendt criticises the conflation of violence with a necessary end in *On Revolution*, pp. 54–5.

69. Ibid. p. 9.
70. For a discussion of Arendt's analysis of evil, see Gavin Rae, *Evil in the Western Philosophical Tradition* (Edinburgh: Edinburgh University Press, 2019), ch. 9. For an engagement with her analysis of the relationship between evil and political resistance, see Gavin Rae, 'Hannah Arendt, Evil, and Political Resistance,' forthcoming in *History of the Human Sciences*.
71. Hannah Arendt, 'On the Nature of Totalitarianism', pp. 342–3, in *Essays in Understanding, 1930–1954*, ed. Jerome Kohn, (New York: Schocken Books, 1994), pp. 328–60.
72. Arendt, *The Origins of Totalitarianism*, p. 457.
73. Ibid. p. 457.
74. Hannah Arendt and Karl Jaspers, *Correspondence: 1932–1969*, ed. Lotte Kohler and Hans Sander (New York: Harcourt, 1992), p. 166.
75. The description of the gestation period that led to the publication of *On Violence* is based on the description found in Elisabeth Young-Bruehl, *Hannah Arendt: For Love of the World*, 2nd edn (New Haven: Yale University Press, 2004), pp. 412–21.
76. Arendt, *On Violence*, p. 12.
77. Ibid. p. 12.
78. Ibid. p. 20. For a critical account of Arendt's analyses of Sartre's and Fanon's views on violence, see Elizabeth Frazer and Kimberly Hutchings, 'On Politics and Violence: Arendt contra Fanon', *Contemporary Political Theory*, 7:1, 2008, pp. 90–108.
79. Arendt, *On Violence*, p. 18.
80. Ibid. p. 20.
81. Ibid. p. 8.
82. Ibid. p. 35.
83. Ibid. p. 35.
84. Ibid. pp. 35–6.
85. Ibid. p. 36.
86. Ibid. p. 36.
87. Ibid. p. 36.
88. Ibid. p. 36.
89. Ibid. p. 37.
90. Ibid. p. 38.
91. Ibid. p. 38.
92. Ibid. p. 39.
93. Ibid. p. 39.
94. Ibid. p. 40.
95. Ibid. p. 40.
96. Ibid. p. 40.
97. Ibid. p. 40.
98. Ibid. p. 40.
99. Ibid. pp. 40–1.
100. Ibid. p. 41.
101. Ibid. p. 41.
102. Ibid. p. 41.
103. Ibid. p. 41.
104. Maurizio Passerin d'Entrèves, *The Political Philosophy of Hannah Arendt* (Abingdon: Routledge, 1994), p. 19.
105. Christian Volk, 'Towards a Critical Theory of the Political: Hannah Arendt on Power

and Critique', *Philosophy and Social Criticism*, 42:6, 2015, pp. 549–75 (p. 552).
106. Ibid. p. 552.
107. Arendt, *On Violence*, p. 42.
108. Ibid. p. 42.
109. Ibid. p. 43.
110. Christopher Finlay, 'Hannah Arendt's Critique of Violence', *Thesis Eleven*:97, May, 2009, pp. 26–45 (p. 42).
111. Ibid. p. 42.
112. Arendt, *On Violence*, p. 44.
113. Ibid. p. 44.
114. Ibid. p. 44.
115. Ibid. p. 44.
116. Ibid. p. 44.
117. Ibid. p. 44.
118. Ibid. p. 44.
119. Ibid. pp. 44–5.
120. Ibid. p. 45.
121. Ibid. p. 45.
122. Ibid. p. 45.
123. Ibid. p. 45.
124. Ibid. p. 45.
125. Ibid. p. 46.
126. Ibid. p. 46.
127. Ibid. p. 47.
128. Keith Breen, 'Violence and Power: A Critique of Hannah Arendt on the "Political"', *Philosophy and Social Criticism*, 33:3, 2007, pp. 343–72 (p. 358).
129. Arendt, *On Violence*, p. 47.
130. Ibid. p. 47.
131. Ibid. p. 48.
132. Ibid. p. 48.
133. Ibid. p. 49.
134. Ibid. p. 49.
135. Ibid. p. 49.
136. Ibid. p. 50.
137. Ibid. p. 50.
138. Ibid. p. 51.
139. Ibid. p. 51.
140. Ibid. p. 51.
141. Ibid. p. 51.
142. Ibid. p. 52.
143. Ibid. p. 52.
144. Ibid. p. 52.
145. Ibid. p. 52.
146. Ibid. p. 79.
147. Ibid. p. 52.
148. Ibid. p. 52.
149. Ibid. p. 52.
150. Ibid. p. 53

151. Ibid. p. 53
152. Ibid. p. 64.
153. Ibid. p. 80.
154. Frazer and Hutchings, 'On Politics and Violence', p. 104.
155. Arendt, *On Violence*, p. 53.
156. Ibid. p. 53.
157. Ibid. p. 54.
158. Ibid. p. 55.
159. Ibid. p. 55.
160. Ibid. p. 55.
161. Ibid. p. 55.

CHAPTER 4

Disrupting Sovereignty: Deleuze and Guattari on the War Machine

Deleuze and Guattari's work on the war machine was long neglected, but has garnered much recent attention as scholars attempt to work out the political implications of these authors' thought. Dating from, at least, the mid-1960s, when it formed an important part of Guattari's thinking, the notion of the war machine found expression in their collaborative works of the 1970s.[1] The most condensed and systematic discussion of it, however, is found in the 12th plateau, '1227: Treatise on Nomadology – The War Machine', of their 1980 work *A Thousand Plateaus*.[2]

The notion itself has been called 'the most remarkable but also puzzling feature'[3] of their thought, which is, perhaps, one reason why it has been interpreted so differently. There are, at least, two dominant interpretations in the literature. The first understands the concept 'war machine' in primarily ontological terms, so that the chaotic differentiation of the war machine undermines and usurps the identity of the State. For this reason, Paul Patton explains that 'the real object of Deleuze and Guattari's war-machine concept is not war but the conditions of creative mutation and change'.[4] On this understanding, the war machine is not related to war, but is an ontological principle or function that disrupts ontological identity, which, of course, harks back to Deleuze's affirmation of difference over identity in *Difference and Repetition*.[5] How this occurs, however, has led to much contestation in the literature to the extent that we are told that the war machine (1) 'expresses a specific type of social cohesion'[6] distinct from that which binds the State; (2) 'escapes codes and codings on all sides'[7] and so is the excess that cannot be codified and incorporated by the State; and/or (3) describes 'the opposition (war-machine/State, difference/identity, smooth/striated) between two tendencies in any assemblage'.[8] Despite these differences, the common theme underlying this line of interpretation is that the war machine is primarily an ontological principle. As such, at least one commentator has concluded that 'it is a concept which is betrayed by its name since it has little to do with war and only a paradoxical and indirect relation to armed conflict';[9] a conclusion that might be thought to call into question the validity of incorporating a discussion of it here.

This ontological interpretation has, however, been challenged by a political reading that emphasises the relationship between the war machine, armed conflict, and the State. For example, Nathan Widder[10] compares and contrasts Deleuze and Guattari's notion of the war machine to Hegel's conception of the State, while Guillaume Silbertin-Blanc not only relates Deleuze and Guattari's notion to Clausewitz's concept of 'absolute war', but also claims that the war machine arises 'when a group becomes heterogeneous to the State apparatuses . . . to the reciprocal determination of the State's power and of the specific spatiotemporal formation in which it actualises itself',[11] and so identifies its relationship to political exclusion and struggle. Similarly, Gregg Lambert makes the claim that the notion of the war machine is inherently political because 'the nature of violence deployed by the war machine is not conservative, but essentially destructive: to vanquish, destroy, thereby to ruin the organs of State power',[12] which Julian Reid expands on by producing a detailed and nuanced understanding of the relationship between violence and the war machine to make the strong claim that 'the concept of war is absolutely fundamental to Deleuze's philosophy'.[13]

That Deleuze and Guattari's concept can be interpreted in different ways is, of course, not surprising. They always emphasised that philosophy is and should be problem-orientated with the consequence that it will lead to different conclusions and interpretations. My aim in this chapter is to develop a compatibilist understanding that shows that their concept of the war machine is both ontological and political. I develop this by taking seriously their claim that 'the State is sovereignty'[14] to focus on the war-machine–sovereignty relationship. By grounding sovereignty in differential ontological flows and relations, I argue that Deleuze and Guattari offer a subtle but radical rejection of the classic-juridical claim that sovereignty is singular and indivisible; for them, it is always multiple and divisible, which ensures its vitality and power. They do, however, continue to focus on the ways in which the war machine disrupts the juridical order, thereby revealing that their thinking continues to be bound to the classic-juridical model.

THE STATE AND THE *URSTAAT*

The plateau '1227: Treatise on Nomadology – The War Machine' is structured around three axioms, three problems, and nine propositions. The first axiom states that '*The war machine is exterior to the State apparatus.*'[15] The war machine is not then the State *per se*, but is other than the State, which gives rise to the question: what do Deleuze and Guattari mean by the State? To respond, we need to turn from *A Thousand Plateaus* to *Anti-Oedipus* and, in particular, its discussion of 'The *Urstaat*'.[16]

Once we do, we find Deleuze and Guattari turning to theology and the city of Ur, 'the point of departure of Abraham or the new alliance'.[17] They reject the notion that the State was created in progressive stages; 'it appears fully armed, a master stroke executed all at once; the primordial *Urstaat*, the eternal model of everything the State wants to be and desires'.[18] At this stage, it is not clear if Deleuze and Guattari affirm that the *Urstaat* was *actually* created in a single blow or rather was simply understood to be thus created so as to lay down a mythic foundation for all subsequent States, but, in any case, they hold that the *Urstaat* 'is the basic formation, on the horizon throughout history'[19] because the *Urstaat* is a despotic regime that continues to underpin all subsequent ones. Thus, 'under every Black and every Jew there is an Egyptian, and a Mycenean under the Greeks, an Etruscan under the Romans. And yet their origin sinks into oblivion, a latency that lays hold of the State itself, and where the writing system sometimes disappears.'[20]

The key reason for this is the stratification inherent in the *Urstaat*: land is divided up among those loyal to the regime with the consequence that the State is stratified into regions. In turn, this leads to private property and exchange. From this, '*classes* appear, inasmuch as the dominant classes are no longer merged with the State apparatus, but are distinct determinations that make use of this transformed apparatus'.[21] All subsequent States share and take over this stratification, which is not to say that they do so in the same ways.

Indeed, the problem of understanding how the *Urstaat* operates through newer State-formations is that

> on the one hand, the ancient city-state, the Germanic commune, and feudalism presuppose the great empires, and cannot be understood except in terms of the *Urstaat* that serves as their horizon. On the other hand, the problem confronting these forms is to reconstitute the *Urstaat* insofar as possible, given the requirements of their new distinct determinations.[22]

This does not simply involve imposing social codes and orders on previous ones, but entails '*the breakdown of codes*'.[23]

For Deleuze and Guattari, societies are not substances, but are coding machines that determine meaning and, through this, order. Different codes produce different orders. Furthermore, societies are heterogeneously composed of different codes, which are in constant flux 'internally' and in relation to one another. This means that dominant codes constantly encounter others that 'pour over the socius, crossing it from one end to the other'.[24] It is not then a case, as it was for the initial *Urstaat*, of stratifying and territorialising virgin flows. Rather, modern societies 'must invent specific codes for flows that are increasingly deterritorialised'.[25] This requires that the new State put 'despotism in the service of the new class relations; integrating the relations of wealth and power, of commodity and labour; reconciling market money and money from revenues; everywhere stamping the mark of *Urstaat* on the new state of things'.[26] Through this, and despite the new forms it took, the stratification of the *Urstaat* continued to shape the State.

Insisting that the *Urstaat* delineates the foundation of subsequent States appears to introduce a foundation for all States that risks grounding their differences in a singular point of origin. This would reduce all States to a point of singular emanation and so re-instantiate the logic that privileges the identity that Deleuze rejects in *Difference and Repetition*. For this reason, Deleuze and Guattari note that 'the special situation of the State – oblivion and return – has to be explained'[27] by recognising 'that the primordial despotic State is not a historical break like any other'.[28] The *Urstaat* never was an actual State *per se*, nor is it '*one formation amongst others*, [or] *the transition from one formation to another*'.[29] Rather, the *Urstaat*

> appears to be set back at a remove from what it transects and from it resects, as though it were giving evidence of another dimension, a cerebral ideality that is added to, superimposed on the material evolution of societies, a regulating idea or principle of reflection (terror) that organises the parts and the flows into a whole.[30]

It is, in other words, an ideal, mythic creation that 'only appears fully armed in the brain of those who institute it'.[31] This explains why 'Marxism didn't quite know what to make of it: it has no place in the famous five stages: primitive communism, ancient city-states, feudalism, capitalism, and socialism'.[32]

The despotic regime of the *Urstaat* transects, alters, and over-codes that which 'comes before ... the territorial machine, which it reduces to the state of bricks, of working parts henceforth subjected to the cerebral idea'.[33] Deleuze and Guattari are suggesting that the earth – that which exists prior to the stratification of the *Urstaat* – is 'constituted' by flows and fluxes. These are, initially, smooth, before being delineated and defined in terms of space and meaning through the *Urstaat*. The way in which this occurs both emanates from and defines the codes, structures, and processes of the State. Thus, the *Urstaat* is the origin of the State, but it is not the foundation, insofar as it depends on, by way of capturing and configuring, the flows and fluxes subtending it. This capturing is not substantial – it does not entail a 'thing' opposing itself to the flows – but is, rather, an ideal construction used to explain the transition from these flows to the State. It 'is in this sense [that] the despotic State is . . . the origin, but the origin as an abstraction that must include its differences with respect to the concrete beginning'.[34] It is also why Deleuze and Guattari link the *Urstaat* to myth.

With this, they continue Benjamin's thinking on the relationship between violence and law in two ways: first, they agree that the creation of law is a violent act. They extend Benjamin's thinking, however, by developing the ontological categories to explain how this occurs: the originary fluxes and flows are channelled into structures and meanings by the *Urstaat*, the despotic regime.

Second, they also agree that this founding act is a mythic one. As a consequence, violence founds law through the mediation of myth. Again, however, they go beyond Benjamin by explaining how myth relates to the pre-mythic time it emanates from and replaces. To do so, they make two claims: first, 'myth always expresses a passage and a divergence'.[35] Myth is the mediation from one point or state or another; a transition that entails not an imposition, but a displacement. Thus, 'the primitive territorial myth of the beginning expressed the divergence of a characteristically intense energy . . . in relation to the social system in extension that it conditioned, passing back and forth between alliance and filiation'.[36]

Second, and linked to this, the mythic origin is only able to arise from the origin itself. It is not imposed on that which preceded it, but is an effect of that origin:

> the divergence of this [mythic] beginning [emanates] from the origin itself, the divergence of the extension from the idea, of the genesis from the order and the power (the new alliance), and also what repasses from filiation to alliance, what is taken up again by filiation.[37]

The problem, of course, is that if the (mythic) beginning were to simply emanate from the pre-mythic 'origin', there would be no need for myth. Myth is needed, however, to explain and legitimise the rise of the State. There appears, then, to be a tension between the notion that myth is needed to explain the beginning of the State and the claim that the State results from the self-divergence of its origin.

To resolve this, Deleuze and Guattari appeal to the work of Jean-Pierre Vernant to conclude that this apparent problem is generated from the function and structure of myth. Because myth is incapable of admitting 'a law of immanence that is immanent in the universe',[38] it 'need[s] to posit and internalise this difference between the origin and the [mythic] beginnings, between the sovereign power and the genesis of the world',[39] and does so by imposing its narrative on the origin. What initially appeared to be a straightforward linear explanation for the rise of the State that moved from ontological flows and fluxes to a territorial machine to the *Urstaat* is actually revealed to be a complicated process, wherein myth not only mediates the movement from the originary flows and fluxes to the State and so acts as a beginning of the latter, but also is that which depends upon, is an effect of, and, indeed, imposes itself on the originary flows and fluxes to create the *Urstaat*. As a consequence, 'one no longer really knows what comes first, and whether the territorial machine does not in fact presuppose a despotic machine from which it extracts the bricks or that it segments in its turn'.[40]

Nevertheless, the movement from origin to mythic beginnings instantiates a despotic regime, one that continues to accompany subsequent State formations, not as an inner core, but as 'the abstraction that is realised – in imperial formations, to be sure – only as an abstraction'.[41] In other words, the spirit of the *Urstaat* focuses the unity that emanates from the flows and fluxes subtending the State. This occurs differently in the various subsequent regimes, but each State-formation is orientated towards creating order out of the originary flows and fluxes that ground its mythic beginning.

Indeed, Deleuze and Guattari note that whereas 'the State was first [an] abstract unity that integrated subaggregates functioning separately; it is now subordinated to a field of forces whose flows it co-ordinates and whose autonomous relations of domination and subordination it expresses'.[42] Rather than being at the apex of the social system controlling what was beneath it, the State is now merely a nodal point in a social system absent a controlling point. Rather than imposing itself on the system as a whole to maintain control and reduce other aspects to itself, the State

> is no longer the transcendent law that governs fragments; it must fashion as best it can a whole to which it will render its law immanent. It is no longer the pure signifier that regulates its signifieds; it now appears behind them, depending on the things it signifies. It no longer produces an overcoding unity; it is itself produced inside the field of decoded flows.[43]

For this reason, the State 'no longer of itself forms a ruling class or classes; it is itself formed by these classes, which have become independent and delegate it to serve their power and their contradictions, their struggles and their compromises with the dominated class'.[44] The State is now not only a bit-part player in maintaining and creating order out of the flows and fluxes that subtend the social world, but, as such, comes into constant contact and, potentially, conflict with the other nodal points and power structures that seek to define, control, and shape the flows and fluxes subtending the social world. It is from this background that Deleuze and Guattari's notion and discussion of the war machine arises.

THE WAR MACHINE

In *A Thousand Plateaus*, Deleuze and Guattari develop their previous analysis of the *Urstaat* by linking it explicitly to violence in the form of the war machine. Whereas the State apparatus stratifies its subtending ontological flows and fluxes to produce order, the war machine disrupts this effort from the outside. Appealing to the work of Georges Dumézil, they explain that political sovereignty has two heads – the magician-king and the jurist-priest – that work in sync to produce binary distributions and an internal structure 'that makes the State apparatus into a *stratum*'.[45] This ordering entails a form of violence, but it is a violence that is significatory rather than physical. The State itself is defined not by physical violence but by an ordering violence, wherein stratification is imposed on smooth space to divide it up in particular ways. Crucially, then,

> war is not contained within this [State] apparatus. *Either* the State has at its disposal a violence that is not channelled through war – either it uses police officers and jailers in place of warriors, has no arms and no need of them, operates by immediate, magical capture, 'seizes' and 'binds', preventing all combat – *or*, the State acquires an army, but in a way that presupposes a juridical integration of war and the organisation of a military function.[46]

The State employs violence through its institutions either to prevent war from breaking out against another State or by incorporating, through legal means, violence into its socius so that it becomes integral to the functioning of the State. Both actions are, however, always additive to the State. War is not a function of the State apparatus *per se*, even though the State can always deploy war once it has appropriated a war machine for itself.

The war machine is, then, 'irreducible to the State apparatus'.[47] It is 'outside of sovereignty and prior to its law: it comes from elsewhere'.[48] Appealing to the warrior God, Indra, Deleuze and Guattari explain that He is different to Varuna, the God of water, and Mitra, the God of friendship or pacts. Indra does not, however, entail a third God in relation to the other two: He 'is like a pure and immeasurable multiplicity, the pack, an irruption of the ephemeral and the power of metamorphosis. *He unites the bond just as he betrays the pact.*'[49] In other words, Indra is conditioned by a different logic to that of sovereignty: 'He brings a *furor* to bear against sovereignty, a celebrity against gravity, secrecy against the public, a power (*puissance*) against sovereignty, a machine against the apparatus'.[50] Whereas sovereignty is defined in terms of being, understood as static and unchanging, Indra 'sees all things in relations of *becoming*'.[51] As a consequence, 'in every respect, the war machine is of another species, another nature, another origin than the State apparatus'.[52]

Deleuze and Guattari further distinguish the war machine and State apparatus by their different relationships to space and number.[53] They outline the first through a comparison of the games of chess and Go. The former is 'a game of State, or of the court ... Chess pieces are coded; they have an internal nature and intrinsic properties from which their movements, situations, and confrontations derive.'[54] Each chess piece has a specific power to move in a particular way and each piece has its own relative internal power. In contrast, Go is far more complicated. First, the pieces are not defined individually: they 'are pellets, disks, simple arithmetic units, and have only an anonymous, collective, or third-person function'.[55] Each piece is indistinguishable from the next and only has power in relation to the others on the board, never in-itself.

Second, the spatial relations between pieces in the two games are different. Deleuze and Guattari claim that, in chess, space is tightly controlled with a defined structure, whereas 'a Go piece has only a milieu of exteriority, or extrinsic relations with nebulas or constellations, according to which it fulfils functions of insertion or situation, such as bordering, encircling, shattering'.[56] Whereas chess is striated, Go is disruptive, based on 'smooth' space; that is, space that has no striation. As a consequence, 'chess is indeed a war, but an institutionalised, regulated, coded war, with a front, a rear, battles'.[57] In contrast, 'what is proper to Go is war without battle lines, with neither confrontation nor retreat, without battles even: pure strategy, whereas chess is a semiology'.[58]

Deleuze and Guattari return to the spatial component of the war machine, namely its emphasis on smooth space, in their discussion of nomadism. Indeed, they go so far as to claim that 'the war machine is the invention of the nomads (insofar as it is exterior to the State apparatus and distinct from the military institution'.[59] The notion of the nomad or nomadic was raised in *Difference and Repetition*, where Deleuze, distinguishing between types of distribution, explains that a nomadic one is 'completely without property, enclosure or measure. Here, there is no longer a division of that which is distributed but rather a division among those who distribute *themselves* in an open space – a space which is unlimited, or at least without precise limits.'[60]

While a number of commentators have mistakenly claimed that Deleuze and Guattari's discussion of 'nomadism' refers to or aims to offer an empirical anthropology,[61] 'nomadism' is, for them, a *philosophical concept* that refers to and describes a particular distribution of space.[62] While the nomad exists in space and so moves between points, these 'points', including their meaning, are unique. Rather than being defined by co-ordinates of sedimentary locations through which it moves, the nomad is defined by the 'between' joining each location. As such, the nomad emphasises the continuous journey between the points rather than the arrival at a point. For this reason, the nomad is defined by becoming rather than being. This distinguishes the nomad from the migrant because whereas the former continuously moves between points and is defined by that movement, the latter 'goes principally from one point to another, even if the second point is uncertain, unforeseen, or not well localised'.[63]

Importantly, while the nomad's trajectory may follow trails or paths, it does not do so in a closed manner; that is, by distributing a closed space to people. Rather, 'it *distributes people (or animals) in an open space*, one that is indefinite and noncommunicating'.[64] From this, Deleuze and Guattari distinguish between two forms of space: 'sedentary space is striated, by walls, enclosures, and roads between enclosures, while nomad space is smooth, marked only by "traits" that are effaced and displaced with the trajectory'.[65] Whereas the State is based on striation and the delineation of strict, linear divisions along homogeneous directions, 'the nomad distributes himself in a smooth space; he occupies, inhabits, holds that space; that is his territorial principle'.[66] However, as Nathan Widder explains, it would be a mistake to think that 'nomadology is defined . . . by movement as such'.[67] It is defined 'rather by its distribution in and occupation of smooth space, whereby it remains "exterior" to the State by virtue of its "intensive becomings"'.[68]

To understand why this is so requires a word on the distinction between 'movement' and 'speed'. For Deleuze and Guattari,

> movement is extensive; speed is intensive. Movement designates the relative character of a body considered as 'one', and goes from point to point: *speed, on the contrary, constitutes the absolute character of a body whose irreducible parts (atoms) occupy or fill a smooth space in the manner of a vortex*, with the possibility of springing up at any point.[69]

Nomadism refers, then, to an *intensive*, not extensive, distribution within an open, smooth space. In turn, intensity is linked to speed, with the consequence that nomadism refers to a particular form of movement based on intensive speed and distribution through vectors, rather than lines, of smooth space. For this reason, the nomadic war machine not only continuously alters itself at a far higher degree than do States, but also distributes itself in space differently. Indeed, the war machine releases 'such a vector of speed so specific to it that it needs a special name; it is not only the power of destruction, but "dromocracy" (= *nomos*)'.[70] In other words, the speed depended upon and released by the war machine re-instantiates a fundamentally new order and people to that of the State; 'this is its sole and veritable positive object (*nomos*)'.[71]

Their intensive speed means that nomads 'have no points, paths, or land, even though they do by all appearances'.[72] They are, rather, the 'de-territorialised par excellence'.[73] De-territorialisation refers to the ways in which territories alter and are altered through the movement of their different component parts. Through this process, the territory of a society alters, changes, and becomes anew. Normally, de-territorialisation entails an immediate re-territorialisation.[74] Nomadism is different, however, in that 'there is no reterritorialisation *afterward* as with the migrant, or upon *something else* as with the sedentary (the sedentary's relation with the earth is mediatised by something else, a property regime, the State apparatus)'.[75] To say, then, that nomads are 'de-territorialisation par excellence'[76] is simply to say that they are not defined by fixed points, stability, or identity; they are continuous intensive becomings wherein the nomad constantly moves intensively and what it moves on is always changing.

Crucially, however, the nomad does not cross the smooth space in the same way. Not only is the space itself constantly changing, but this change defines how the nomad relates to it. For example, 'the sand desert has not only oases, which are like fixed points, but also rhizomatic vegetation that is temporary and shifts location according to local rains, bringing changes in the direction of the crossings'.[77] Indeed, this 'variability, this polyvocality of directions, is an essential feature of smooth spaces of the rhizome type, and it alters their cartography'.[78]

In contrast to smooth nomadic space, is the striated space of the State: 'one of the fundamental tasks of the State is to striate the space over which it reigns, or to utilise smooth spaces as a means of communication in the service of striated space'.[79] The State is designed to capture the smooth space and over-code it, linguistically, culturally, and normatively, to provide it with meaning and secure ownership and control over it. Thus, it aims to establish 'fixed paths in well-defined directions, which restrict speed, regulate circulation, relativise movement, and measure in detail the relative movements of subjects and objects'.[80]

The State's relationship to nomadism is, then, inherently oppressive and violent, insofar as the State aims to impose itself on the nomad to co-opt and so control it. Deleuze and Guattari explain that, for this reason, 'it is a vital concern of every State not only to vanquish nomadism but to control migrations and, more generally, to establish a zone of rights over an entire "exterior", over all of the flows traversing the ecumenon'.[81] Following Paul Virilio, they claim that this is achieved through the political power of the

State, the police, the management of the public highways, as well as the levies, duties, and fees that need to be paid before admittance is granted, all of which filter the masses and slow them down.[82]

The battle between the nomadic war machine and the State is, then, a battle over different approaches to space. The State striates the smooth space of the nomads, while the subsequent actions of the nomads against the State aim to smooth that striation:

> each time there is an operation against the State – insubordination, rioting, guerrilla warfare, or revolution as act – it can be said that a war machine has revived, that a new nomadic potential has appeared, accompanied by the reconstitution of a smooth space or a manner of being in space as though it were smooth.[83]

This disrupts the regimentation of the State apparatus and, in so doing, permits an alternative course of movement and organisation. It is always, however, a disruption from outside the State apparatus.

Deleuze and Guattari also distinguish the war machine from the State apparatus by the arithmetic underpinning both. In relation to the State, they explain that 'arithmetic, the number, has always had a decisive role in the State apparatus'.[84] This is true in the early imperial bureaucracies, which were based on 'census, taxation, and election',[85] but is more so in modern societies, given the influence of mathematical science on politics (polling, demography, organisation, and so on), where the aim is for number 'to gain mastery over matter, to control its variations and movements, in other words, to submit them, to the spatiotemporal framework of the State'.[86]

To distinguish between the arithmetic underpinning the war machine and that of the State, Deleuze and Guattari introduce a distinction between the '*numbered* number'[87] of the State, which works through specific quantities and fixed relations that generate order, and the '*Numbering Number*',[88] which they associate with the war machine. Whereas the numbered number of the State apparatus is concerned with 'dividing up space or distributing space itself',[89] the numbering number of the war machine is concerned with the distribution of 'something in space'.[90]

Crucially, this distribution is not the result of abstraction from or imposition of number on space, but is a direct consequence 'of the concrete nature of smooth space, which is occupied without itself being counted'.[91] The numbering number is 'no longer a means of counting or measuring but of moving: it is the number itself that moves through smooth space'.[92] For this reason, the numbering number does not move through space, but is disruptive of space itself.[93]

With this, Deleuze and Guattari identify two definitive characteristics of numbering number: first, it is 'a complex of numbers every time'.[94] Complexity is also, of course, a feature of State organisation:

> The Roman legion was made up of numbers, articulated in such a way that the segments became mobile, and the figures geometrical, changing, transformational. The complex or articulated number comprises not only men but necessarily weapons, animals, and vehicles.[95]

The difference is that, in the numbering number of the war machine, this complexity is far more organic and heterogeneous. Whereas the Roman legions were based on homogenous principles of assemblage, the numbering number is a becoming that spreads out in diffuse ways. Its numbering system 'always has several bases at the same time'.[96]

Second, 'the war machine displays a curious process of arithmetic replication or doubling'.[97] This occurs through two simultaneous processes: '*on the one hand*, the lineages are indeed organised and reshuffled numerically',[98] but '*on the other hand*, men are simultaneously extracted from each lineage to form a special numerical body'.[99] The language is highly abstract, but Deleuze and Guattari's basic point is that the war machine is organised around two principles: first, the organisation of itself into lineages or orders. This it shares with the numbered number of the State apparatus, although as previously noted, how exactly this functions is slightly different. But, having divided itself in such a fashion, it then, second, performs another division, one in which some individuals are extracted from their lineages to form another 'special' unit. This does not so much create a distinction between an 'inner' core and an outer membership, but acts to re-enforce the structure of the war machine by providing it with an intensifying force missing from the straightforward division of the State apparatus.

Deleuze and Guattari call the first operation – the division into lineages – 'the number of the body',[100] and the second, the further division into a special unity, 'a body of the number'.[101] Both must be operationalised for the war machine to function. For example, when Genghis Khan undertook his takeover of the steppe, he numerically organised the lineages and fighters in each, before extracting 'from each arithmetici[s]ed lineage a small number of men who were to constitute his personal guard, in other words, a dynamic formation comprising a staff, commissars, messengers, and diplomats ("antrustions")'.[102] Similarly, when 'Moses undertook his great composition of the desert . . . he took a census of each tribe and organi[s]ed them numerically'[103] before decreeing a law 'according to which the firstborn of each tribe at that particular time belonged by right to Yahweh'.[104] Obviously, these firstborn were too young to fight, so their special role was transferred 'to a special tribe, the Levites, who provided the body of the Number or the special guard of the ark'.[105] These special bodies form 'an essential constituent of the war machine'[106] and, indeed, are the aspect of nomadic existence 'that implies the most variety and originality'[107] because they 'drive' the war machine on; they are, after all, composed of its most committed components.

These spatial and numerical differences point to two different forms of assemblage. Whereas the State apparatus is ordered around extension and hierarchy, and proceeds regularly in a linear fashion, the war machine is based on an intensive conception of number and vectors and speeds, with the consequence that it is dynamic and horizontal. This is not to say that one is better than the other, 'only that [war machines] animate a fundamental indiscipline of the warrior, a questioning of hierarchy, perpetual blackmail by abandonment or betrayal, and a very volatile sense of honour, all of which . . . impedes the formation of the State'.[108]

The problem, of course, is that, while the war machine and the State are conceptually and ontologically different, they do have a relationship with one another. The State must appropriate a war machine to survive, while the war machine comes into contact and (potential) conflict with States. Their relationship is, however, 'difficult to conceptualise'[109] for, at least, two reasons: first, while the war machine is exterior to the State, the heterogeneity of the former means that it is not always clear how they relate to one another. For example, the war machine can take the form of 'huge worldwide machines [that have] branched out over the entire *ecumenon* at a given moment, which enjoy a large measure of autonomy in relation to the State'[110] – examples include multinational organisations, industrial complexes, and even religious institutions – or it can entail 'the local mechanisms of bands, margins, minorities, which continue to affirm the rights of segmentary societies in opposition to the organs of State power'.[111] These two groups are not necessarily distinct – for example, 'a commercial organisation is also a band of pillage, or piracy, for part of its course and in many of its activities; or it is in bands that a religious formation begins to operate'[112] – but more often than not they are, meaning that it is not clear what form the war machine takes or how it relates to the State.[113]

From an epistemological perspective, Brent Adkins explains that the notions of 'interior' and 'exterior' are linked to Deleuze's discussion of the image of thought in *Difference and Repetition*.[114] The analysis is complex, but, very simply, Deleuze argues that thought has historically been guided by certain presuppositions that (1) are based on fixed foundations, which (2) shape how the object under consideration is perceived, understood, and analysed, and (3) provide a singular, fixed conclusion.[115] Rather than describing the differential structure of the world, the image of thought is premised on a prior model of ontological identity to be represented.

The problem, of course, is that the understanding of the world generated does not actually correspond to the world, but is based purely on the image of thought itself. It is, in other words, a purely internal, self-referential creation of thought based on its own presupposed affirmation of identity. Similarly, the State affirms such identity and so is understood to be a self-referential construction concerned only with itself. It has, therefore, 'a tendency to reproduce itself, remaining identical to itself across its variations and easily recognisable within the limits of its poles, always seeking public recognition (there is no masked State)'.[116] On the contrary, the war machine is based on the ontological principle of becoming so that it is never based on fixity or presuppositions. Rather it occurs through a different logic to the State.[117]

However, from the perspective of the State, the exterior disruption of the war machine appears to be a purely negative function, with the consequence that

> it is not enough to affirm that the war machine is external to the apparatus. It is necessary to reach the point of conceiving the war machine as itself a pure form of exteriority, whereas the State apparatus constitutes the form of interiority we habitually take as a model, or according to which we are in the habit of thinking.[118]

The war machine must, then, be thought in terms of pure exteriority or non-representationally; that is, as pure becoming. The problem is that the dominance of the image of thought makes this extremely difficult; it is all too easy to slip into the image of thought and so think of the war machine in purely negative, destructive terms.

Furthermore, while the war machine and State apparatus are distinct, the 'extrinsic power of the war machine tends, under certain circumstances, to become confused with one of the two heads of the State apparatus. Sometimes it is confused with the magic violence of the State, at other times with the State's military institution.'[119] When this occurs, the war machine is understood to be an appendage of the State. For example, whereas the war machine 'invents speed and secrecy',[120] these attributes, albeit in a secondary sense, can find expression in the State. As a consequence, there is 'a great danger of identifying the structural relation between the two poles of political sovereignty, and the dynamic interrelation of these two poles, with the power of war'.[121] When this occurs, 'everything gets muddled',[122] with the consequence that we must carefully tease out the relationship between the two.

THE STATE AND THE WAR MACHINE

Whereas Benjamin and Schmitt link violence and sovereignty and Arendt insists on the absolute analytical opposition between the two, Deleuze and

Guattari offer a compatibilist understanding: on the one hand, they recognise that '*the State apparatus has no war machine of its own*',[123] and so agree with Arendt that violence – the war machine – and the State apparatus – sovereignty – are distinct. But, on the other hand, they recognise that the State apparatus 'can appropriate [a war machine] in the form of a military institution',[124] thereby linking violence and sovereignty. They do, however, contribute to the entwinement model – manifested in the thought of Benjamin and Schmitt – by recognising that the incorporation of the war machine *within* the State apparatus 'will continually cause it problems'.[125] It is not the case that the military exists harmoniously with the State apparatus that houses it. The various parts of the social apparatus and, by extension, the State apparatus are multiplicities and so are amalgamations of heterogeneous elements. Rather than harmony and homogeneity, there is only ever heterogeneous movement that constantly reconfigures all aspects of the multiplicity.

The first thing to note is that the war machine does not 'necessarily have war as its object'.[126] War results 'because the war machine collides with States and cities, as forces (of striation) opposing its positive object: from then on, the war machine has as its enemy the State, the city, the [S]tate and urban phenomenon, and adopts as its objective their annihilation'.[127] It is only once the war machine encounters the striation of the State that 'the war machine becomes war'.[128] It is only at this point that the positive action of the nomadic war machine – smoothing of space, existence at speed, opening up of alternatives – turns into (the) negative annihilation of/against the State. War is then a synthetic aspect of the war machine. It 'is neither the condition nor the object of the war machine, but necessarily accompanies or completes it'.[129]

But this does not mean that war is a condition of the State. Deleuze and Guattari explain that 'States were not the first to make war: war, of course, is not a phenomenon one finds in the universality of Nature, as nonspecific violence . . . War is not the object of States, quite the contrary.'[130] Indeed, 'the most archaic States do not even seem to have had a war machine, and their domination . . . was based on other agencies (comprising, rather, the police and prisons)'.[131] While their initial encounter with the nomadic war machine 'was one of the mysterious reasons for their sudden demise',[132] the early States learnt and adapted quickly to this new threat by incorporating a war machine into themselves. This gave rise to the military, although Deleuze and Guattari are careful to note that the military is not a pure form of war machine, 'but the form under which it is appropriated by the State'.[133]

However, when the State incorporates a war machine, it does not simply add it to its matrix. Because the nomadic war machine is exterior to the State – its smoothness runs counter to the striation of the State – any incorporation of it by and within the State must necessarily alter both the State and the war machine. 'This explains the mistrust [that] States have toward their military institutions, in that the military institution inherits an extrinsic war machine.'[134]

The State is, however, able to appropriate the war machine because of the internal dynamics of the war machine itself: it simply hesitates about what to do. Because war is synthetic to the war machine, the war machine must 'think' about when it is appropriate to employ war, what form it takes, and how it will be constrained. This hesitation 'proves fatal'[135] because 'the State apparatus . . . is able to lay hold of war and thus turn the war machine back against the nomads'.[136] Lest we be in any doubt about the hesitation of the nomads, Deleuze and Guattari assure us that it is 'legendary',[137] and gives rise, for example, to the question:

> What is to be done with the lands conquered and crossed? Return them to the desert, to the steppe, to open pastureland? Or let a State apparatus survive that is capable of exploiting them directly, at the risk of becoming, sooner or later, simply a new dynasty of that apparatus.[138]

From the perspective of the war machine, then, it is the engagement with the State apparatus that risks turning the nomadic war machine into a State apparatus.

On the other side of the equation, the incorporation of the war machine into the State causes the State problems. It must, for example, find some way to release its war machine against others so that it does not destroy the State apparatus from within. This requires that the State decide on the shape, networks of organisation, and place of the war machine within it. It also requires that it establish logistical, support networks to finance, organise, and move the war machine. These alter the dynamics of the State itself; for example, they require 'fiscal regimes [that] determine both the nature of the services and taxes owed by the beneficiary warriors, and especially the kind of civil tax to which all or part of society [will be] subject for the maintenance of the army'.[139]

It must be remembered, however, that the State cannot integrate a 'pure' nomadic war machine; the State's striation means that the nomadic war machine must be striated to be incorporated within the State. As such, the State's war machine is always 'the heavier and more unproductive since it exist[s] only as the empty form of appropriation of that machine'.[140] The incorporation of the war machine into the State not only introduces something that lies uneasily with the striation of the State; it also means that the State must find some way to release the war machine productively. Not only does this place the State in danger as it battles the nomadic war machine, but it means that the State becomes subordinate to the war machine. As a consequence, 'turning the war machine back against the nomads may constitute for the State a danger as great as that presented by nomads directing the war machine against States'.[141]

It is here that Deleuze and Guattari turn to Carl von Clausewitz's famous formula that 'war is the continuation of politics by other means'.[142] They note that it is based on three premises: (1) 'there is a pure concept of war as absolute, unconditioned war, an Idea not given in experience';[143] (2) 'what is given are real wars as submitted to State aim';[144] and (3) 'real wars swing between two poles, both subject to State politics: the war of annihilation, which can escalate to total war . . . and tends to approach the unconditioned concept via an ascent to extremes; and limited war [which] effects a descent toward limiting conditions'.[145]

They focus on the Ideal/Real distinction underpinning these points. Deleuze and Guattari accept the distinction, but reject the implication emanating from it that the nomad can be identified with real war. Rather, the nomadic war machine is 'the content adequate to the Idea, the invention of the Idea, with its own objects, space, and composition of the *nomos*'.[146] The nomads were simply the first to realise the Idea of the war machine. Indeed, Deleuze and Guattari suggest that it is the nomads who are the truly abstract. Not only are nomads always moving assemblages, meaning that it is not possible to identify a 'pure' nomad/ism, but the nomadic war machine always comes up against and so is intimately entwined with the State. 'The question is therefore less the realisation of war than the appropriation of the war machine'[147] by the State. Contrary to Clausewitz's claim that war and politics are entwined, Deleuze and Guattari remind us that this only occurs if the State incorporates the war machine within it. War and politics, violence and sovereignty are not necessarily linked. Only a particular form of political sovereignty, one that has arisen from a State with a war machine, generates war.

This form of politics arises when the State goes 'from figures of encastment to forms of appropriation proper . . . from limited war to so-called total war, and [in so doing] transform[s] the relation between aim and object'.[148] The clearest contemporary example of the movement towards an absolute State war machine is

> closely connected to capitalism: it has to do with the investment of constant capital in equipment, industry, and the war economy, and the investment of variable capital in the population in its physical and mental aspects (both as warmaker and as victim of war).[149]

Capitalism and the State war machine complement one another: the former provides the spiritual and material conditions through which the antagonism of the war machine can be played out for the purposes of the State. By searching for new markets, capitalism expresses the competitive spirit of the nomadic war machine, while also providing the weapons that permit the State apparatus to secure its dominance. Politics and violence are not, then, simply tied to questions of law and sovereignty; there is an economic aspect to the violence–sovereign relationship that has all too often been ignored.

Deleuze and Guattari's point is that 'total war is not only a war of annihilation but arises when annihilation takes as its "centre" not only the enemy army, or the enemy State, but the entire population and its economy'.[150] Total war is not an exception, but an aspect of the everyday in modern capitalist societies. It is fundamental to the structures, norms, and processes governing everyday interaction to the point where, on Deleuze and Guattari's telling, we exist within a total war. Paradoxically, capitalism's total war depends upon a limited war to permit the stable conditions that facilitate production on a sufficiently large scale. Only once it has the means to wage total war – means that can only be created when war is, at least, limited – can the capitalist war machine 'develop total war'.[151] This dynamic points to a fundamental tension at the heart of the capitalist State apparatus: on the one hand, the State must appropriate the war machine to defend itself against nomadic structures, but, on the other hand, when doing so it has to ensure that the war machine is subordinated to political ends.

However, while politics may orientate the war machine to a political end, it cannot control how the war machine achieves this. Ground conditions, for example, may move too quickly to obtain bureaucratic clearance from the State apparatus. Granting autonomy to the war machine does not resolve this because it would risk 'unleash[ing], [and] reconstitut[ing], an immense war machine of which [the State] is no longer anything more than the opposable or apposed parts'.[152] Having appropriated the war machine, the State would become an appendage of it.

According to Deleuze and Guattari, this can take two forms: 'first, that of fascism, which makes war an unlimited movement with no aim other than itself; but fascism is only a rough sketch, and the second, postfascist, figure is that of a war machine that takes peace as its object directly, as the peace of Terror or Survival'.[153] While fascism is the clearest indication that a State has moved towards total war, it is not the only kind and, indeed, is a rather unsophisticated manifestation of total war.[154] Deleuze and Guattari point out that the defeat of fascism does not mean the defeat of total war: when war defines society to the extent that the war machine comes to dominate so that political discourse is defined by Terror or Survival, society has moved to a total war footing.

War does not, then, have to be the explicit aim of the State for total war to be realised; a more sophisticated version of total war arises when the norms of the State are orientated around questions of war and, in particular, when political discourse is defined by terror threats or issues – such as the values of other States, minority groups, and immigration – that, so it is claimed, are sure to bring about imminent annihilation. Once this occurs, States become 'no more than objects or means adapted to the machine'.[155] This is why Clausewitz's dictum must be reversed: not war as the continuation of politics, but politics understood as the continuation of the war machine, wherein 'having appropriated a war machine, and having adapted it to their aims, [States] reimport a war machine that takes charge of the aim, appropriates the States, and assumes increasingly wider political functions'.[156] Having been exterior to the State, the appropriated war machine now directs the State and, by extension, worldwide politics.

With this, Deleuze and Guattari suggest that violence and a war mentality come to shape and govern the State apparatus, even when the State is not engaged in a physical war. Its continuous war footing means that violence conditions its existence. Not only does this ensure that 'the war machine grows stronger and stronger'[157] until it has 'as its objective a peace still more terrifying than fascist death',[158] but it also leads to the development of 'a new type of enemy, no longer another State, or even another regime, but the "unspecified enemy"'.[159] With this, the war machine has created the conditions for its own brutality and the justification for its continuation: because the enemy is unspecified, there can always be an enemy to be defeated.

But we have to remember that, for Deleuze and Guattari, being is differential becoming; change, fluidity, flux, and alteration are constitutive of things. Indeed, 'things' are never singular; they are multiplicities. For this reason, they cannot be reduced to one aspect – in this case, a negative, oppressive understanding of the war machine. While the State's appropriation of the war machine in a capitalist economy has led to total war,

> the very conditions that make the State or World war machine possible, in other words, constant capital (resources and equipment) and human variable capital, continually recreate unexpected possibilities for counterattack, unforeseen initiatives determining revolutionary, popular, minority, mutant machines.[160]

Deleuze and Guattari see two reasons for this: not only has 'the war machine ... many varied meanings',[161] but '*the war machine has an extremely variable relation to war itself*'.[162] While the war machine, especially as it is appropriated by the State, 'takes war for its object and forms a line of destruction prolongable to the limits of the universe',[163] this does not define the 'essence' of the war machine. As noted, the war machine smooths space, disrupts striation, order, and regimentation. From the perspective of the State, this is an inherently negative act, but, when looked at in itself, a different conclusion arises: 'the war machine, with infinitely lower "quantities", has as its object not war but the drawing of a creative line of flight, the composition of a smooth space and of the movement of people in that space'.[164] The smoothing of space, the disruption of sovereignty and order, open the possibility not just for alternatives, but for radically creative forms of expression and political action 'directed against the State and against the worldwide axiomatic expressed by States'.[165]

CONCLUDING REMARKS

By pointing out that many types of war machine are possible and that they can always disrupt the repressive war machine of capitalist society, Deleuze and Guattari appeal to an ontological principle, namely that each assemblage is a multiplicity of competing flows and forces, to offer the possibility of political action against the capitalist State war machine. While they are clear that this possibility arises from the deterritorialisations inherent in any and all formations, meaning that the enclosure aimed for by the State war machine will never be total, they also insist that the war machine is not an instrument for individual use; it is a pre-personal assemblage. Agents, themselves multiplicities, are effects of the creative disruption of the war machine. For this reason, 'it is not the nomad who defines this constellation of characteristics; it is this constellation that defines the nomad, and at the same time the essence of the war machine'.[166] War machines come in many guises to disrupt the established order, but they are spontaneous, pre-individual events.

While this ensures that the total war of capitalist State war machines will necessarily be challenged by the continuous ontological flows and fluxes subtending them, with this creating gaps and pores for alternatives to rise through, it is not clear what, if anything, political agents – themselves effects of pre-personal forces – can do to facilitate this process. Nevertheless, Deleuze and Guattari's conception of the war machine contributes much to our understanding of violence and, in particular, the ways in which violence disrupts established sovereign structures, practices, and norms. Whereas Benjamin, Schmitt, and Arendt identify the intimate relationship between violence and sovereignty/State, but tend to reduce society to the State, Deleuze and Guattari decentre the State from social existence to claim that it is one assemblage amongst others. These assemblages are constantly moving, meaning that the components and relations of society are heterogeneous and in conflict with one another; a premise that emphasises how violence operates throughout society at large. Indeed, Deleuze and Guattari also offer us a particular conception of the State, where, rather than being a single entity, it is conceived as a flux of competing components that is, initially, devoid of violence. War and violence are additive to the State rather than constitutive of it. Different conceptions of the violence-sovereignty, violence-State relationship are then possible. Indeed, by linking this relationship to the question of economy, Deleuze and Guattari introduce a new dimension to thinking on the topic and show how political violence manifests itself economically to the extent that it imperceptibly defines and creates the norms and values of society.

Yet, for all the innovation inherent in their analysis of the disruption caused by the war machine to the State and, indeed, their original conception of the State apparatus as an assemblage that expresses flows of ontological forces that constantly change, their notion of the State apparatus is still, fundamentally, juridical: it is understood as one assemblage – albeit one that is constantly becoming – that aims for the creation of order from chaos and faces off against the violence of the war machine that tries to disturb its order. With this, Deleuze and Guattari radically disrupt the notion of sovereignty underpinning the classic-juridical model, but maintain the end that defines that model. For all their talk of difference and heterogeneity, they continue to see sovereignty as being orientated to the creation/maintenance/disruption of juridical order.

However, at around the same time as they were developing their conception of sovereignty, another strand of post-structuralist thought claimed that fundamental historical changes had taken place in the last two centuries that undermined the claim that sovereignty is orientated towards the establishment and preservation of juridical order. The next chapter engages with Michel Foucault's 1976 lecture course on racism, arguing that it marks the point of transition from critical accounts of the classical-juridical model based on the radical-juridical paradigm to those founded on a biopolitical model. In so doing, we move from critical analyses that conceive of violence as being external to or an instrument of sovereignty as it seeks to establish juridical order, to ones that hold that sovereignty generates internal divisions and conflicts within society to better regulate life.

NOTES

1. For example, Guattari mentions it in a 1965 lecture, subsequently published as 'Causality, Subjectivity and History', p. 262, in *Psychoanalysis and Transversality*, trans. Ames Hodges (Cambridge, MA: MIT Press, 2015), pp. 235–80, and again in 1972 in 'Machine and Structure', p. 321, in *Psychoanalysis and Transversality*, pp. 318–30. Deleuze appears to first mention it in 1972 in the preface – 'Three Group-Related Problems', pp. 199–201, in *Desert Islands and Other Texts, 1953–1974*, ed. David Lapoujade, trans. Michael Taomini (New York: Semiotext, 2004), pp. 193 – to Guattari's *Psychoanalysis and Transversality*. Deleuze then discusses it in the 1973 essays 'Nomadic Thought', pp. 254, 259–60, in *Desert Islands and Other Texts, 1953–1974*, pp. 252–61; 'On Capitalism and Desire', p. 267, in *Desert Islands and Other Texts, 1953–1974*, pp. 262–73; and 'Five Propositions in Psychoanalysis', p. 279, in *Desert Islands and Other Texts, 1953–1974*, pp. 274–80; his 1977 book with Claire Parnet, *Dialogues II*, trans. Hugh Tomlinson

and Barbara Habberjam (London: Continuum, 2006), pp. 31–2, 58, 119, 123, 140–6; and the 1977 letter to Michel Foucault, published as 'Desire and Pleasure', pp. 133–4, in Gilles Deleuze, *Two Regimes of Madness: Texts and Interviews, 1975–1995*, ed. David Lapoujade, trans. Ames Hodges and Mike Taormina (New York: Semiotext, 2007), pp. 122–34.
2. Gilles Deleuze and Felix Guattari, *A Thousand Plateaus*, trans. Brian Massumi (London: Continuum, 2004), pp. 387–467.
3. Paul Patton, *Deleuzian Concepts: Philosophy, Colonisation, Politics* (Stanford: Stanford University Press, 2010), p. 3.
4. Paul Patton, *Deleuze and the Political* (Abingdon: Routledge, 2000), p. 109.
5. The purpose of *Difference and Repetition* is to think as and from difference, which, as Deleuze explains, means to 'think difference in itself independently of the forms of representation which reduce it to the Same, and which make them pass through the negative'. (Gilles Deleuze, *Difference and Repetition*, trans. Paul Patton [New York: Columbia University Press, 1994], p. xix.) For a critical discussion of this endeavour, see Gavin Rae, *Ontology in Heidegger and Deleuze* (Basingstoke: Palgrave Macmillan, 2014).
6. Eugene W. Holland, *Deleuze and Guattari's A Thousand Plateaus* (London: Bloomsbury, 2013), p. 50.
7. Nathan Widder, *Political Theory after Deleuze* (London: Continuum, 2012), p. 132.
8. Brent Adkins, *Deleuze and Guattari's A Thousand Plateaus: A Critical Introduction and Guide* (Edinburgh: Edinburgh University Press, 2015), p. 191.
9. Patton, *Deleuze and the Political*, pp. 109–10.
10. Nathan Widder, 'State Philosophy and the War Machine', in *At the Edges of Thought: Deleuze and Post-Kantian Philosophy*, ed. Craig Lundy and Danielle Voss (Edinburgh: Edinburgh University Press, 2015), pp. 190–211.
11. Guillaume Sibertin-Blanc, 'The War-Machine, the Formula, and the Hypothesis: Deleuze and Guattari as Readers of Clausewitz', *Theory and Event*, 13:3, 2010: https://muse.jhu.edu/article/396505. See also Guillaume Sibertin-Blanc, *State and Politics: Deleuze and Guattari on Marx*, trans. Ames Hodges (New York: Semiotext, 2016).
12. Gregg Lambert, 'The War-Machine and "a people who revolt"', *Theory and Event*, 13:3, 2010: https://muse.jhu.edu/article/396506.
13. Julian Reid, 'Deleuze's War Machine: Nomadism against the State', *Millennium: Journal of International Studies*, 32:1, 2003, pp. 57–85 (p. 62).
14. Deleuze and Guattari, *A Thousand Plateaus*, p. 397.
15. Ibid. p. 387.
16. Gilles Deleuze and Felix Guattari, *Anti-Oedipus: Capitalism and Schizophrenia*, trans. Robert Hurley, Mark Seem, and Helen R. Lane (London: Continuum, 2004), pp. 237–41.
17. Ibid. p. 237.
18. Ibid. p. 237.
19. Ibid. p. 237.
20. Ibid. p. 237.
21. Ibid. p. 237.
22. Ibid. pp. 237–8.
23. Ibid. p. 238.
24. Ibid. p. 238. 'Socius' here delineates the intensive 'field' from and through which social activity, including the generation of meaning, takes place.
25. Ibid. p. 238.
26. Ibid. p. 238.

27. Ibid. p. 238.
28. Ibid. p. 238.
29. Ibid. p. 238.
30. Ibid. p. 238.
31. Ibid. p. 238.
32. Ibid. p. 238.
33. Ibid. p. 239.
34. Ibid. p. 239.
35. Ibid. p. 239.
36. Ibid. p. 239.
37. Ibid. p. 239.
38. Ibid. p. 239.
39. Ibid. p. 239.
40. Ibid. p. 239.
41. Ibid. p. 240.
42. Ibid. p. 241.
43. Ibid. p. 241.
44. Ibid. p. 241.
45. Deleuze and Guattari, *A Thousand Plateaus*, p. 388.
46. Ibid. p. 388.
47. Ibid. p. 388.
48. Ibid. p. 388.
49. Ibid. p. 388.
50. Ibid. p. 388.
51. Ibid. p. 388.
52. Ibid. p. 389.
53. Space constraints prevent a discussion of these, but Deleuze and Guattari also insist that the State apparatus and war machine are distinguished by their relations to affectivity, which also entails discussions of the weapons/tool division and metallurgy. The fundamental difference between the State apparatus and the war machine is, however, sufficiently revealed by focusing on their different relationships to space and number.
54. Deleuze and Guattari, *A Thousand Plateaus*, p. 389.
55. Ibid. p. 389.
56. Ibid. p. 389.
57. Ibid. p. 389.
58. Ibid. p. 389.
59. Ibid. p. 419.
60. Deleuze, *Difference and Repetition*, p. 36.
61. Caren Kaplan, *Questions of Travel: Postmodern Discourses of Displacement* (Durham: Duke University Press, 1996), p. 90; Christopher L. Miller, 'Beyond Identity: The Postidentarian Predicament of *A Thousand Plateaus*', in *Nationalists and Nomads: Essays on Francophone African Literature and Culture* (Chicago: University of Chicago Press, 1998), pp. 171–244.
62. Einat Bar-on Cohen makes the same point in relation to Deleuze and Guattari's notion of the State: 'The Deleuzian concept of the "State" is not equivalent to the nation-State; it is a philosophical concept indicating a striated logic of operation.' (Einat Bar-on Cohen, 'Events of Organicity: The State Abducts the War Machine', *Anthropological Theory*, 11:3, 2011, pp. 259–82 [p. 262].)
63. Deleuze and Guattari, *A Thousand Plateaus*, p. 419.

64. Ibid. p. 420.
65. Ibid. p. 420.
66. Ibid. p. 420.
67. Widder, 'State Philosophy and the War Machine', p. 200.
68. Ibid. p. 200.
69. Deleuze and Guattari, *A Thousand Plateaus*, pp. 420–1.
70. Ibid. p. 436.
71. Ibid. p. 460.
72. Ibid. p. 421
73. Ibid. p. 421.
74. For a discussion of the notion of de-/re-territorialisation, see Gavin Rae, 'Violence, Territorialisation, and Signification: The Political from Carl Schmitt and Gilles Deleuze', *Theoria and Praxis: International Journal of Interdisciplinary Thought*, 1:1, 2013, pp. 1–17.
75. Deleuze and Guattari, *A Thousand Plateaus*, p. 421.
76. Ibid. p. 421.
77. Ibid. p. 421.
78. Ibid. pp. 421–2.
79. Ibid. p. 425.
80. Ibid. p. 425.
81. Ibid. p. 425.
82. Ibid. p. 426. Virilio's analysis is found in his *Speed and Politics*, trans. Mark Polizzoti (New York: Semiotext, 1986), pp. 12–13.
83. Deleuze and Guattari, *A Thousand Plateaus*, p. 426.
84. Ibid. p. 429.
85. Ibid. p. 429.
86. Ibid. p. 429.
87. Ibid. p. 431, emphasis added.
88. Ibid. p. 429.
89. Ibid. p. 429.
90. Ibid. p. 429.
91. Ibid. pp. 429–30.
92. Ibid. p. 430.
93. Ibid. p. 430.
94. Ibid. p. 431.
95. Ibid. p. 431.
96. Ibid. pp. 431–2.
97. Ibid. p. 432.
98. Ibid. p. 432.
99. Ibid. p. 432.
100. Ibid. p. 432.
101. Ibid. p. 432.
102. Ibid. p. 432.
103. Ibid. p. 432.
104. Ibid. p. 432.
105. Ibid. p. 433.
106. Ibid. p. 432.
107. Ibid. p. 433.
108. Ibid. p. 395.

109. Ibid. p. 390.
110. Ibid. p. 397.
111. Ibid. p. 397.
112. Ibid. p. 397.
113. Ibid. p. 397.
114. Adkins, *Deleuze and Guattari's A Thousand Plateaus*, p. 194.
115. For a more extensive discussion, see Rae, *Ontology in Heidegger and Deleuze*, pp. 146–52.
116. Deleuze and Guattari, *A Thousand Plateaus*, p. 397.
117. Deleuze and Guattari expand on this in their discussion of the difference between nomadic, war-machine science and royal science. See ibid. pp. 398–412.
118. Ibid. p. 390.
119. Ibid. pp. 390–1.
120. Ibid. p. 391
121. Ibid. p. 391
122. Ibid. p. 391
123. Ibid. p. 391.
124. Ibid. p. 391
125. Ibid. p. 391
126. Ibid. p. 460.
127. Ibid. p. 460.
128. Ibid. p. 460.
129. Ibid. p. 460.
130. Ibid. p. 461.
131. Ibid. p. 461.
132. Ibid. p. 461.
133. Ibid. p. 461.
134. Ibid. p. 391
135. Ibid. p. 461.
136. Ibid. p. 461.
137. Ibid. p. 461.
138. Ibid. pp. 461–2.
139. Ibid. p. 463.
140. Ibid. p. 462.
141. Ibid. p. 462.
142. Ibid. p. 463. Clausewitz's famous dictum actually reads: 'We see, therefore, that war is not merely an act of policy but a true political instrument, a continuation of political intercourse, carried on with other means.' (Carl von Clausewitz, *On War*, ed. and trans. Michael Howard and Peter Paret [Princeton: Princeton University Press, 1984], p. 87.)
143. Deleuze and Guattari, *A Thousand Plateaus*, p. 463.
144. Ibid. p. 463.
145. Ibid. p. 463.
146. Ibid. p. 463.
147. Ibid. p. 463.
148. Ibid. p. 464.
149. Ibid. p. 464.
150. Ibid. p. 464.
151. Ibid. p. 464.
152. Ibid. p. 465.
153. Ibid. p. 465.

154. For an extended discussion of Deleuze and Guattari's analysis of the relationship between nomadism and fascism, see Eugene W. Holland, 'Schizoanalysis, Nomadology, Fascism', in *Deleuze and Politics*, ed. Ian Buchanan and Nicholas Thorburn (Edinburgh: Edinburgh University Press, 2008), pp. 74–97; and the essays collected in Brad Evans and Julian Reid, eds, *Deleuze and Fascism: Security, War, Aesthetics* (Abingdon: Routledge, 2015).
155. Deleuze and Guattari, *A Thousand Plateaus*, p. 465.
156. Ibid. p. 465.
157. Ibid. p. 465.
158. Ibid. p. 465.
159. Ibid. p. 465.
160. Ibid. p. 465.
161. Ibid. p. 465.
162. Ibid. pp. 465–6.
163. Ibid. p. 466.
164. Ibid. p. 466.
165. Ibid. p. 466.
166. Ibid. p. 466.

PART II

The Biopolitical Critique

CHAPTER 5

From Law to Life: Foucault, Sovereignty, and Biopolitical Racism

Throughout the 1970s, Michel Foucault produced significant genealogical studies – that is to say, analyses of the history of concepts or thought-schemas to determine how they came to dominance – of the productive role that power plays in a range of fields, including the lecture series *Psychiatric Power*,[1] given in 1973-4, and *Abnormal*[2] in 1974-5, and the major studies *Discipline and Punish*,[3] published in 1975, and the first volume of *The History of Sexuality*[4] from 1976.

In between the publication of the last two books, Foucault gave a series of lectures, between 7 January and 17 March 1976, at the Collège de France, published as *Society Must Be Defended*,[5] where he 'develops a two-fold problematic, testing to what extent war can serve as a principle of historical intelligibility, while developing a genealogy of nineteenth and twentieth century racism',[6] which, in the final lecture, is linked to the notion of biopower. The lecture series is not, then, so much a study of war *per se* as an analysis of a particular conception of power relations, and the way in which that conception may be suitable as a means of showing how Western European States and societies came, in the nineteenth century, to be defined by and function through the logic of racism. Specifically, Foucault shows how shifting historical power relations in the sixteenth and seventeenth centuries led to the development of the notion of race, which became politically important in the nineteenth and twentieth centuries by generating a new conception of power and politics called biopower/biopolitics.

Prior to engaging further with this lecture course, we have to deal with two methodological issues: first, there is the troubling status of the 1976 lecture series within Foucault's thinking. John Marks, for example, points out that *Society Must Be Defended* can be read from the viewpoint of

Foucault's wider project or as independent studies of particular topics. If the former is emphasised, the lectures 'mark the point at which Foucault begins to shift his focus from a genealogy of power-knowledge ... to think of power in new ways'.[7] On this reading, the lecture series marks something of a methodological and conceptual turning point for Foucault; one that, in some respects, was just as quickly rejected. After all, as Beatrice Hanssen points out, 'Foucault, after the 1976 lecture course, more or less gave up on the figure of war.'[8] Similarly, Ansgar Allen and Roy Goddard argue that these lectures 'mark the transition from his conception of power-as-war to the revised (now dominant) framework of power-as-government',[9] while Paul Patton simply talks of 'the crisis of 1976'.[10] If Foucault quickly abandoned the conclusions arrived at in the 1976 lecture series, should we not leave it for his later work? After all, is it not there that he developed his thinking to his satisfaction?

The problem is that it is not clear that he did reject the conclusions reached in the lecture course. Other commentators have, after all, pointed out that the lectures were a place to work out ideas that would later find expression in different form. On this reading, there is no radical break from them; merely, a reworking of the ideas found within. For example, Johanna Oksala argues that 'Foucault's move from discipline to government was ... not a conceptual substitution, but an extension',[11] presumably with the analysis of war playing a role in this transition. Similarly, Stuart Elden argues that the notion of 'population' introduced in these lectures was carried over into his later work on governmentality,[12] while Elizabeth Frazer and Kimberly Hutchings focus not on the various forms that violence takes, but on the conclusion that Foucault defends – violence is ubiquitous:

> The significance of violence for politics for Foucault shifts with a chronological development from an early pervasive emphasis on the violence of order and power . . . to a more complex set of accounts of the interaction of forms of violence with forms of [S]tate and social organisation.[13]

If this is the case, then the inquiry into the relationship between war and power undertaken in the 1976 lecture course provides unique insights into this issue and those related to it.

This confirms Marks's alternative point that, rather than providing insights into Foucault's wider project, the lectures 'can be read, in isolation, as an exploration of one of the key themes of his work; namely, the way in which – reversing Clausewitz's formula – politics is a continuation of war by other means'.[14] Taking off from this interpretative approach, this chapter is guided by the contention that the 1976 lecture course on war offers important insights into the nature of power, demonstrates that what Foucault calls racism is key to this conception of power, and shows that the racism–power relationship develops a new conception of biopower/biopolitics.

Linked to this, I argue that Foucault's study also delineates an important move away from conceptions of sovereignty that link it directly to the creation, maintenance, or disruption of the juridical order, to *biopolitical* conceptions that emphasise the ways in which sovereign violence regulates life through the creation of insider/outsider groups. In so doing, Foucault shows how a form of power distributes itself throughout society to create and constitute its normative claims and values. The benefit of this is, as Hidefumi Nishiyami notes, that it 'br[ings] critical insight into the operation of modern racism not so much in terms of traditional prejudice or discrimination but in terms of the way in which racism [is] constitutive of the formation of modern society in Europe'.[15]

Foucault's analysis therefore outlines the logical (racist) structures underpinning modern Western European societies *and* offers a radical conception of power that not only breaks decisively with the classic-juridical notion of sovereignty, but also shows that violence has a positive, creative role to play in the construction of social and individual norms. *Contra* Deleuze and Guattari's claim that violence enters the State through the exteriority of the war machine, Foucault points out how violence, in the form of conflictual power relations, underpins all social relations, including those of the State. To show this, a brief word on the notion of 'power' underpinning Foucault's analyses of racism and biopolitics will be helpful.

CONCEPTUALISING POWER

In the first lecture, given on 7 January 1976, Foucault notes the new organisational arrangements for the lecture series. The Collège de France is unique within (French) academia. It does not award degrees or hold classes *per se*, but is an institution composed of around fifty individuals who are selected by the professors themselves to do 'pure' research. The only stipulation is that each professor must teach for twenty-six hours per year on the original research they are conducting; classes are free and open to everyone. Foucault was nominated for a position in 1969 subsequent to the death of Jean Hyppolite and, on 12 April 1970, was elected to the chair in the History of Systems of Thought. He gave his inaugural lecture on 2 December 1970 and continued to lecture every year, apart from a sabbatical in 1977, until his death in 1984. Foucault's lectures were initially held on Wednesday afternoon and filled two theatre rooms. Their unwieldy size appeared to bother him to the extent that, in 1976, he changed the time of the lecture to 09:30 hours because he had been told that 'students are no longer capable of getting up at nine-thirty'.[16] It did not have the desired effect.

This organisational change is mirrored by a number of alterations to the way he approached the content of his lectures. In the first lecture, he summarises the orientation of his previous lecture courses in rather dismissive fashion – 'bits and pieces of research . . . A few remarks on the history of penal procedure; a few chapters on the evolution, the institutionalisation of psychiatry in the nineteenth century; considerations on sophistry or Greek coins; an outline history of sexuality'.[17] The basic problem was that he felt that they were 'fragmented, repetitive, and discontinuous'.[18]

He notes that this could be defended by claiming that it was part of a contemporary trend – manifested through developments in antipsychiatry, existentialism, Deleuze and Guattari's *Anti-Oediupus*, and neo-Marxism – towards localisation, fragmentation, and minor narratives opposed to the totalising structures and epistemological structures of modernity.[19] This methodology resembles something like 'a sort of autonomous and noncentralised theoretical production . . . that does not need a visa from some common regime to establish its validity'.[20] It multiplies the number of discourses without tying them to a totalising centre or unifying principle.

The great benefit of this multiplication is that it led to the study of 'subjugated knowledges',[21] which had previously been ignored, made subservient to dominant ones, or 'been disqualified as nonconceptual knowledges, as insufficiently elaborated knowledges: naïve knowledges, hierarchically inferior knowledges, knowledges that are below the required level of erudition or scientificity'.[22] These subjugated knowledges were always crucial to 'the functional and systematic ensembles, but . . . were masked'.[23] This, however, brings forth the reason for their exclusion. Foucault explains that, rather than being a consequence of a 'natural' failure on their part, their subjugated status was the consequence of having lost out in the power struggle for domination. We need, therefore, to study the historical processes that led to their exclusion.[24]

In 1971, Foucault published his famous essay 'Nietzsche, Genealogy, History',[25] in which he outlines the genealogical method for the first time. He returns to this in 1976 to explain that 'genealogy is certainly not a matter of contrasting the abstract unity of theory with the concrete multiplicity of the fact',[26] nor is it 'some form or other of scientism that disqualifies speculation by contrasting it with the rigor of well-established bodies of knowledge',[27] or 'an empiricism . . . in the normal sense of the word'.[28] Rather, genealogy

> is a way of playing local, discontinuous, disqualified, or nonlegitimised knowledges off against the unitary theoretical instance that claims to be able to filter them, organise them into a hierarchy, organise them in the name of a true body of knowledge, in the name of the rights of a science that is in the hands of a few.[29]

For this reason, genealogies are not forms of positivist science, but 'antisciences'.[30]

This does not mean that they ignore knowledge or affirm ignorance, but they question and, in so doing, undermine the power structures supporting and affirming dominant knowledge. Genealogy is, then, a form of insurrection 'against the centralising power-effects that are bound up with the institutionalisation and workings of any scientific discourse organised in a society such as ours'.[31]

For example, to the question of whether Marxism is a science or not, Foucault questions why it is important that Marxism is understood in such fashion:

> What types of knowledge are you trying to disqualify when you say that you are a science? What speaking subject, what discursive subject, what subject of experience and knowledge are you trying to minorize when you begin to say: 'I speak this discourse, I am speaking a scientific discourse, and I am a scientist.'[32]

Genealogy seeks to uncover the normative assumptions and power relations that legitimise and privilege a particular discourse. This will, he contends, 'desubjugate historical knowledges, to set them free, or in other words to enable them to oppose and struggle against the coercion of a unitary, formal, and scientific theoretical discourse'.[33]

To return to the question as to why he did not continue the contemporary affirmation of fragmentation, Foucault contends that this question is largely irrelevant – 'the battle no longer looks quite the same'[34] – because the rise of local discourses and fragmentation has fundamentally changed the playing field: the unitary power structures, norms, and discourses that once ruled have been usurped, deposed, and fragmented. To simply continue affirming fragmentation would not, then, permit us to understand the new configurations that have resulted.

The danger, of course, is that without this continuous emphasis on difference, the identity previously fragmented could always simply return, but Foucault thinks that the contemporary affirmation of heterogeneous discourses reveals something else: namely, that the subtending relation between the heterogeneous discourses is 'a battle'[35] and, as such, is intimately linked to power. For this reason, he notes that the 1976 lecture 'should try . . . to specify or identify what is at stake when knowledges begin to challenge, struggle against, and rise up against the institution and the power- and knowledge-effects of scientific discourse'.[36]

This, however, depends upon an understanding of what power is, which cannot be derived from a purely abstract exercise as this would risk producing a definition that privileges the abstract universal over the concrete particular. To get round this, Foucault suggests that the analysis of power must be concretely situated and grounded in particular histories. By studying historical formations, the aim 'is to determine what are, in their mechanisms, effects, their relations, the various power-apparatuses that operate at various levels of society, in such very different domains and with so many different extensions?'[37]

Foucault argues that this depends upon and points to a particular conception of power, one that challenges the model of power-sovereignty that has long dominated Western thinking. Specifically, he maintains that 'the classic juridical theory of power'[38] is based on the assumption that

> power is . . . a right which can be possessed in the way one possesses a commodity, and which can therefore be transferred or alienated, either completely or partly, through a juridical act or an act that founds a right – it does not matter which, for the moment – thanks to the surrender of something or thanks to a contract.[39]

Because it conceives of power through an exchange model, Foucault claims that the classic-juridical model of sovereignty is premised on the notion that power is a thing that is possessed. It can therefore be surrendered to another, 'either as a whole or in part, so as to constitute a power or a political sovereignty',[40] and is 'modelled on a juridical operation similar to an exchange of contracts'.[41]

Marxism is slightly different, insofar as it is based not on contracts but on economic functionality, where 'the role of power is essentially both to perpetuate the relations of production and to reproduce a class domination that is made possible by the development of the productive forces and the ways they are appropriated'.[42] Rather than conceive of power in terms of exchange, Marxism is underpinned by a notion of power that operates from and through the entire economy. Foucault, however, rejects the fundamental link between power and economy – or, put differently, thinking power through economics – that underpins this analysis because it continues to think of 'power' as a thing to be distributed for particular ends.

Rather than a possession, he understands power to be 'a relationship of force'.[43] However, this immediately raises the questions of what power consists of and how it is exercised. Foucault offers 'off-the-cuff'[44] remarks that identify 'two grand hypotheses'.[45] On the one hand, he holds that analyses have tended to affirm what he calls 'Reich's hypothesis':[46] 'power is essentially that which represses'.[47] Foucault points out, however, that this is a very traditional conception of power that seems inadequate to conceptualise the dynamics of power-force. On the other hand, there is 'Nietzsche's hypothesis'[48] that is underpinned by the following position:

If power is indeed the implementation and deployment of a relationship of force, rather than analysing it in terms of surrender, contract, and alienation, or rather than analysing it in functional terms as the reproduction of the relations of production, shouldn't we be analysing it first and foremost in terms of conflict, confrontation, and war?[49]

Thus, if Reich's hypothesis holds that power is repressive, the Nietzsche hypothesis claims that 'power is war, the continuation of war by other means'.[50] With this, Foucault inverts Carl von Clausewitz's famous dictum to 'say that politics is the continuation of war by other means'.[51]

This leads to three points: first, political organisation is structured according to and from war and, indeed, was instantiated at a particular moment wherein the structure of war was transposed to politics.[52] Second, politics must be understood in terms of war; that is, shifting alliances, movements, oppositional struggles, and so on.[53] Third, and most controversially, politics is dependent on 'a trial by strength in which weapons are the final judges'.[54] The implication is that 'the last battle would put an end to politics'[55] because it 'would at last . . . suspend the exercise of power as continuous warfare'.[56] This final point would, ultimately, prove highly problematic for Foucault, who very quickly rejected the notion that war and, hence, power could somehow come to an end in a moment of great political refusal.[57]

Foucault's inversion of Clausewitz's dictum does, however, reveal an important difference with Deleuze and Guattari's inversion of it. Specifically, the latter maintained that it only applies once the war machine has been incorporated into the State apparatus; only then does politics conform to war. Foucault, in contrast – and writing four years prior to Deleuze and Guattari – claims that war relations always subtend the political. This is a consequence of the different ways in which they situate the disruption of war to the State: for Deleuze and Guattari, the war machine is external to the State and has to be internalised by it for politics to take on warlike form. For Foucault, in contrast, the power relations upon which the State depends are warlike, with the consequence that war is always 'internal' to the State; indeed, the State is nothing but an effect of power-as-war. For Deleuze and Guattari, therefore, violence is contingent to the State, whereas for Foucault it is constitutive, which is not to say that it is always explicit. Rather, 'the role of political power is perpetually to use a sort of silent war to reinscribe that relationship of force, and to reinscribe it in institutions, economic inequalities, language, and even the bodies of individuals'.[58] Power-as-war is not, strictly speaking, repressive, but expressive.

With this, Foucault identifies three models of power relations: (1) the contractual model, which he claims dominated the seventeenth century, and which holds that power is a right that is surrendered and constrains sovereignty through contract; (2) the war-repression schema – based on Reich's hypothesis – which maintains that power is inherently repressive; and (3) a model that he aims to use in the 1976 lecture course, where power is understood not in terms of contract or repression, but as 'what is rumbling away and what is at work beneath political power . . . essentially and above all a warlike relation'.[59]

In turn, this involves a radical reorientation of the notion of political sovereignty. Specifically, Foucault rejects 'the juridico-political theory of sovereignty'[60] that has dominated Western societies since the Middle Ages. He points out that this model was all-pervasive, so that even when sovereignty was no longer explicitly grounded in a particular figure – the King – the juridical model of sovereignty and power that underpinned it continued to exist: for example, it was no longer the King securing law, but the singularity of the populace. In other words, despite altering the name of the founding principle, the logic underpinning it remained the same: (1) an instrumental account of power is offered (2) that holds that power is used by and to secure the position of the sovereign (the founding principle), with the consequence that (3) the exercise of power is inherently repressive.[61]

In contrast to this model, Foucault affirms one more attuned to the dispersed 'nature' of power relations. Rather than focusing on sovereignty as the singular, stable ground of power, he insists that we focus on the relationship between domination and subjugation emanating from the power-as-war model. This prefigures his famous claim – made in the interview 'Truth and Power' conducted in June 1976 – that 'we need to cut off the [K]ing's head'.[62]

Foucault aims to achieve this by rethinking 'domination' so that, rather than describing

> the brute fact of domination of the one over the many, or of one group over another, [it depicts] the multiple forms of domination that can be exercised in society; so, not the king in his central position, but subjects in their reciprocal relations; not sovereignty in its one edifice, but the multiple subjugations that take place and function within the social body.[63]

Instead of being understood 'as a phenomenon of mass and homogeneous domination – the domination of one individual over others, of one group over others, or of one class over others',[64] power must be 'analysed as something that circulates, or rather as something that functions only when it is part of a chain'.[65] For this reason, power is not controlled by individuals, nor are individuals the foundational locus of power; 'the individual is a power-effect, and at the same time, and to the extent that he is a power-effect, the individual is a relay: power passes through the individual it has constituted'.[66]

With this, Foucault argues that, rather than being the point of entry for studies of power and politics, sovereignty must be understood as an effect of multiple, pre-individual power relations: 'we have to study power outside the model of Leviathan, outside the field dominated by juridical sovereignty and the institution of the State. We have to analyse it by beginning with the techniques and tactics of domination.'[67]

This, in turn, requires that we start from a different standpoint wherein '[rather] than asking subjects how, why, and by what right they can agree to being subjugated, [we show] how actual relations of subjugation manufacture subjects'.[68] Power is not then in the 'hands' of a sovereign individual, but is the effect of a complex matrix of pre-personal forces that must be thought in terms of the relations of domination. From this, Foucault aims to 'identify the technical instruments that guarantee that [things] function'[69] to show the means by which a particular form of domination and, hence, power structure arises and secures its pre-eminence.

PERPETUAL WAR AND RACISM

In the third lecture, given on 21 January 1976, Foucault returns to the Nietzschean hypothesis to expand on its fundamental claim that society is structured by perpetual war relations. This first involves a discussion of Clausewitz's dictum, highlighting that it was based on the inversion of a prior understanding that was closer to the fundamental claim of the Nietzsche hypothesis; before, second, showing that the conception of power relations underpinning the Nietzschean hypothesis was not and could not be thought from the perspective of Machiavelli or Hobbes – two classic thinkers of sovereign power – but is justified by examining an often ignored discourse on race that arose in the nineteenth century and continues to shape European conceptions of society to the present day.

For Foucault, the 'juridical model of sovereignty was not . . . able to provide a concrete analysis of the multiplicity of power relations'[70] because it 'establishes the political relationship between subject and subject'[71] and 'assumes from the outset the existence of a multiplicity of powers that are not powers in the political sense of the term; they are capacities, possibilities, potentials'[72] that can only be constituted as political powers through 'a moment of fundamental and foundational unity'.[73] This foundational unity 'takes on the face of the monarch'[74] or some other organ of the State, with the consequence that it is both the point of emanation for the disparate powers and that which provides them with unity. Furthermore, the juridical model of sovereignty, as understood by Foucault, is based on a certain relationship to law underpinned by a certain notion of legitimacy. Putting the three aspects together, he concludes that the juridical model of sovereignty is based on three questionable assumptions: 'the theory of sovereignty presupposes the subject; its goal is to establish the essential unity of power, and it is always deployed within the pre-existing element of law'.[75]

Foucault sets himself apart from this model, claiming that 'the general project . . . is to try to release or emancipate this analysis of power from three assumptions – of subject, unity, and law – and to bring out, rather than these basic elements of sovereignty, what I would call relations or operators of domination'.[76] This requires a methodological inversion: rather than derive sovereignty from power relations, 'we should be extracting operators of domination [i.e. sovereignty] from relations of power'.[77] Rather than starting with subjects and monadic elements that are prior to any relationship, we must start with the power relationship(s) subtending them.

This, however, brings forth the question of how 'power' should be thought. In this lecture course, Foucault inquires as to whether 'war [can] really provide a valid analysis of power relations'.[78] This does not mean that he thinks that power and war are synonymous; rather, he claims to simply be considering 'an extreme [case] to the extent that war can be regarded as the point of maximum tension, or as force-relations laid bare'.[79] The basic guiding question is whether 'if we look beneath peace, order, wealth, and authority, beneath the calm order of subordination, beneath the State and State apparatuses, beneath the laws, and so on, will we hear and discover a sort of primitive and permanent war?'[80]

Foucault responds affirmatively and defends the notion that the State is grounded in a subterranean permanent war through a historical methodology that leads to another question: 'how, when, and why was it noticed or imagined that what is going on beneath and in power relations is war?'[81] More specifically, he turns to the genesis of Carl von Clausewitz's claim that war is the continuation of politics, to suggest that the claim existed long before Clausewitz; indeed, Clausewitz's statement was an inversion of 'a sort of thesis that had been in circulation since the seventeenth and eighteenth centuries and which was both diffuse and specific'.[82] Thus, Foucault's inversion of Clausewitz's doctrine is not to radically depart from the tradition; it is to return to the understanding of power relations that long defined Western thinking: politics (or power) is war by another name.

Alexander Barder and François Debrix point out that this reversal was unthinkable for other theorists of sovereign power who, while making war subservient to power, did not follow Foucault's conception of power relations. Barder and Debrix argue that Schmitt, for example, 'could not accept such a reversal . . . because for him it would have implied that the sovereign's decision had lost control of the friend–enemy distinction'.[83] While the 'internal' politics of the constitutional State is, for Schmitt, conflictual, this conflict is (1) always relative to the potential(ly) (far more serious) warfare that can/must be waged against its perceived 'external' enemy, and (2) premised on the homogeneity of the constituting-power regarding its foundational norms. Whereas Foucault maintains that the State is an effect of warlike power relations, Schmitt warns that, if that were true, the constituting-power would be unable to agree on the foundational norm of the constitutional State, with the consequence that the populace would be stuck in the (violent) chaos of the pre-constitutional state, or the constitutional State would descend into civil war. In either case, juridical order would not be possible. For Schmitt, the constituting-power and constitution are defined in opposition to a designated external enemy, but the decision about the enemy and the day-to-day discussions internal to the constitutional State are dependent on and respectful of the homogeneity and acclamation of the constituting-power. For this reason, Schmitt's conception of power is a classic-juridical one because it remains based on a single subject, whether in the form of the constitutional sovereign or that of the homogeneity of the constituting-power.

Barder and Debrix also point out that Foucault's claim would be unacceptable to Arendt, who maintains that the political is defined by co-action between agents based on discursive agreement. For Arendt, politics is grounded in the plurality of the populace who found the State based on discussion and agreement rather than warfare. If politics were underpinned by a warlike struggle, it simply would not be possible to form a stable polity. Preventing this lies behind her insistence that violence and power must be held apart.[84]

Foucault, however, rejects the notion that sovereignty is ever stable. It is always underpinned by warlike power relations and so is inherently conflictual. For this reason, he rejects the juridical-philosophical notion of sovereignty underpinning both Schmitt's and Arendt's analyses. The nature and distribution of power relations are far more important than the question of sovereignty, which is 'merely' an effect of the former.

To develop this, Foucault returns to the question of the relationship between war and the State. Tracing a very general overview that starts with the Middle Ages, he claims that the nature of war changed, both in-itself and in relation to the State. Initially, 'the practices and institutions of war were ... concentrated in the hand of a central power'[85]: the State, headed by a sovereign. As a consequence, 'it transpired that in both de facto and de jure terms, only State powers could wage wars and manipulate the instruments of war. The State acquired a monopoly on war.'[86] Whereas the State monopolised legal warfare against other States, 'what might be called day-to-day warfare, and what was actually called "private warfare", was eradicated from the social body, and from relations among men and relation among groups'.[87] The latter, which had up to then dominated, was gradually 'cleansed'[88] from the social body so that legal State warfare came to dominate and, indeed, became synonymous with war. War was no longer central to the functioning of the State – it was no longer day-to-day – but was pushed to the margins; a movement that gave rise 'to the emergence of something that did not exist as such in the Middle Ages: the army as institution'.[89]

While this appears to be a straightforward replacement of one model of social organisation with another, Foucault suggests that more is going on: 'when war was expelled to the limits of the State, or was both centralised in practice and confined to the frontier, a certain discourse appeared. A new discourse, a strange discourse'.[90] It was new because it was not only 'the first historico-political discourse on society',[91] as opposed to a section of it, but also 'a discourse on war, which was understood to be a permanent social relationship, the ineradicable basis of all relations and institutions of power'.[92]

Foucault locates this movement not in the civil wars of the sixteenth century that gave rise to Hobbes's *Leviathan* – which he takes to be the classic philosophical statement of the juridico-philosophical conception of sovereignty – but 'at the beginning of the civil wars of seventeenth-century England, at the time of the English bourgeois revolution'.[93] It subsequently reappeared in France at the end of that century through figures including Boulainvilliers, Comte d'Estaing, Freret, and Sieyés, before finding final expression 'in the racist biologists and eugenicists of the late nineteenth century'.[94]

The basic point uniting these figures is that 'no matter what the philosophico-juridical theory may say, political power does not begin when the war ends'.[95] War does not stop once the physical confrontation between States is over. While the State is born of war, this does not mean that 'society, the law, and the State are like armistices that put an end to wars, or that they are the product of definitive victories'.[96] *Contra* Arendt and Schmitt, violence does not stop for law to be founded: 'beneath law, war continues to rage in all the mechanisms of power, even in the most regular. War is the motor behind institutions and order. In the smallest of its cogs, peace is waging a secret war.'[97] Rather than war instantiating a regime of peace, 'a war runs through the whole of society, continuously and permanently, and it is this battlefront that puts us all on one side or the other. There is no such thing as a neutral subject. We are all inevitably someone's adversary.'[98]

Two aspects of this stand out: first, society is based not on agreement or unity, but on conflict and division. Second, 'a binary structure runs through society',[99] insofar as each thing is structured through its conflict with another. No one and nothing escapes this; all are linked in a relation of conflict to another. Whereas the classic-juridical model holds that the sovereign unifies society, Foucault claims that this only applies to a particular historical period that no longer exists. Rather, society is now organised around a 'binary conception of society . . . There are two groups, two categories of individuals, or two armies, and they are opposed to each other.'[100]

Whereas Roberto Esposito[101] claims that this binary structure underpins all Western philosophical thought, Foucault argues that it only starts to develop in the Middle Ages before becoming *philosophically* explicit in the sixteenth and seventeenth centuries and *politically* so in the nineteenth and twentieth centuries. This is not to say that it did not have political importance prior to this time, but its political importance during the sixteenth and seventeenth centuries was an implicit one 'kept in the margins'.[102] This gradually changed until, at the end of the nineteenth century and start of the twentieth century, it dominated in a specific form: 'the war that is going on beneath order and peace, the war that undermines our society and divides it in a binary mode is, basically, a race war'.[103] More specifically, an evolutionary – albeit non-Darwinian – discourse, supported by a particular philological reading, gave 'birth to the theory of races'.[104] This was accompanied and underpinned by a number of fundamental epistemic alterations that made war between races possible: 'ethnic differences, differences between languages, different degrees of force, vigour, energy, and violence; the differences between savagery and barbarism; the conquest and subjugation of one race by another'.[105]

Initially, this was 'a very ambiguous theory',[106] located in the latent nationalist movements in Europe, specifically the Russian and Austrian ones, who were looking for ways to undermine 'the great State apparatuses',[107] before it found expression in the nineteenth century in terms of class. For Foucault, the Marxist notion of class division is simply based on the logic of binary opposition transposed from the divide underpinning the racial discourses of the early nineteenth century.[108]

Crucially, however, the social division is not defined by a clash of two races, but entails the 'splitting of a single race into a superrace and a subrace'.[109] This is not imposed on the society from without, but is the condition upon which it defines itself. Through this racial splitting, a division is created between those fit and those unfit, those pure and those impure. In turn, this rift and the struggle it entails are understood to perpetuate a battle

> that has to be waged not between races, but by a race that is portrayed as the one true race, the race that holds power and is entitled to define the norm, and against those who deviate from that norm, against those who pose a threat to the biological heritage.[110]

This was re-enforced by two simultaneous occurrences: first, the rise of particular 'biological-racist discourses of degeneracy'[111] that sanctioned, perpetuated, and affirmed the division between the races and where the emphasis was no longer on the entire society, but only on those members who belonged to the dominant race and who had to be defended against others. Thus, the social norm was no longer underpinned by the desire, found in classical liberalism, to defend the individual against society, but by the desire to 'defend society against all the biological threats posed by the other race, the subrace, the counterrace that we are, despite ourselves, bringing into existence'.[112]

Second, this was accompanied and re-enforced by 'all those institutions within the social body which ma[d]e the discourse of race struggle function as a principle of exclusion and segregation and, ultimately, a way of normalising society'.[113] We see this if we turn to the previous year's lecture course, *Abnormal*, where Foucault points to the ways in which race discourse became instantiated and supported by psychiatry, which not only came to think in terms of racial differences, but also purposefully excluded those deemed to belong to the so-called subrace: 'it is a racism ... whose function is not so much the prejudice or defence of one group against another as the detection of all those within a group who may be the carriers of a danger to it'.[114]

Psychiatry played a key role in fostering, supporting, and legitimising this logic, insofar as it designated who was 'normal' and who was not and so who was to be designated as a threat to society. This hygiene function was quickly taken up by and tied to anti-Semitism without the two necessarily being intertwined. For Foucault, then, all the Nazis did was combine the hygiene function associated with psychiatry and the 'ethnic racism that was endemic in the nineteenth century'.[115] This is why 'we should not be surprised that German psychiatry functioned so spontaneously within Nazism'.[116]

We should not, however, think that this racist logic only underpins Nazism. For Foucault, it underpins all contemporary Western European societies. The combination of a racist bifurcation between an inner and outer group, in combination with the creation of discourses and institutions supporting and affirming it, generated a particular social and State organisation:

> We see the appearance of State racism: a racism that society will direct against itself, against its own elements and its own products. This is the internal racism of permanent purification, and it will become one of the basic dimensions of social normalisations.[117]

Foucault's notion of 'racism' is, then, of a specific variety. Robert Bernasconi[118] criticises it for failing to distinguish between different concrete forms of racism, but it has, in reality, little to do with providing a study of ethnicities or racial theory *per se* and even less to do with prejudice, irrationality, or ideology, and more to do with the logic defining a social discourse. Racism, on Foucault's understanding, simply entails an inner division within society, based on supposed biological characteristics that distinguish one 'race' from a supposedly degenerate one.

To explain this further, we can appeal to the distinction between 'hetero-referential' and 'auto-referential' forms of racism, wherein the former 'typically negates the value of the other and follows a logic of domination, whereas auto-referential racism affirms the supreme value of the self and follows a logic of exclusion'.[119] Rather than defining itself by its relation to an external other, Foucault's notion of 'internal' racism describes the ways in which society orientates/orientated itself from and around an internal division posed in terms of those who have the 'correct' bio-racial characteristics and so can be said to rightfully belong and those who do not. It distinguishes between those who, we might say, are 'pure' and so entitled and welcome to belong to the society and those who are considered 'impure' and so not welcome. This initial bifurcation permits a justification for killing the latter and for the degraded ways in which they will be treated that feeds into Foucault's discussion of the difference between sovereignty and biopower. Through this self-bifurcation, itself supported by discourses and institutions, society came to normalise and create itself around a particular logic.

Racism is not then grounded in nature or biology; it describes a particular logical discourse of bifurcation created through and from a specific configuration of the warlike power relations of which it is an effect. Contemporary racist societies are inherently violent, not only because of the continuous operation of the warlike power relations subtending them, but also because they express these power relations in a particular fashion; namely by dividing the populace biologically, thereby excluding those deemed to be racially inferior.

RACISM AND BIOPOWER

In the final lecture, given on 17 March 1976, Foucault examines the ways in which power relations operate throughout contemporary society and, crucially, the role that racism plays in that. Taking off from his claim that the nineteenth century saw a turn towards biological explanations, he insists that this generated and was accompanied by a fundamental alteration in how power operated.

Whereas prior to the nineteenth century, power was disciplinary, insofar as it operated on individual bodies to discipline them in accordance with particular norms, the nineteenth-century discourses on racial biology inaugurated a fundamental alteration so that power took hold over life itself. Rather than focus on disciplining individual bodies for an infraction of sovereign power, power came to focus on 'man [a]s a living being',[120] so 'that the biological came under State control, [and] there was at least a certain tendency that leads to what might be termed State control of the biological'.[121] To explain this, he contrasts it with what the classic-juridical notion of sovereignty says about the relationship between sovereign power and life and death.

According to Foucault, classical theories understand sovereignty to be defined by 'the right of life and death'.[122] With this, the sovereign is taken to have the legitimate power to permit an individual to live or not. Foucault claims that this actually means that the sovereign's power 'is always tipped in favour of death'.[123] It comes into effect 'only when the sovereign can kill',[124] meaning that 'the very essence of the right of life and death is actually the right to kill: it is at the moment when the sovereign can kill that he exercises his right over life'.[125] The sovereign's function is, then, defined negatively, by the capacity to kill. In the nineteenth century, this gradually changed so that whereas 'the right of sovereignty was the right to take life or let live ... this new right ... established ... the right to make live and to let die'.[126] Understanding why this is so requires an engagement with the historical process through which it arrived.

Foucault notes that, in the seventeenth and eighteenth centuries, discussions of power were orientated from and around a more efficient distribution of bodies, information, and operations, with this being realised through disciplinary functions and processes. This changed in the latter half of the eighteenth century as 'a new technology of power'[127] arose that, while not completely usurping the former, differed from it while also dovetailing with the disciplinary matrix. The fundamental difference between the two forms of power related to the conception of the 'subject' relied upon *and* the means through which that subject was operated on:

> discipline tries to rule a multiplicity of men to the extent that their multiplicity can and must be dissolved into individual bodies that can be kept under surveillance, trained, used, and, if need be, punished. And that the new technology that is being established is addressed to a multiplicity of men, not to the extent that they are nothing more than their individual bodies, but to the extent that they form, on the contrary, a global mass that is affected by overall processes characteristic of birth, death, production, illness, and so on.[128]

By focusing on the general populace and regulating its processes of life, there was a movement from a politics concerned with discipline backed up by the threat of death to a politics concerned with the management of life itself – a biopolitics.

Biopolitics involves a distinct conception of politics orientated around and from a specific series of activities and processes, including concern for and management over 'the ratio of births to death, the rate of reproduction, the fertility of a population, and so on'.[129] This depends upon and is supported by new epistemological techniques for tracking, delineating, and measuring the population, and an interventionist approach to manipulating and managing these figures.

With regard to life, this occurs, for example, through the control over contraception and maintenance of a birth registry; with regard to death, it occurs through the tracking of longer-term health issues that shape the configuration of the populace, which is contrary to the previous emphasis on short-term events, such as cholera outbreaks and earthquakes. It also led to a focus on endemic illnesses, which do not necessarily cause death but are difficult to eradicate, and were, more often than not, considered to be 'permanent factors which ... sapped the population's strength, shortened the working week, wasted energy, and cost money, both because they led to a fall in production and because treating them was expensive'.[130]

This was accompanied by an alternation in the understanding of death. Rather than an external event that disrupted life in a single blow, death 'was now something permanent, something that slips into life, perpetually gnaws at it, diminishes it and weakens it'.[131] Warding it off required more subtle, but total, means of intervention than had been necessary in the disciplinary model. Not only did this give rise to a whole set of financial instruments, such as 'insurance, individual and collective savings, safety measures, and so on',[132] but it also created a whole industry and discourse concerning the environment, specifically the realisation that, with the rise of urbanisation, the environment is an artificial one and so can and should be altered, changed, and reshaped to manage the population.

With this, Foucault identifies three basic alterations that were brought forth by biopolitics: first, rather than being based on an individual–individual relationship as found in classic-juridical theories of sovereignty, or individual–society as found in disciplinary models, biopolitics ushered in a new concept to focus on, a multiple body called the population: 'Biopolitics deals with the problem of population, with the population as a political problem, as a problem that is at once scientific and political, as a biological problem and as power's problem.'[133]

Second, biopolitics concerned itself with what happens to this mass – the population – over a period of time and takes into account a range of phenomena to tackle the 'problem' from various angles: biological, economic, educative, medical, social, political, and so on.

Third, biopolitics introduced a different epistemology to the study and management of the population, which required not only detailed records, but also 'forecasts, statistical estimates, and overall measures'.[134] Crucially, these do not operate at the individual or local level, but 'intervene at the level at which these general phenomena are determined . . . The morality rate has to be modified or lowered; life expectancy has to be increased; the birth rate has to be stimulated.'[135] The aim is to maintain and secure the average, which requires the management of power relations. This is orientated not to individual phenomena, but to

> using overall mechanisms and acting in such a way as to achieve overall states of equilibrium or regularity; it is, in a word, a matter of taking control of life and the biological processes of man-as-species and of ensuring that they are not disciplined, but regularised.[136]

Through these processes, functions, and alterations, power operates in a different fashion for an alternative end to that which previously governed disciplinary societies. It is no longer located in a fixed point of sovereignty and exercised through great displays of 'his' power and ability. Power is distributed throughout the social body, is exercised against the population on a continuous basis, and is the regularised 'force' that shapes processes and structures to anonymously determine who lives, how they will live, and who dies.

That biopolitics depends upon and ushers in a new configuration of power relations has consequences for the way(s) in which violence operates. Rather than being explicit, focused on individuals, and direct, Johanna Oksala explains that

> the violence it uses has to be hidden away or called something else because it presents a problem in the rationality of biopolitics, the explicit aim of which is the organisation and enhancement of life. The connection with violence has to be mediated: biopolitical violence must pass through the regime of knowledge/power and it must be given a scientific legitimacy compatible with the aim of biopolitics.[137]

As a management system, biopolitics cannot simply rely, as was the case with classic disciplinary conceptions of sovereignty, on explicit uses of violence to achieve its ends. The violence of biopolitics is both everywhere and non-localisable; subtle, but insidious. It constantly works to manage the equilibrium by working on the population through policies, distribution of resources, management of expectations, and so on. It does not repress a pre-formed population, but squeezes the population in particular ways to form a particular mass, one that it continues to regulate. Through this process, norms arise which re-enforce the power relations underpinning them.

This does, however, give rise to the following questions: if biopolitics regulates and creates life to prolong and maintain it, how is it that it also comes to kill? How 'is it possible for a political power to kill, and to call for deaths, to demand deaths, to give the order to kill, and to expose not only its enemies but its own citizens to the risk of death?'[138]

Foucault's response is tied to his analysis of racism, which he holds to be fundamental to biopolitics. Indeed, he claims that 'the modern State can scarcely function without becoming involved with racism at some point, within certain limits and subject to certain conditions'.[139] As we previously saw, Foucault understands 'racism' to entail the introduction of division, based on biological considerations, into the population, to separate those considered 'pure' and welcome from those considered 'impure' and so not:

> the appearance within the biological continuum of the human race of races, the distinction among races, the hierarchy of races, the fact that certain races are described as good and that others, in contrast, are described as inferior: all this is a way of fragmenting the field of the biological that power controls.[140]

Through this fragmentation, conceptions of each race are created, the 'proper' relations with other races established, and the field of existence demarcated with particular rules, regulations, and norms, both explicit and implicit. But racism goes beyond simply demarcating the population into competing races. Racism's relation to biopower means that it is also concerned with regulating and managing the deaths of the races.

While biopolitics is concerned with the regulation of life, Foucault points out that in dividing the races and managing their lives according to their perceived worth, biopolitics introduces a 'break between what must live and what must die'.[141] By managing the distribution of resources and the expectations for each race in accordance with his racist division, biopolitics permits a race to live or die. This is not a direct, physical form of control, but a subtle, insidious one that appears to control anonymously. Racism provides the norm for the distribution of biopower, while also being re-enforced by that distribution. Indeed, so important is racism to biopower that Foucault explains that 'racism is the indispensable precondition that allows someone to be killed'[142] and 'the precondition for exercising the right to kill'.[143]

The division and discrimination of racism in conjunction with biopower's concern for the regulation of life are potent partners that create society according to a particular logic: the populace is divided into 'pure' and 'impure' races with the latter understood to be not simply different to the former, but a threat to it. As such, the 'impure' race must be disappeared, not because it is a political enemy who simply offers up an alternative, competing way of life, but because it is a threat 'either external or internal, to the population and for the population'.[144]

Somewhat paradoxically then biopower's concern for life translates into and even demands the death of those considered a threat to it, which, when perceived through the lens of racism, entails the 'impure' race(s). This does not simply remove a threat: 'the death of the other, the death of the bad race, of the inferior race (or the degenerate, or the abnormal) is something that will make life in general healthier: healthier and purer'.[145] By performing its hygiene function and causing the death of the other, the dominant race perpetuates its own life, both insofar as it no longer encounters the perceived other, and also because it moves within a more rarefied environment where the threat of contamination from the other is removed.

However, it is important to note that, while the death of the other can be physical, Foucault expressly points out that 'I do not mean murder as such, but also every form of indirect murder: the fact of exposing someone to death, increasing the risk of death for some people, or, quite simply, political death, expulsion, rejection, and so on.'[146] The violence associated with enforcing racism comes in many varieties, not all of which are physical. Generally speaking, however, the form of violence used is underpinned by the same aim: to remove the 'impure' race as a threat to the 'pure' one. Racism is, then, intimately related to violence, insofar as it is based on a violent cleavage of the races and depends upon further violence to annihilate and contain the impure race to secure the purity of the superior race.

That sovereignty is an effect of power relations means that, with the movement to biopower and racism, the notion of sovereignty must also change. The sovereign does not function by imposing himself on the populace as the juridical theory of sovereignty insists; the biopolitical sovereign is an effect of the war inherent in the power relations subtending him. Thus, the biopolitical State 'is obliged to use race, the elimination of races and the purification of the race, to exercise its sovereign power'.[147]

Indeed, Foucault claims that once we understand the intimate relationship between racism and biopolitics, we see why 'the most murderous States are also, of necessity, the most racist'.[148] This brings him to the twentieth century, where the relationship between biopolitics and racism came to the fore most explicitly and devastatingly with Nazism. For Foucault, Nazism combined two aspects: disciplinary power with biopower. Not only was there an unyielding emphasis on discipline and order, but this order was entwined with a concern over the health of the populace to the extent that 'controlling the random element inherent in biological processes was one of the regime's immediate objectives'.[149] This biopolitical control over the population was also combined with 'the old sovereign right to take life'.[150] As such, Nazism was a combination of biopolitics, including its racism, and the right to take life inherent in classic theories of sovereignty.

What was new about this was that the right to take life was not located in the sovereign alone, but permeated the entire populace so that 'ultimately, everyone in the Nazi State had the power of life and death over his or her neighbours, if only because of the practice of informing, which effectively meant doing away with the people next door, or having them done away with'.[151] The emphasis on murder and destruction of 'undesirables' was understood as necessary to maintain the health and purity of the population.

In turn, this was supported by the glorification of war, whereby it was understood that only by 'exposing the entire population to universal death . . . could [it] truly constitute itself as a superior race and bring about its definitive regeneration once other races had been either exterminated or enslaved forever'.[152] Transferring the sovereign's traditional right over life to the entire populace, in combination with a reliance on the hygiene function inherent in racism and insistence that war is the testing ground for its own superiority, brought Nazism to develop 'an absolutely racist State, an absolutely murderous State, and an absolutely suicidal State'.[153]

Foucault's judgement of the Nazi State is not particularly controversial. What is controversial is his claim that the Nazis State was not an anomalous political form, but simply the most explicit and extreme form of the biopolitical racism underpinning *all* contemporary States. In the 1979 lecture course *The Birth of Biopolitics*,[154] Foucault studies the relationship between biopolitics and neoliberal capitalism, but towards the end of the final lecture of the 1976 course he turns to the socialist States to claim that, while they are supposedly based on equality, as biopolitical entities they are just as 'marked by racism as the workings of the modern State, of the capitalist State'.[155] With this, he demonstrates just how important the violence of racism is to the establishment and continuation of *all* modern States.

CONCLUDING REMARKS

Foucault's analysis of the way in which war, racism, and biopolitics intertwine to create modern European societies departs fundamentally from the juridical models of sovereignty and, in so doing, offers a particularly innovative understanding of sovereign violence. This is not, however, to say that there are not problems with it. Beyond the Eurocentric focus of his study, his claim[156] that racism and colonisation developed together means that prior to the end of the nineteenth century, when racism became explicit, his theory holds that there was no colonialism based on race. This seems to downplay centuries of colonial experiences and actions that were precisely based on race; the transportation of African slaves to the New World being a case in point.[157]

Besides this historical issue, lies a conceptual one, insofar as it is not exactly clear what Foucault means by 'war'. This is central to his point in these lectures and, indeed, his notion of power, but is never discussed at any length, nor is it defined. It is not clear therefore whether it works as a historical example or a fundamental aspect of all forms of power.

Indeed, the notion of 'war' also seems to divide society into only two factions, which, of course, feeds nicely into Foucault's analysis of racism, but downplays the emphasis he otherwise places on the heterogeneity of society and power relations. Linked to this is the danger of conceptualising the relationship between the two groups in terms of a victor–vanquished relation. Again, this feeds into the binary opposition inherent in his understanding of racism, but it also points to the notion that, with a final decisive victory, the impure other can be vanquished once and for all, thereby putting an end to war and, by extension, power and all its effects.

Nevertheless, Foucault's lectures on biopolitics and racism reconfigure the notion of sovereign violence away from a single locus to the conflictual logic subtending its concrete manifestations. Beneath the veneer of the apparent stability of sovereign States lies a maelstrom of conflicting power relations that continuously threaten to disrupt that veneer. Rather than something imposed on the State/society from without, violence is a necessary, constitutive, and 'internal' aspect of each modern society; one that functions to create and sustain it. This cannot be thought in terms of sheer repression but, as evidenced by the discussion of racism, operates through the configuration of power relations – themselves conditioned by violent struggle – that creates the structures, values, and norms that define our world. Foucault's lesson is then that violence is constitutive of our social world, cannot be avoided or overcome because it continues to subtend our social institutions, and has a productive, rather than repressive, function, insofar as it generates the racist divisions from which social norms, structures, and values are created.

However, given that Foucault's analysis of biopolitics emphasises the necessary and creative force of internal rupture, it should be no surprise to find that biopolitical theory itself gave rise to a creative caesura. In the next chapter, I explore this by turning to Giorgio Agamben's work on sovereignty, before linking it to his little-discussed analysis of civil war. This will show that Agamben not only challenges Foucault's historical account, but also rejects Foucault's claim that the fundamental division of Western politics is racial. For Agamben, it is that between household and city, private and public.

NOTES

1. Michel Foucault, *Psychiatric Power: Lectures at the Collège de France, 1973–1974*, ed. Jacques Lagrange, trans. Graham Burchell (Basingstoke: Palgrave Macmillan, 2008).
2. Michel Foucault, *Abnormal: Lectures at the Collège de France, 1974–1975*, ed. Valerio Marchetti and Antonella Salomoni, trans. Graham Burchell (New York: Picador, 2003).
3. Michel Foucault, *Discipline and Punish: Birth of the Prison*, trans. Alan Sheridan (New York: Vintage, 1995).

4. Michel Foucault, *A History of Sexuality, vol. 1*, trans. Robert Hurley (New York: Vintage, 1990).
5. Michel Foucault, *Society Must Be Defended*, ed. Mauro Bertani and Alessandro Fontana, trans. David Macey (London: Penguin, 2003).
6. Jospeph Tanke, 'Michel Foucault at the Collège de France, 1974–1976', *Philosophy and Social Criticism*, 31:5–6, 2005, pp. 687–96 (p. 688).
7. John Marks, 'Michel Foucault: Biopolitics and Biology', p. 88, in *Foucault in an Age of Terror: Essays on Biopolitics and the Defence of Society*, ed. Stephen Morton and Stephen Bygrave (Basingstoke: Palgrave Macmillan, 2008), pp. 88–105.
8. Beatrice Hanssen, *Critique of Violence: Between Poststructuralism and Critical Theory* (Abingdon: Routledge, 2000), p. 148.
9. Ansgar Allen and Roy Goddard, 'The Domestication of Foucault: Government, Critique, War', *History of the Human Sciences*, 27:5, 2004, pp. 26–53 (p. 33).
10. Paul Patton, 'From Resistance to Government: Foucault's Lectures 1976–1979', p. 174, in *A Companion to Foucault*, ed. Christopher Falzon, Timothy O'Leary, and Jana Sawicki (London: Wiley-Blackwell, 2013), pp. 172–88.
11. Johanna Oksala, 'From Biopolitics to Governmentality', p. 326, in *A Companion to Foucault*, ed. Christopher Falzon, Timothy O'Leary, and Jana Sawicki (London: Wiley-Blackwell, 2013), pp. 320–36.
12. Stuart Elden, *Foucault's Last Decade* (Cambridge: Polity, 2016), p. 41.
13. Elizabeth Frazer and Kimberly Hutchings, 'Avowing Violence: Foucault and Derrida on Politics, Discourse, and Meaning', *Philosophy and Social Criticism*, 37:1, 2011, pp. 3–23 (p. 6).
14. Marks, 'Michel Foucault', p. 88.
15. Hidefumi Nishiyami, 'Towards a Global Genealogy of Biopolitics: Race, Colonialisation, and Biometrics beyond Europe', *Environment and Planning D: Society and Space*, 33:2, 2015, pp. 331–46 (p. 331).
16. Foucault, *Society Must Be Defended*, p. 3.
17. Ibid. p. 4.
18. Ibid. p. 4.
19. Ibid. pp. 5–6.
20. Ibid. p. 4.
21. Ibid. p. 7.
22. Ibid. p. 7.
23. Ibid. p. 7.
24. Ibid. p. 8.
25. Michel Foucault, 'Nietzsche, Genealogy, History', in *The Foucault Reader*, ed. Paul Rabinow (New York: Vintage, 2010), pp. 76–100.
26. Foucault, *Society Must Be Defended*, pp. 8–9.
27. Ibid. p. 9.
28. Ibid. p. 9.
29. Ibid. p. 9.
30. Ibid. p. 9.
31. Ibid. p. 9.
32. Ibid. p. 10.
33. Ibid. p. 10.
34. Ibid. p. 11.
35. Ibid. p. 12.
36. Ibid. p. 12.

37. Ibid. p. 13.
38. Ibid. p. 13.
39. Ibid. p. 13.
40. Ibid. p. 13.
41. Ibid. p. 13.
42. Ibid. p. 14.
43. Ibid. p. 15.
44. Ibid. p. 15.
45. Ibid. p. 16.
46. Ibid. p. 16.
47. Ibid. p. 15.
48. Ibid. p. 16.
49. Ibid. p. 15.
50. Ibid. p. 15.
51. Ibid. p. 15.
52. Ibid. p. 15.
53. Ibid. p. 16.
54. Ibid. p. 16.
55. Ibid. p. 16.
56. Ibid. p. 16.
57. Foucault, *A History of Sexuality*, vol. *1*, pp. 92–102.
58. Foucault, *Society Must Be Defended*, p. 16.
59. Ibid. p. 17.
60. Ibid. p. 34.
61. Ibid. p. 25.
62. Michel Foucault, 'Truth and Power', p. 122, in *Power: Essential Works of Foucault, 1954–1984, vol. 3*, ed. James D. Faubion, trans. Robert Burchell and others (London: Penguin, 2000), pp. 111–33.
63. Foucault, *Society Must Be Defended*, p. 27.
64. Ibid. p. 29.
65. Ibid. p. 29.
66. Ibid. p. 30.
67. Ibid. p. 34.
68. Ibid. p. 45.
69. Ibid. p. 46.
70. Ibid. p. 43.
71. Ibid. p. 43.
72. Ibid. p. 43.
73. Ibid. p. 44.
74. Ibid. p. 44.
75. Ibid. p. 44.
76. Ibid. pp. 44–5.
77. Ibid. p. 45.
78. Ibid. p. 46.
79. Ibid. p. 46.
80. Ibid. pp. 46–7.
81. Ibid. p. 47.
82. Ibid. p. 48.
83. Alexander Barder and François Debrix, 'Agonal Sovereignty: Rethinking War and

Politics with Schmitt, Arendt, and Foucault', *Philosophy and Social Criticism*, 37:7, 2011, pp. 775–93 (p. 783).
84. Ibid. p. 783.
85. Foucault, *Society Must Be Defended*, p. 48.
86. Ibid. p. 48.
87. Ibid. p. 48.
88. Ibid. p. 48.
89. Ibid. p. 49.
90. Ibid. p. 49.
91. Ibid. p. 49.
92. Ibid. p. 49.
93. Ibid. p. 49.
94. Ibid. p. 50.
95. Ibid. p. 50.
96. Ibid. p. 50.
97. Ibid. p. 50.
98. Ibid. p. 51.
99. Ibid. p. 51.
100. Ibid. p. 51.
101. Roberto Esposito, *Two: The Machine of Political Theology and the Place of Thought*, trans. Zakiya Hanafi (New York: Fordham University Press, 2015).
102. Foucault, *Society Must Be Defended*, p. 58.
103. Ibid. pp. 59–60.
104. Ibid. p. 60.
105. Ibid. p. 60.
106. Ibid. p. 60.
107. Ibid. p. 60.
108. Ibid. p. 60.
109. Ibid. p. 61.
110. Ibid. p. 61.
111. Ibid. p. 61.
112. Ibid. pp. 61–2.
113. Ibid. p. 61.
114. Foucault, *Abnormal*, p. 317.
115. Ibid. p. 317.
116. Ibid. p. 317.
117. Foucault, *Society Must Be Defended*, p. 62.
118. Robert Bernasconi, 'The Policing of Race Mixing: The Place of Biopower within the History of Racisms', *Journal of Bioethical Inquiry*, 7:2, 2010, pp. 205–16 (p. 206).
119. Kim Su Rasmussen, 'Foucault's Genealogy of Racism', *Theory, Culture, and Society*, 28:5, 2011, pp. 34–51 (p. 38).
120. Foucault, *Society Must Be Defended*, p. 240.
121. Ibid. p. 241.
122. Ibid. p. 240.
123. Ibid. p. 240.
124. Ibid. p. 240.
125. Ibid. p. 240.
126. Ibid. p. 241.
127. Ibid. p. 242.

128. Ibid. pp. 242–3.
129. Ibid. p. 243.
130. Ibid. p. 244.
131. Ibid. p. 244.
132. Ibid. p. 244.
133. Ibid. p. 245.
134. Ibid. p. 246.
135. Ibid. p. 246.
136. Ibid. pp. 246–7.
137. Oksala, 'From Biopolitics to Governmentality', p. 322.
138. Foucault, *Society Must Be Defended*, p. 254.
139. Ibid. p. 254.
140. Ibid. p. 255.
141. Ibid. p. 254.
142. Ibid. p. 256.
143. Ibid. p. 256.
144. Ibid. p. 256.
145. Ibid. p. 255.
146. Ibid. p. 256.
147. Ibid. p. 258.
148. Ibid. p. 258.
149. Ibid. p. 259.
150. Ibid. p. 259.
151. Ibid. p. 259.
152. Ibid. p. 260.
153. Ibid. p. 260.
154. Michel Foucault, *The Birth of Biopolitics: Lectures at the Collège de France, 1978–1979*, ed. Michel Senellart, trans. Graham Burchell (Basingstoke: Palgrave Macmillan, 2008).
155. Ibid. p. 261. Little attention has been paid to Foucault's comments on the relationship between biopolitics and State socialism, but an interesting discussion is found in Sergei Prozorov, 'Foucault and Soviet Biopolitics', *History of the Human Sciences*, 27:5, 2014, pp. 6–25.
156. Foucault, *Society Must Be Defended*, p. 257.
157. For an overview of the relationship between colonialism and racism prior to the nineteenth century in this context, see Alan Taylor, *American Colonies: The Settling of North America* (London: Penguin, 2002).

CHAPTER 6

Life Excluded from Law: Agamben, Biopolitics, and Civil War

While Giorgio Agamben's 1970 essay – sent with a letter to Hannah Arendt – 'On the Limits of Violence'[1] contains discussions of many of the themes that will later occupy him – including Benjamin's violence essay, the nature of violence itself, the relationship between violence and law, and the possibility of a new political beginning – his most developed engagements with the question of sovereignty, violence, and biopolitics are found in *Homo Sacer*[2] (published in 1995) and *State of Exception* (published in 2003).[3] In these texts, he rejects the classic-juridical conception of sovereignty to develop a biopolitical one that (1) breaks down the opposition that Foucault instantiates between biopolitics and sovereignty, (2) outlines how the violence associated with biopolitical sovereignty fulfils both a creative *and* a destructive function, and (3) demonstrates that biopolitical sovereignty operates at the nexus between the 'inside' and 'outside' of the juridical-political order.

While this reveals that biopolitical sovereignty is a non-substantive nexal relation binding the various – specifically, juridical, political, and biological – aspects of society, I develop it by turning to Agamben's analysis of civil war – *stasis* – outlined in a lecture of that name given at Princeton University in October 2001.[4] This concept and lecture have received relatively scant attention in the literature despite dealing with a topic that is explicitly linked to both the figure of *homo sacer* and the state of exception. I argue that Agamben's analysis of civil war is important because it reveals that *stasis* is not a result of a sovereign decision, but an ontological concept delineating the conflict that lies at the 'foundation' of biopolitical sovereignty, and that it is to this conflictual logic that his critical comments on biopolitics are orientated.

Whereas Foucault roots biopolitical struggle in the racist discourses of the nineteenth century, Agamben claims that biopolitical conflict and hence violence, in the form of *stasis*, are fundamental to the ontological structure of Western political system generally. Western biopolitical sovereignty functions by politicising life itself and dividing populations into those included and those excluded, with the latter being subjected to increasing terror and even death. Agamben maintains that such exclusion and killing, rather than being contingent aspects of biopolitics, are integral to its operation. By way of conclusion, I engage with Agamben's critical comments on biopolitics, paying particular attention to his claim that its logic needs to be deactivated to permit the movement to what he calls the coming politics.

SOVEREIGNTY AND THE STATE OF EXCEPTION

Agamben's analysis of sovereignty is conditioned by Foucault's insight that the historically dominant juridical conception needs to be replaced with a biopolitical one. As noted, the classic-juridical conception is premised on the notion that sovereignty is indivisible and orientated towards the maintenance of law. Agamben rejects this: sovereignty is dispersed throughout the social body and not necessarily located in law. This points to 'the paradox of sovereignty'[5] wherein 'the sovereign is, at the same time, outside and inside the juridical order'.[6] This place – termed the state of exception – *between* the inside and outside of law reveals much about the sovereignty–law and, by extension, sovereignty–violence relationships.

Agamben claims that the notion of the state of exception goes back to the French Revolution,[7] but has been largely overlooked by political and, indeed, legal theory. Instead, both theory and practice are conditioned by two rather blunt approaches to the issue where one attempts to regulate the exception and the other claims that it is not possible to do so.[8] Agamben takes up this theoretical and practical divide to determine which side, if any, is correct: 'the essential task is not simply to clarify whether [sovereignty] has a juridical nature or not, but to define the meaning, place, and modes of its relation to the law'.[9]

While recognising that Schmitt brought forth the question of the relationship 'between state of exemption and juridical order',[10] Agamben rejects his claim that the state of exception describes the chaos prior to the establishment of law: 'the state of exception is . . . not the chaos that precedes order but rather the situation that results from its suspension'.[11] For Schmitt, the state of exception is the situation prior to the establishment of law; he, therefore, starts from the absence of law to show how law results from it. In contrast, Agamben starts from law to show how the state of exception arises from its *suspension*, which does not mean its absence. Holding that the suspension of law creates a space between law and chaos, Agamben maintains that 'the state of exception is not a special kind of law (like the law of war); rather, insofar as it is a suspension of the juridical order itself, it defines law's threshold or limit concept'.[12] This disrupts the binary logic upon which Schmitt's understanding of the law–state-of-exception relationship depends.

The state of exception is, then, intimately tied to 'a kind of exclusion',[13] wherein 'the most proper characteristic of the exception is that what is excluded in it is not, on account of being excluded, absolutely without relation to the rule'.[14] This is because the state of exception does not annihilate law; it *suspends* it: 'what is excluded in the exception maintains itself to the rule in the form of the rule's suspension'.[15] Specifically, *'the rule applies to the exception in no longer applying, in withdrawing from it'*.[16] Because the state of exception is outside the law, it still, somewhat paradoxically, maintains a tentative link to law.

Indeed, because the state of exception points to an exclusion from law, it can only operate by defining itself against law: 'the state of exception (with its necessary indistinction of Bia and Dikē) is not external to the *nomos* but rather, even in its clear delimitation, included in the *nomos* as a moment that is in every sense fundamental'.[17] This is because, for Agamben, the state of exception is a relational rather than substantive concept; there is always a relation to law, even if that relation is a negative one:

> the state of exception is neither external nor internal to the juridical order, and the problem of defining it concerns precisely a threshold, or a zone of indifference, where inside and outside do not exclude each other but rather blur with each other. The suspension of the norm does not mean its abolition, and the zone of anomie that it establishes is not (or at least claims not to be) unrelated to the juridical order.[18]

Existing between law and the absence of law, the state of exception creates and occupies a mediating place – a zone of indistinction – that 'displaces a contrast between two juridical demands into a limit relation between what is inside and what is outside the law'.[19] Thus, the instantiation of a state of exception does not establish a dictatorship, whether commissarial or sovereign, as Schmitt contends,[20] but creates 'a space devoid of law, a zone of anomie in which all legal determinations – and above all the very distinction between public and private – are deactivated'.[21]

However, while the state of exception creates a space between law and its absence, we have to be careful how we understand the notion of 'space' attached to it. Agamben warns that 'the state of exception is . . . not so much a spatiotemporal suspension as a complex topological figure in which not only the exception and the rule but also the state of nature and law, outside and inside, pass through one another'.[22] The state of exception is not a static space, but a nexus whereby law fluctuates between its application and its suspension, between that which is included and that which is excluded from it. This paradoxical location provides the tools from which to rethink the notion of sovereignty in terms other than a straightforward association with law.

Sovereignty, for Agamben, is then always linked to law, but this linkage can take, at least, two logical forms: (1) the establishment and defence of law as in traditional conceptions of sovereignty, or (2) a far more nuanced and subtle relationship to law through the instantiation of the ambiguity of the state of exception; a locus that allows the sovereign to simultaneously be inside and outside, within and beyond the law. Affirming the later, Agamben notes that within the state of exception, the sovereign is not defined by a simple absence-of-law; the sovereign continues to be bound to law through its suspension of law. This, however, depends on the claim that the non-juridical is a condition of law, meaning that to suspend the law is not to abandon it.

Explaining this through an analogy with language, Agamben tells us that

> just as language presupposes the nonlinguistic as that with which it must maintain itself in a virtual relation . . . so that it may later denote it in actual speech, so the law presupposes the nonjuridical . . . as that with which it maintains itself in a potential relation in the state of exception.[23]

In a very strong sense then Agamben holds that the law is always dependent on its interaction with the non-juridical; a dependence that comes to the fore in the state of exception, wherein law suspends itself to enter into and control the non-juridical. For this reason, he explains that law 'nourishes itself on th[e] exception and is a dead letter without it'.[24]

Sovereign power does not, therefore, dissipate by virtue of operating within the state of exception; it is amplified because the sovereign has the force-of-law without being constrained by law *per se*. It is this that Agamben tries to capture by writing 'force-of-~~law~~'[25]:

> The state of exception is an anomic space in which what is at stake is a force of law without law (which should therefore be written: force-of-~~law~~). Such a 'force-of-~~law~~', in which potentiality and act are radically separated, is certainly something like a mystical element, or rather a *fictio* by means of which law seeks to annex anomie itself.[26]

Having removed itself from law, the sovereign in the state of exception continues to exert authority, a distinction that Agamben first links to Derrida's notion of the mystical element of law,[27] before rethinking it around the stronger claim that the sovereign is based on a fiction rather than a mystical foundation. The reason for the alteration is never spelled out, but it allows Agamben to remove any trace of foundationalism from sovereignty to emphasise its pure relationality.

To develop his non-foundational, fictitious notion of sovereignty, he plays on the distinction between *auctoritas* and *potestas*, where, as Steven DeCaroli points out, '*potestas* refer[s] to the power or ability to achieve certain ends, [whereas] *auctoritas* refer[s] to a claim of legitimacy, the right to exercise power. One who possessed *auctoritas* held the capacity to confirm, or to give, a thing its completeness.'[28] While it is not clear how one gains *auctoritas* – indeed, Agamben's claim that sovereignty is a fiction would seem to indicate that it is something believed in rather than achieved – Agamben explains that it is fundamental to the state of exception and, by extension, to sovereignty because '*auctoritas* seems to act as *a force that suspends* potestas *where it took place and reactivates it where it was no longer in force*. It is a power that suspends or reactivates law, but is not formally in force as law.'[29]

From this, Agamben draws a number of conclusions: first, sovereignty is structured around two heterogeneous elements, 'one that is normative and juridical in the strict sense (which we can for convenience inscribe under the rubric *potestas*) and one that is anomic and metajuridical (which we can call by the name *auctoritas*)'.[30] The former needs the latter to be applied, while the latter can only assert itself by affirming or suspending the former. Because sovereignty is conditioned by this dialectic, one that can break down at any moment, we see that, second, 'the ancient dwelling of law is fragile and, in straining to maintain its own order, is always already in the process of ruin and decay'.[31] As a consequence, third, the state of exception is 'the device that must ultimately articulate and hold together the two aspects of the juridico-political machine by instituting a threshold of undecidability between anomie and *nomos*, between life and law, between *auctoritas* and *potestas*'.[32] The two distinct aspects are, fourth, bound together by the fictional notion that the sovereign is that which stands at the nexus between the two points, uniting them in their difference.

As long as the sovereign maintains the two moments in such a way that they 'remain correlated yet conceptually, temporally, and subjectively distinct ... their dialectic – though founded on a fiction – can nevertheless function in some way'.[33] The problem arises when the two moments collapse so that, rather than being the mediation between the two moments, the sovereign manifests both in him. When this occurs, his actions become synonymous with law: he is able to seamlessly move between law and its suspension, upholding law one moment before subsequently suspending it the next; actions that permit him to control all aspects of life and death. When this becomes the rule, as Agamben insists it is in contemporary society, 'the juridico-political system transforms itself into a killing machine'.[34]

With this, Agamben makes a practical point regarding the danger inherent in contemporary politics and draws a theoretical conclusion regarding the nature of sovereignty: sovereignty cannot properly be said to belong to law, politics, or the non-juridical in general; it is a nexal fiction operating in a zone of indistinction *between* law, politics, and the non-juridical.[35] This permits sovereignty to take control of life, condition it based on the inclusion–exclusion structure, and determine how one lives and who is left to die.[36] Through the state of exception the sovereign reveals and affirms its fundamental relationship with biopolitics.

SOVEREIGNTY AND BIOPOLITICS

Agamben analyses this relationship by returning to the ancient Greek distinction between two senses of 'life': *zoē* and *bios*. The former 'expressed the simple fact of living common to all living beings (animals, men, or gods)',[37] while the latter 'indicated the form or way of living proper to an individual or a group'.[38] Having noted how this distinction plays out in Plato and Aristotle, he turns to contemporary thinkers, specifically Foucault and Arendt.

Whereas Foucault was able to understand the fundamental relationship between biology and politics, Agamben complains that he 'never dwelt on the exemplary places of modern biopolitics: the concentration camp and the structure of the great totalitarian [S]tates of the twentieth century'.[39] Arendt, in contrast, did focus on the camps and totalitarian structures, but failed to examine the two from 'a biopolitical perspective'.[40] Agamben aims to overcome the lacunae in both by developing a biopolitical perspective that shows how sovereignty operates on bare life – life removed from the juridical schema – with this operation finding its most explicit manifestation through the paradigm of the concentration camps.

Noting that Foucault criticised juridical-philosophical conceptions of sovereignty to affirm biopolitics and, in so doing, maintained a distinction between the two, Agamben disrupts this opposition to suggest that the two intersect. His aim is to show that, while Foucault is correct to note the importance of biopolitics, he is wrong to claim that it is a modern phenomenon. By focusing on the point where sovereignty and biopolitics overlap, Agamben aims to demonstrate that sovereignty has always been biopolitical: 'the inclusion of bare life in the political realm constitutes the original – if concealed – nucleus of sovereign power. *It can even be said that the production of a biopolitical body is the original activity of sovereign power.*'[41]

This explanation requires a word on the distinction and relationship between bare life, *zoē*, and *bios*. As Kevin Attell explains, 'bare life is not natural, biological life [*bios*] or *zoē*; it is precisely the politicised *zoē* that has been identified and inclusively excluded in the body of the human subjected to sovereign power'.[42] Whereas *bios* is associated with natural life, *zoē* describes the politicised life, with bare life describing a particular way in which life is excluded from *zoē* to exist in the state of exception. Sovereign power is that which creates a particular form of life (*zoē*), including conceptions of bare life, from the *bios* common to all beings. It is for this reason that sovereignty is biopower. Through its operations, specifically how it divides the populace into those included and excluded from law, the sovereign structures *zoē* into bare life.

To explain the relationship between sovereignty and biopolitics further, Agamben turns to the obscure Roman figure of '*homo sacer* (sacred man), who may be killed and yet not sacrificed'.[43] This figure is first mentioned in *Language and Death*, published in 1982, where Agamben explains that

> the sacred is necessarily an ambiguous and circular concept. (In Latin *sacer* means vile, ignominious, and also august, reserved for the gods; both the law and he who violates it are sacred: *qui legem violavit, sacer esto*.) He who has violated the law, in particular by homicide, is excluded from the community, exiled, and abandoned to himself, so that killing him would not be a crime.[44]

While Agamben's reading of *homo sacer* has been criticised – Frederiek Depoortere insists that it is 'at odds with historical reality and . . . nothing but a fanciful creation'[45] – the claim that *homo sacer* is conditioned by a double exclusion is the cornerstone of his understanding of the term, one that he repeats thirteen years later in *Homo Sacer: Sovereign Power and Bare Life*.

It is important to note, however, that *homo sacer*'s double exclusion is not simply due to the semantic ambiguity of the term 'sacred', which, as Leland de la Durantaye notes, can mean anything from 'that which is treasured as most pure and precious to that which is most contemptible and must be cast out of the community so as to preserve it from contamination'.[46] The double exclusion afflicting *homo sacer* comes from his status between the human and divine: in being excluded by the sovereign, he is excluded from human law, but, in being killed but not sacrificed, he is also excluded from the divine. By 'subtracting itself from the sanctioned forms of both human and divine law, this violence opens a sphere of human action that is neither the sphere of *sacrum facere* nor that of profane action'.[47] The exclusion from sovereign law places him in an ambiguous place between human and divine, inside and outside of law. This is because, even while he is excluded from sovereign law, his excluded status still binds him to sovereign law. He is, therefore, between law and the absence of law.

The consequences of this for *homo sacer* are dramatic:

> The daily struggle for survival for those who remain outside the *polis* entails not only periodic encounters with the caprice of nature's fury but continual encounters with the violence of the [S]tate stemming from the fact that the [S]tate and the political life it sustains, ruthlessly pursues a survival of its own.[48]

By being placed outside the protection of the sovereign and placed under the constant threat of death, the *homo sacer* lives a precarious life conditioned by violence.

Agamben's discussion of *homo sacer* is important, not just because it brings to light an interesting facet of and figure in Roman law, but also because he claims that, in pointing to a 'place' beyond the law that is not quite absent law, this figure reveals a crucial and often-overlooked structural dimension of Western juridical systems; namely, the fundamental role that the state of exception plays within them. The state of exception does not simply open a lacuna in law, but is the 'place' where sovereignty and biopolitics meet. Through the suspension of law inherent in the state of exception, life becomes politicised.

This is not because law is applied to life, but because through the suspension of law, life is subject to 'Abandonment'.[49] The ban underpinning this act of abandonment has a relational rather than substantial structure, in that it establishes a relation of excluded-inclusion: 'what has been banned is delivered over to its own separateness and, at the same time, consigned to the mercy of the one who abandons it – at once excluded and included, removed and at the same time captured'.[50] Crucially, the ban does not just reveal how *homo sacer* is excluded by the sovereign; it also demonstrates that both figures have a similar structural relation to law: 'the sovereign is the one with respect to whom all men are potentially *homines sacri*, and *homo sacer* is the one with respect to whom all men act as sovereigns'.[51] This is because both the sovereign and *homo sacer* point to a sphere of existence *between* the human and divine. For Agamben, this is 'the first properly political space of the West distinct from both the religious and profane sphere, from both the natural order and the regular juridical order'.[52]

The political sphere is, then, not linked to the juridical, natural, profane, or theological, but is the 'space' between them. Because it is conditioned by the ban structure, the political is able to both include and exclude these various aspects all at once. Far from a contingent relation, however, 'the relation of ban has constituted the essential structure of sovereign power from the beginning'.[53]

For this reason, the ban structure is more originary than Schmitt's insistence that the friend–enemy structure defines the political. According to Agamben, the Schmittian friend–enemy structure is an effect of the ban structure, insofar as the '"estrarity" of the person held in the sovereign ban is more intimate and primary than the extraneousness of the foreigner'.[54] Whereas the foreignness of the Schmittian enemy means that it is wholly external from the beginning, the sovereign ban structure makes into an external 'enemy' one who was initially a 'friend' internal to the juridical sovereign structure. While it is questionable whether the Schmittian political decision starts from a privileging of the friend – Derrida, for example, famously criticises Schmitt for privileging the enemy[55] – Agamben claims that the friend's initial close contact means that Schmitt starts from a privileging of juridical law which permits exclusions. The sovereign ban structure, however, precedes the friend/enemy distinction; it is that 'place' from which the designations of 'friend' or 'enemy' arise. As a consequence, Agamben concludes that all sovereignty is biopolitical, which is not to say that all effects of biopolitical sovereignty are the same.

Indeed, Agamben claims that contemporary politics has witnessed a growing intensification of biopolitical sovereign action through the explicit and extensive use of bans and states of exception:

> The realm of bare life – which is originally situated at the margins of the political order – gradually begins to coincide with the political realm, and exclusion and inclusion, outside and inside, *bios* and *zoē*, right and fact, enter into a zone of irreducible indistinction.[56]

What was previously implicit or reduced to the margins has become explicit and paradigmatic, so that 'what confronts us today is a life that as such is exposed to a violence without precedent precisely in the most profane and banal ways'.[57] '[B]are life is no longer confined to a particular place or a definite category. It now dwells in the biological body of every living being.'[58] The Jews in the Nazi concentration camps were the clearest manifestation of this increasing politicisation and control of bare life – 'a flagrant case of a *homo sacer* in the sense of a life that may be killed but not sacrificed'[59] – but contemporary politics has extended the conditions of the camp beyond the camps themselves so that they condition contemporary society.

Thus, while the concentration camp describes 'the most absolute biopolitical space ever to have been realised, in which power confronts nothing but pure life, without any mediation',[60] it does not necessarily indicate or refer to a particular location, but a *logic* that comes to condition the normal order; namely, one in which the state of exception rules. For this reason, it can take the form of a refugee camp, indefinite detention without legal trial, and even, as Agamben notes, 'the *zones d'attentes* of our airports and certain outskirts of our cities'.[61] It is simply shorthand for the spaces where law is legally suspended, with the consequence that individuals find themselves between the inside and outside of law: 'to an order without localisation (the state of exception, in which law is suspended) there now corresponds a localisation without order (the camp as permanent space of exception)'.[62] Agamben concludes that 'we are all virtually *homines sacri*'.[63]

One of the key ways in which this status is controlled contemporarily is through the delineation of rights. Altering Schmitt's famous dictum that 'sovereign is he who decides on the exception',[64] Agamben claims that

> in modern biopolitics, sovereign is he who decides on the value or the non-value of life as such. Life – which, with the declarations of rights, had as such been invested with the principle of sovereignty – now itself becomes the place of a sovereign decision.[65]

In modern biopolitics, law takes on something of an 'organic', ever-changing form where it is constantly altering to define acceptable forms of life: 'once *zoē* is politicised by declarations of rights, the distinctions and thresholds that make it possible to isolate a sacred life must be newly defined'.[66] Thus, rights are not a neutral discourse that protect against sovereign power, but a mechanism of sovereign power that distinguishes between those included and excluded from law. This is why the status of refugees is so important: they call into question the limit-status of the fundamental categories defining national sovereignties – namely the link between citizenship, natality, and right – and, in so doing, bring to the fore their constructed nature. The entrance of refugees into the *polis* reveals that 'rights', rather than being universal and ahistoric, are granted and so bound to particular sovereign regimes.

This discovery is tied to and, in part, defined by the notion of 'the people'.[67] Refugee status becomes an issue because the individual does not initially belong to the right people, but must apply for that status. The decision regarding how to treat him/her is, then, a decision about who or what defines the people. The problem is that the notion of 'the (right) people' is inherently ambiguous. There are practical implications of this, but Agamben claims that they are rooted in the ambiguity of its meaning:

> it is as if what we call 'people' were in reality not a unitary subject but a dialectic oscillation between two opposite poles: on the one hand, the set of the People as a whole political body, and on the other, the subset of the people as a fragmentary multiplicity of needy and excluded bodies.[68]

The notion of 'the people' does not then signify a unity; it 'is a polar concept that indicates a double movement and a complex relation between two extremes'.[69] Indeed, using 'the people' in political discourse brings to the fore the fundamental division that mirrors the other political categories of contemporary biopolitics – 'bare life (people) and political existence (People), exclusion and inclusion, zoē and bios'[70] – so that 'the "people" always already carries the fundamental biopolitical fracture within itself'.[71] 'The people' refers to both the whole and the part, a bind that generates 'the contradictions and aporias ... every time that it is evoked and put into play on the political scene. It is what always already is and yet must, however, continually be redefined and purified through exclusion, language, blood, and land.'[72] For this reason, 'the people always contains a division more originary than that of friend–enemy, an incessant civil war that divides it more radically than every conflict and, at the same time, keeps it united and constitutes it more securely than any identity'.[73]

By showing the intimate relation between biopolitical sovereignty and the notion of 'the people', Agamben is, on the one hand, appealing to Foucault's notion of racism to highlight how a populace is divided between those considered acceptable and those excluded, while, on the other hand, departing from Foucault in claiming that this racist division did not arise from developments in the nineteenth century but is constitutive of all historical appeals to 'the people' in Western political discourse.

While this division was historically accepted and incorporated into the *polis*, with the Romans dividing the populace between the *populus* and plebs, and the Middle Ages distinguishing between the *popolo minute* (artisans and tradespeople) and the *popolo grasso* (commercial classes), Agamben argues that, starting with the French Revolution, this duality has increasingly been rejected and unity affirmed. The *People* as a unitary whole has become synonymous with sovereignty, while the *people* has been 'transformed into an embarrassing presence'.[74]

Contemporary biopolitics has gone further, insofar as it does not simply leave alone that which is excluded, but through 'the implacable and methodical attempt to overcome the division dividing the people [aims] to eliminate radically the people that is excluded'.[75] This occurs through multiple means, such as the socio-economic management of resources to the disadvantage of those in the excluded groups, or the transformation of 'the entire population of the Third World into bare life'[76] to be used for the so-called First World. The basic point is that the excluded group is not accepted with a space made for them within society, but is excluded from society and subject to strategies and actions of elimination. For this reason, contemporary biopolitical sovereignty is conditioned by a fundamental, if often ignored, civil war between the included and excluded aspects of the populace; a civil war that is increasingly global in nature.

CIVIL WAR

That Agamben links biopolitical sovereignty to civil war through both the state of exception and the internal division marking biopolitics indicates that the concept plays a fundamental role in his analysis of biopolitical sovereignty. It is surprising to find then that, while a number of commentators mention it,[77] there is no detailed engagement with what he understands by the term. In what follows, I start to remedy this by focusing on the lecture that Agamben gave on the topic at Princeton University in October 2001. This will demonstrate that the biopolitical sovereign decision is conditioned by the violence inherent in *stasis*, before showing that this *stasis* 'ground' continuously disrupts the unity which sovereignty aims for and depends upon. Crucially, this subtending tension provides structural openings for social transformation and 'the coming politics'.[78]

Agamben notes that while 'there exists, today, a "polemology", theory of war, and an "irenology", a theory of peace ... there is no "stasiology", no theory of civil war'.[79] Strangely, however, 'this absence does not seem to concern jurists and political scientists too much'.[80] When civil war is discussed, Agamben claims that it is not to offer a theory of civil war, but, more often than not, to determine 'the conditions under which an international intervention becomes possible'.[81] This, however, 'seems [to be] incompatible with the serious investigation of a phenomenon that is at least as old as Western democracy'.[82]

That the question of the meaning and nature of civil war has largely bypassed serious philosophical discussion is all the more troubling because, following Arendt and Schmitt, Agamben claims that civil war has become global to the extent that it has largely replaced traditional forms of warfare. However, no sooner does he complain about the lack of theorising about civil war in the literature than he explains that 'a theory of civil war is not among the possible objectives of this text'.[83] What he aims to do is restrict himself to the phenomenon as it appears in ancient Greece, before using this historical example to bring to light certain lacunae in our historical understanding.

To do so, he turns to the work of Nicole Loraux, in particular her influential text *The Divided City: On Memory and Forgetting in Ancient Athens*,[84] because he finds in it a theory that 'situates the problem in its specific locus, which is to say, in the relationship between the *oikos*, the family or household, and the *polis*, the city'.[85] The tension between both and, indeed, the space between them is crucial to Agamben's analysis of the phenomenon. Specifically, he suggests that what Loraux points out is that we have to redefine the relationship between the household and the city. Contrary to what is commonly thought, civil war is not marked by 'an overcoming of the family in the city, of the private in the public and of the particular in the general';[86] it is a state conditioned by 'a more ambiguous and complex relation'[87] between the two.

Agamben develops this by noting Loraux's claim that the ambiguity of *stasis* is linked to that of *oikos*, insofar as, initially, *stasis* was tied to the 'conflict particular to the *phylon*, to blood kinship'.[88] This was to such an extent that, initially, civil war was synonymous with '*ta emphylia* (literally, "the things internal to the bloodline)"'.[89] However, 'precisely because it is what lies at the origin of the *stasis*, the family is also what contains its possible remedy'.[90] The family is both the location of civil war, namely the division inherent in civil war, and that which remedies that division. For this reason, civil war is a familial issue that, by virtue of the family–city relationship, becomes a city one; although it is important to note that it continues to remain a fundamentally familial conflict as it engulfs the *polis*.

From this brief summary, Agamben develops three theses: first, a study of *stasis* 'calls into question the commonplace that conceives Greek politics as the definitive overcoming of the *oikos* in the *polis*'.[91] Second, 'in its essence, *stasis* or civil war is a "war within the family", which comes from the *oikos* and not from outside. Precisely insofar as it is inherent to the family, the *stasis* acts as a revealer; it attests to its irreducible presence in the *polis*.'[92] Third, that the civil war of the *polis* is conditioned by the conflict within the *oikos* reveals the latter to be 'essentially ambivalent: on the one hand, it is a factor of division and conflict; on the other, it is the paradigm that enables the reconciliation of what it has divided'.[93] The family is, then, both the provoker of civil war and that which heals the division.

Agamben notes that all these theses are premised on certain oppositions: *oikos* and *polis*, division and reconciliation, conflict and non-conflict. What links them is the notion of *stasis*, which is not a substance, but rather a nexal concept that, on the one hand, 'remains in the shadows',[94] but, on the other hand, 'is . . . a "revealer" of the *oikos*'.[95] Analysing *stasis* does not then lead to the study of the *polis* as might typically be thought – it might seem reasonable after all to conclude that civil war is a war between two *political* factions within the *polis* – but to the study of the *oikos* as the real source of *stasis*.

However, if an understanding of *stasis* is always dependent on other phenomena, such as the meaning of *oikos* and its relationship to the *polis*, the nature and meaning of *stasis* are always deferred. As a nexal concept, it depends on others, but, in depending on others, it can never be revealed: 'reduced . . . to the element from which it originates [*oikos*] and to whose presence in the city it can only attest, its own definition ultimately remains elusive'.[96] Thus, if Loraux's analysis points in this direction, the key is to develop it to bring to light the elusive moment.

Starting with the first aforementioned thesis – *stasis* calls into question the claim that the Greek *polis* overcame the *oikos* – Agamben maintains that rather than a binary opposition between the *oikos* and the *polis*, the *oikos*/*polis* distinction needs to be linked to the *zoē*/*bios* dichotomy introduced in *Homo Sacer*. These lie 'at the foundation of Western politics [but] need to be rethought from scratch'.[97] This should not fixate on the opposition 'between *zoē* and the *oikos* [or] *polis* and political *bios*',[98] but focus on the relation between them, which should be interpreted to show that 'the former must be included in the latter through an exclusion'.[99] In other words, Agamben does not so much provide an answer to the *oikos*–*polis* relationship as, by linking it to the *zoē*/*bios* division, conclude that it demonstrates that the ban structure applies to both. Understood in this way, both *stasis* and biopolitics entail 'a complicated and unresolved attempt to capture an exteriority and to expel an intimacy'.[100]

If the first thesis confirms the *zoē*/*bios* division of his earlier work on *homo sacer*, the latter two theses 'appear [to be] more problematic'.[101] The second holds that stasis results from a conflict within the family, while the third insists that there is an ambiguity to the family's relationship to *stasis*: it is the cause and cure for it. The problem is that Agamben is not, initially, sure why the family 'entail[s] conflict at its centre'[102] or how the *oikos* can play both roles. Rather than respond directly to these issues, he turns to the etymology of *stasis* '(from *histemi*)'[103] to explain that it 'designates the act of rising, of standing firm upright (*stasimos* is the point in the tragedy when the chorus stands still and speaks; *stas* is the one who swears the oath while standing)'.[104]

The question then becomes 'where does the stasis "stand"?'[105] Agamben responds by turning to a section in Plato's *Laws* (869c–d) – 'The brother [*adelphos*, the blood brother] who kills his brother in combat during civil war ... will be held pure [*katharos*] as if he had killed an enemy [*polemios*]; the same will happen when a citizen has killed a citizen in the same conditions, or a stranger a stranger'[106] – to reject Loraux's claim that *stasis* results in the death of the immediate family, whose bond is transferred to the city, which becomes the *real* family.[107] Instead, Agamben suggests that Plato's text proposes not a connection between *stasis* and *oikos*, but 'the fact that the civil war assimilates and makes undecidable brother and enemy, inside and outside, household and city'.[108] Through *stasis*, 'the killing of what is most intimate is indistinguishable from the killing of what is most foreign',[109] thereby indicating that 'the *stasis* does not have its place within the household, but constitutes a threshold of indifference between the *oikos* and *polis*, between blood kinship and citizenship'.[110]

This removes *stasis* from the household to relocate it in the zone of indifference *between* the *oikos* and *polis*. Thus, in response to the original question of where *stasis* 'stands', Agamben explains that 'the *stasis* – this is our hypothesis – takes place neither in the *oikos* nor in the *polis*, neither in the family nor in the city; rather, it constitutes a zone of indifference between the unpolitical space of the family and the political space of the city'.[111] *Stasis* disrupts the binary opposition between *oikos* and *polis* that subtends Loraux's analysis; it is not a purely private or public matter, but is located on the threshold between the two:

> in transgressing this threshold, the *oikos* is politicised; conversely, the *polis* is 'economised', that is, it is reduced to an *oikos*. This means that in the system of Greek politics civil war functions as a threshold of politicisation and depoliticisation, through which the house is exceeded in the city and the city is depoliticised in the family.[112]

Agamben does not mention him, but, with this, he is implicitly criticising Schmitt's insistence that Western societies have become increasingly depoliticised. Specifically, Agamben rejects (1) the binary opposition, between politicisation and depoliticisation, underpinning Schmitt's analysis, and (2) the temporality of this movement, wherein Schmitt holds that there was initially a politicised world that has from the sixteenth century become increasingly depoliticised. For Agamben, there has never been a temporal movement from a politicised to a depoliticised world because the history of Western politics is not conditioned by a movement from politicisation to depoliticisation. Rather, Western politics is generated from the tension *between* the political and non-political. Thus, if politics has existed in the West, it has always been conditioned from the tension between both aspects.

Agamben backs this up by appealing to Solon's law, which punishes, with the loss of civil rights, any citizen who has not fought on either side in a civil war. This reveals that 'not taking part in the civil war amount[ed] to being expelled from the *polis* and confined to the *oikos*, to losing citizenship by being reduced to the unpolitical condition of a private person'.[113] This does not mean that politics disappears; only that the status of the individual in relation to the political can change, insofar as he can move from the political to non-political spheres of society; although due to the ban structure he is always related to the other.

Furthermore, Solon's law reveals that it is *stasis* that joins the *polis* to the *oikos*, the political to the private. *Stasis* is not inherently political or non-political; it is the relation *between* the political and non-political that 'functions as a reactant which reveals the political element in the extreme instance as a threshold of politicisation that determines for itself the political or unpolitical character of a certain being'.[114] *Stasis* is fundamental because it links two opposing aspects in such a way as to allow disparate aspects to feed off one another. It is the pivot point around and from which the whole system operates. It is, quite simply, an 'uneliminable part of the Western political system'.[115]

Stasis is not then a local and temporal outbreak of hostilities, but 'a device that functions in a manner similar to the state of exception'.[116] While the state of exception includes *zoē* in the *polis* by excluding it, so 'the *oikos* is politicised and included in the *polis* through the *stasis*'.[117] *Stasis,* like the state of exception, operates as a zone of indistinction wherein the political and non-political, the outside and inside of the juridical, coincide. Western politics is then structured not by a binary opposition, but by a far more complicated structure wherein 'opposing' concepts are united and pass into another through a mediating zone. This zone is not a substance – 'there is no such thing as a political "substance"'[118] – it is 'a field incessantly traversed by the tensional currents of politicisation and depoliticisation, the family and the city'.[119]

How the tension of *stasis* relates to the political and non-political shapes society: 'when the tension toward the *oikos* prevails and the city seems to want to transform itself into a family (albeit of a particular kind), then civil war functions as a threshold in which family relationships are repoliticised'.[120] In contrast, when the tension moves towards the *polis*, 'the *stasis* intervenes to recodify the family relationships in political terms'.[121] The shift in the form that the tension of *stasis* takes and its relationship to the *oikos* and *polis* are, for Agamben, heterogeneous, but they both produce social relations through the different conformations of the *oikos*–*polis* relationship and continuously disrupt them to permit reformation.

There are, then, a number of similarities between the structures of *stasis* and the state of exception: both delineate the zone or threshold between two positions, in the case of *stasis* between *oikos* and *polis*, and in the case of the state of exception between the juridical and non-juridical. Both seem to be conditioned by the ban structure that permits them to include what they exclude, and both are intimately linked to the politicisation of life, insofar as *stasis* points to whether the political or non-political aspect will be privileged and defines what that will look like, while the state of exception does so juridically. In so doing, both define the form that society will take by outlining who is included in and excluded from society.

Finally, similar political consequences result when one aspect of the opposition they unite dominates: while sovereignty normally exists between *potestas* and *auctoritas*, if the distinction is collapsed into a single figure which is simultaneously composed of both aspects, the result is 'a killing machine'.[122] Equally, when the distinction between *oikos* and *polis* is usurped so that 'the *polis* appears in the reassuring figure of the *oikos* . . . *stasis*, which can no longer be situated in the threshold between the *oikos* and the *polis*, becomes the paradigm of every conflict and re-emerges in the form of terror'.[123] The key issue is that the tension between both aspects must be maintained; violence is inherent in the generation of political life created from the structure of *stasis* and the state of exception, but it intensifies to its most extreme – by creating a State killing machine or terrorism – when the distinction is usurped so that one aspect rules.

From this, it may be tempting to conclude that *stasis* and the state of exception are synonyms. After all, Agamben not only claims that they are structured around a similar logic, but also insists that they both work to instantiate the binary logic and the creation of an *archè* that dominates Western thought:

> The *archè* is constituted by dividing the factical experience and pushing down to the origin – that is, excluding – one half of it in order then to rearticulate it to the other by including it as a foundation. Thus, the city is founded on the division of life into bare life and politically qualified life, the human is defined by the exclusion-inclusion of the animal, the law by the *exceptio* of anomie, governance through the exclusion of inoperativity and its capture in the form of glory.[124]

However, while the structure of *stasis* and the state of exception are similar and work to instantiate a similar logic, they are not the same nor can they be reduced to one another. To understand the relationship, we need to tie it to the sovereign decision, which is the mediation between the two. More specifically, the sovereign decision is always subtended by the conflict of *stasis*, with the affirmation of the state of exception being one response to its subtending conflict, insofar as the instantiation of a state of exception determines a particular logic based on which form of life and which side of *stasis* will be excluded. Crucially, in a similar vein to *stasis*, 'sovereignty' is not substantive or located in a singular point, but the name given to the nexus through which the tension-filled, violent, and constantly changing relations subtending, generating, and disrupting society pass.

CONCLUDING REMARKS

In previous chapters, I have shown that critical analyses of the question of sovereign violence have increasingly moved away from emphasising its relationship to juridical order to insisting on its fundamental bond with the notion of life, which, in turn, has entailed a movement away from thinking of sovereignty in terms of a juridical-political agent who uses violence instrumentally to establish and preserve the juridical order, to analyses that maintain that sovereignty is, in some way, decentred from agents. This finds its most extreme formulation in Agamben's claim that it is a nexal 'point' through which the various – juridical, political, biological – relations of society pass. These relations are inherently tension-filled and violent, thereby revealing that violence is not an instrument to be used by sovereignty but fundamental to the relations that pass through sovereignty and the biopolitical machine.

By claiming that biopolitical sovereignty emanates from the violence of *stasis* and acts as the nexus point of the juridical and non-juridical, Agamben argues that violence is both foundational to and constitutive of all aspects of Western society. There simply is no way to escape or be other-than the biopolitical machine; anything 'external' to biopolitical sovereignty is always included in it through its exclusion and so subject to its violence. Any politics of resistance is, then, caught in the machine it seeks to escape from.

Nevertheless, Agamben does not simply abandon us to biopolitical sovereignty, but affirms the need for a new form of politics – and presumably (non-biopolitical) form of sovereignty – which he terms '*the coming politics*'.[125] This notion is complex and contested,[126] but to start to outline what it entails, I will, by way of conclusion, focus on the notions of and relations between 'inoperativity',[127] 'destituent potential',[128] and 'form-of-life'.[129]

These terms are introduced in *The Use of Bodies* in an attempt to point the way to the 'overcoming' of biopolitical sovereignty. Agamben notes that the 'traditional' notion of political change is to hold that it comes about by simply positing an alternative, with this being dependent on 'the concept of a "constituent power"'.[130] We saw this, for example, in the thought of Carl Schmitt. In turn, this is premised on the notion that each constituted-power, such as biopolitics, is underpinned by a constituting-power that generates and sustains it. By changing the constituting-power, the logic of the tradition holds that the constituted power – biopolitics – will also change. Agamben rejects this because, in reality, such action does not undermine the means–end *logic* inherent in biopolitics. Changing the constituting-power might change the form of politics, but the alteration would simply be a *means* to an *end* and so repeat and remain inscribed within the instrumental logic of biopolitics.

To get round this, Agamben claims that '[t]he fundamental ontological-political problem today is not work but inoperativity, not the frantic and unceasing study of a new operativity but the exhibition of the ceaseless void that the machine of Western culture guards at its centre'.[131] To release the void at the heart of Western culture requires not another constituting-power, but 'something that we can provisionally call "destituent potential"'.[132] With this, Agamben not only criticises the whole tradition of Western thought, but also points to a different form of action. However, as he notes, the problem that arises when we try to think this alternative is that we encounter 'the difficulty of thinking a purely destituent potential'.[133]

To start to unravel this concept, we need to understand what Agamben means by 'potential' and 'destituent'. Agamben situates his conception of potentiality within the Aristotelian tradition, before explaining that 'potentiality . . . is not simply the potential to do this or that thing but potential to not-do, potential not to pass into actuality'.[134] Potentiality exists as the *between* that 'exists' prior to the affirmation of doing or not-doing. This 'between' is not a thing, an action, or even passivity, but 'impotentiality',[135] also called 'pure potentiality'.[136] Biopolitics is premised on a particular actualisation of potentiality, whereby the actualisation is understood solely and exclusively through the binary opposition of activity or passivity. To break with this binary logic, Agamben aims to deactivate the binary logic of biopolitics by affirming the 'impotentiality' that 'exists' prior to the active/passive opposition sustaining biopolitics.

As mentioned, however, this cannot be achieved by the positing of and reliance on a constituting-power; that is, a power that simply posits a different means or end to that of biopolitics. Doing so would remain caught in the means–end, active–passive logic of biopolitics. Instead, Agamben affirms a 'destituent potential'[137] because he holds that this undermines the binary logic that holds apart the terms of biopolitics: '[w]here a relation is rendered destitute and interrupted, its elements are in this sense in contact, because the absence of every relation is exhibited between them'.[138] By doing so, the destituent potential collapses the oppositions of biopolitics so that 'what has been divided from itself and captured in the exception – life, anomie, anarchic potential – now appears in its free and intact form'.[139] The key here is that this collapsing does not re-establish anything immediately, but simply deactivates the logic of oppositions underpinning biopolitics.

Indeed, because it merely deactivates that logic, Agamben links the notion of destituent potential to 'the term "inoperativity"'.[140] Specifically, he explains that in both 'what is in question is the capacity to deactivate something and render it inoperative – a power, a function, a human operation – without simply destroying it but by liberating the potentials that have remained inactive in it in order to allow a different use of them'.[141] In other words, the destituent potential does not oppose the constituting or constituted power of biopolitics with an alternative option, but seeks to deactivate or render inoperative the means–end logic of biopolitics to unleash the (im)potentiality inherent in that logic, to subsequently permit alternative actualisations of it. As Agamben puts it: '[w]hat deactivates operativity is certainly an experience of potentiality, but of a potential that, insofar as it holds its own impotential or potentiality-not-to firm, exposes itself in its non-relation to the act'.[142] Crucially, '[a]t the point where the apparatus is ... deactivated, potential becomes a form-of-life and a form-of-life is constitutively destituent'.[143]

Agamben explains that '[w]ith the term *form-of-life* ... we understand a life that can never be separated from its form, a life in which it is never possible to isolate and keep distinct something like a bare life'.[144] Put simply, form-of-life describes 'a life for which its mode of living, its very living is at stake and, in its living, what is at stake is first of all its mode of life'.[145] Form-of-life is 'pure' life devoid 'of all factical vocations'.[146] As such, Agamben claims that 'form-of-life is a being of potential not only or not so much because it can do or not do, succeed or fail, lose itself or find itself, but above all because it is its potential and coincides with it'.[147] If form-of-life is pure potential, forms of life denote how that potential is expressed factically. Biopolitics is then a form of life that structures the form-of-life around a particular means/end dichotomy. Affirming the destituent potential at the 'heart' of biopolitics renders its logic inoperative, while also returning thought to the form-of-life subtending biopolitics to permit the potential that defines form-of-life to be reactivated in alternative (non-biopolitical) ways. For this reason, Agamben concludes that 'form-of-life . . . must become the guiding concept and the unitary centre of coming politics'.[148]

There is obviously a lot more to these concepts, but this brief outline shows how Agamben aims to overcome biopolitics. Specifically, he challenges the long-held assumption that political change arises from the simple positing of alternatives to those present. The notions of destituent potential and inoperativity point to a two-stage model of change wherein political action first seeks to deactivate the logic of biopolitics before looking for ways to move beyond that logic. With this, Agamben does not just posit biopolitical forms of sovereign violence in opposition to the classical and radical-juridical models so long dominant; he also starts to point towards a form of sovereignty that moves beyond that of biopolitics.

The problem, of course, is that his analysis is highly abstract and not particularly clear on what happens once the destituent potential has rendered inoperative the logic of biopolitics. In many respects, it must remain that way so as to prevent the instantiation of a political programme to be followed; an action that would re-inscribe the means–end logic to be overcome. This does, however, give rise to the following questions: if even Agamben – someone who appeared to affirm the biopolitical paradigm – recognises that the biopolitical model must be overcome (and this cannot entail a return to a juridical model), what alternative forms of sovereignty are available? And can we do better than simply positing an ineffable and indeterminate promise of a coming politics? In the next chapter, I respond to these questions by turning to the thought of Jacques Derrida, who first criticises both the juridical and biopolitical models, before affirming a *bio-juridical* model of sovereign violence to overcome the conceptual impasse generated from them.

NOTES

1. Giorgio Agamben, 'On the Limits of Violence', trans. Elisabeth Fay, *Diacritics*, 39:4, 2009, pp. 103–11.
2. Giorgio Agamben, *Homo Sacer: Sovereign Power and Bare Life*, trans. Daniel Heller-Roazen (Stanford: Stanford University Press, 1998).
3. Giorgio Agamben, *State of Exception*, trans. Kevin Attell (Chicago: University of

Chicago Press, 2005).
4. Giorgio Agamben, *Stasis: Civil War as a Political Paradigm*, trans. Nicholas Heron (Edinburgh: Edinburgh University Press, 2015).
5. Agamben, *Homo Sacer*, p. 15.
6. Ibid. p. 15.
7. Agamben, *State of Exception*, p. 11.
8. Ibid. p. 10.
9. Ibid. p. 51.
10. Ibid. p. 33.
11. Agamben, *Homo Sacer*, p. 18.
12. Agamben, *State of Exception*, p. 4.
13. Agamben, *Homo Sacer*, p. 17.
14. Ibid. p. 17.
15. Ibid. pp. 17–18.
16. Ibid. p. 18.
17. Ibid. p. 37. *Bia* signifies force, power, or violence, whereas *Dikē* means justice.
18. Agamben, *State of Exception*, p. 23.
19. Agamben, *Homo Sacer*, p. 23.
20. For Schmitt, commissarial dictatorship entails a dictatorship sanctioned by constitutional law to restore the constitutional norm in the face of an external threat, whereas sovereign dictatorship usurps one constitution to establish a new one. Schmitt claims that there has been a gradual historical movement to the latter form of dictatorship. See Carl Schmitt, *Dictatorship*, trans. Michael Hoelzl and Graham Ward (Cambridge: Polity, 2014), chs 1–4.
21. Agamben, *State of Exception*, p. 50.
22. Agamben, *Homo Sacer*, p. 37.
23. Ibid. pp. 20–1.
24. Ibid. p. 27.
25. Agamben, *State of Exception*, p. 39.
26. Ibid. p. 39.
27. Jacques Derrida, 'Force of Law: The "Mystical Foundation of Authority"', trans. Mary Quaintance, in *Acts of Religion*, ed. Gil Andjar (Abingdon: Routledge, 2002), pp. 230–98.
28. Steven DeCaroli, 'Political Life: Giorgio Agamben and the Idea of Authority', *Research in Phenomenology*, 43:2, 2013, pp. 220–42 (p. 234).
29. Agamben, *State of Exception*, p. 79.
30. Ibid. p. 86.
31. Ibid. p. 86.
32. Ibid. p. 86.
33. Ibid. p. 86.
34. Ibid. p. 86.
35. Agamben, *State of Exception*, p. 28.
36. Agamben notes that, for Foucault, '*to make die and to let live* summarises the procedure of old sovereign power, which exerts itself above all as the right to kill; *to make live and to let die is*, instead, the insignia of biopower'. Agamben goes on to clarify this further by offering 'a formula that defines the most specific trait of twentieth-century biopolitics: no longer either *to make die* or *to make live*, but *to make survive*'. See Giorgio Agamben, *Remnants of Auschwitz: The Witness and the Archive*, trans. Daniel Heller-Roazen (New York: Zone Books, 2012), p. 155.
37. Agamben, *Homo Sacer*, p. 1.

38. Ibid. p. 1.
39. Ibid. p. 4.
40. Ibid. p. 4.
41. Ibid. p. 6, emphasis in original.
42. Kevin Attell, *Giorgio Agamben: Beyond the Threshold of Deconstruction* (New York: Fordham University Press, 2015), p. 132.
43. Agamben, *Homo Sacer*, p. 8.
44. Giorgio Agamben, *Language and Death: The Place of Negativity*, trans. Karen E. Pinkus and Michael Hardt (Minneapolis: University of Minnesota Press, 1991), p. 105.
45. Frederiek Depoortere, 'Reading Giorgio Agamben's *Homo Sacer* with René Girard', *Philosophy Today*, 56:2, 2012, pp. 154–63 (p. 154).
46. Leland de la Durantaye, *Giorgio Agamben: A Critical Introduction* (Stanford: Stanford University Press, 2009), p. 206.
47. Agamben, *Homo Sacer*, pp. 82–3.
48. DeCaroli, 'Political Life', p. 228.
49. Agamben, *Homo Sacer*, p. 29.
50. Ibid. p. 110.
51. Ibid. p. 84.
52. Ibid. p. 84.
53. Ibid. p. 111.
54. Ibid. p. 110.
55. Jacques Derrida, *The Politics of Friendship*, trans. George Collins (London: Verso, 2005), pp. 112–37.
56. Agamben, *Homo Sacer*, p. 9.
57. Ibid. p. 114.
58. Ibid. p. 140.
59. Ibid. p. 114.
60. Ibid. p. 171.
61. Ibid. p. 175.
62. Ibid. p. 175.
63. Ibid. p. 115.
64. Carl Schmitt, *Political Theology: Four Chapters on the Concept of Sovereignty*, trans. Georg Schwab (Chicago: University of Chicago Press, 2005), p. 5.
65. Agamben, *Homo Sacer*, p. 142.
66. Ibid. p. 131.
67. Ibid. p. 177.
68. Ibid. p. 177.
69. Ibid. p. 177.
70. Ibid. p. 177.
71. Ibid. pp. 177–8.
72. Ibid. p. 178.
73. Ibid. p. 178.
74. Ibid. pp. 178–9.
75. Ibid. p. 179.
76. Ibid. p. 180.
77. See, for example, Durantaye, *Giorgio Agamben*, p. 338; David Pan, 'Against Biopolitics: Walter Benjamin, Carl Schmitt, and Giorgio Agamben on Political Sovereignty and Symbolic Order', *The German Quarterly*, 82:1, 2009, pp. 42–62 (p. 59); and Daniel McLoughlin, 'The Fiction of Sovereignty and the Real State of Exception: Giorgio

Agamben's Critique of Carl Schmitt', *Law, Culture and the Humanities*, 12:3, 2016, pp. 509–28 (p. 516).
78. Giorgio Agamben, *The Coming Community*, trans. Michael Hardt (Minneapolis: University of Minnesota Press, 1993), p. 84.
79. Agamben, *Stasis*, p. 1.
80. Ibid. p. 1.
81. Ibid. p. 1.
82. Ibid. p. 1. For a recent history of the notion of civil war, see David Armitage, *Civil Wars: A History in Ideas* (New Haven: Yale University Press, 2017).
83. Agamben, *Stasis*, p. 3.
84. Nicole Loraux, *The Divided City: On Memory and Forgetting in Ancient Athens*, trans. Corinne Pache and Jeff Fort (New York: Zone Books, 2006).
85. Agamben, *Stasis*, p. 1.
86. Ibid. p. 1.
87. Ibid. p. 1.
88. Ibid. p. 5.
89. Ibid. p. 5.
90. Ibid. p. 6.
91. Ibid. p. 8.
92. Ibid. p. 8.
93. Ibid. p. 8.
94. Ibid. p. 8.
95. Ibid. p. 8.
96. Ibid. p. 8.
97. Ibid. p. 9.
98. Ibid. p. 9.
99. Ibid. p. 9.
100. Ibid. pp. 9–10.
101. Ibid. p. 10.
102. Ibid. p. 10.
103. Ibid. p. 10.
104. Ibid. p. 10.
105. Ibid. p. 10.
106. Ibid. pp. 10–11.
107. Ibid. p. 11.
108. Ibid. p. 11.
109. Ibid. p. 11.
110. Ibid. p. 11.
111. Ibid. p. 12.
112. Ibid. p. 12.
113. Ibid. p. 13.
114. Ibid. p. 13.
115. Ibid. p. 15.
116. Ibid. p. 16.
117. Ibid. p. 16.
118. Ibid. p. 17.
119. Ibid. p. 17.
120. Ibid. p. 17.
121. Ibid. p. 17.

122. Agamben, *State of Exception*, p. 86.
123. Agamben, *Stasis*, p. 18.
124. Giorgio Agamben, *The Use of Bodies*, trans. Adam Kotsko (Stanford: Stanford University Press, 2016), p. 265.
125. Agamben, *The Coming Community*, p. 184.
126. For a detailed discussion of it, including of the transition from biopolitics to the coming politics, see Gavin Rae, 'Agency and Will in Agamben's Coming Politics', *Philosophy and Social Criticism*, vol. 44, n. 9, 2018, pp. 978–96.
127. Agamben, *The Use of Bodies*, p. 266.
128. Ibid. p. 266.
129. Ibid. p. 274.
130. Ibid. p. 266.
131. Ibid. p. 266.
132. Ibid. p. 266.
133. Ibid. p. 268.
134. Giorgio Agamben, 'On Potentiality', pp. 178–9, in *Potentialities: Collected Essays in Philosophy*, ed. and trans. Daniel Heller-Rozen (Stanford: Stanford University Press, 1999), pp. 177–85.
135. Ibid. p. 183.
136. Giorgio Agamben, 'Bartleby, or on Contingency', p. 251, in *Potentialities: Collected Essays in Philosophy*, ed. and trans. Daniel Heller-Rozen (Stanford: Stanford University Press, 1999), pp. 243–71.
137. Agamben, *The Use of Bodies*, p. 266.
138. Ibid. p. 272.
139. Ibid. pp. 272–3.
140. Ibid. p. 273.
141. Ibid. p. 273.
142. Ibid. p. 276.
143. Ibid. p. 277.
144. Ibid. p. 207.
145. Ibid. p. 207.
146. Ibid. p. 277.
147. Ibid. p. 207.
148. Ibid. p. 213.

PART III

The Bio-Juridical Critique

CHAPTER 7

Life and Law: Derrida on the Bio-Juridicalism of Sovereign Violence

Foucault's and Agamben's analyses of biopolitical sovereign violence delineate a sharp turn in critical debates regarding the sovereignty–violence relationship, away from accounts that link it primarily to questions of law and order, to ones that tie it to the regulation of life. This is not to say that biopolitical conceptions of sovereignty simply abandon law. As Foucault explains in the first volume of *A History of Sexuality*,

> I do not mean to say that the law fades into the background or that the institutions of justice tend to disappear, but rather that the law operates more and more as a norm, and that juridical institution is increasingly incorporated into a continuum of apparatuses (medical, administrative, and so on) whose functions are for the most part regulatory.[1]

Law has not been usurped to the extent that it has disappeared; the nature of law has changed away from what might be called positive formal law to a more jurisprudential understanding based on norms. This alteration is somewhat difficult to capture in English, which tends to collapse both senses into the same word ('law'), whereas other European languages distinguish between the two. For example, French distinguishes between *droit* and *loi*, while German differentiates between *Recht* and *Gesetz*; the former in each pair referring to statute law, with the latter referring to a more general, fluid, and ambiguous sense that encompasses the former. Foucault's point is that biopolitics has not abolished law *per se*, but increasingly operates through social-moral norms (*loi/Gesetz*) rather than through juridical formal law (*droit/Recht*). This allows it to seep into every facet of existence and is why it is far more insidious and omnipotent than juridical conceptions of sovereignty.

Agamben, by comparison, continues to tie biopolitical sovereignty to the juridical order through the ban structure inherent in the state of exception. But, somewhat paradoxically, this exclusion from the juridical order continues to include the one excluded. Importantly, however, *homo sacer* is no longer covered by the legal system, with the consequence that the sovereign does not need to pass through it to regulate his life. Therefore, while Agamben's notion of biopolitical sovereignty continues to work through the juridical order, its use of law is designed to exclude individuals from law to permit life to be more fully regulated. In so doing, Agamben downgrades the status and importance of the juridical order; the aim is to pass through law to create the conditions where the sovereign will no longer have to appeal to or be bound by the juridical order when regulating life.

By transitioning from juridical-philosophical conceptions of sovereignty to biopolitical ones, we have moved from analyses that emphasise the use of violence to establish and/or uphold (formal) law, to conceptions that aim to regulate life through juridical exclusion and the management of social norms and values. Put schematically, we transitioned from conceptions of sovereignty that privilege law over life to ones that bind sovereignty to the regulation of life excluded from law.

In this chapter, I call into question the logic of binary opposition (between law and life) underpinning the classical/radical-juridical and biopolitical models by engaging with Jacques Derrida's analysis of the death penalty. Derrida's thinking has always been intimately tied to the question of violence and latterly became increasingly associated with the nature of and relationship between sovereignty and law. For example, in the early *Of Grammatology*, Derrida outlines three different senses of violence to not only identify an originary violence associated with the designation of meaning and signification, but also show that violence is a ubiquitous and subterranean facet of social existence.[2] Throughout the 1980s and 1990s, in texts including 'Before the Law'[3] and the seminal 'Force of Law',[4] he turned to discuss the relationship between violence and law, showing how law is far from being that which tames violence but is underpinned by an originary violence that conditions law. These discussions were supplemented in the 1990s by analyses of sovereignty in *Rogues*[5] and of its symbolic importance in the final seminar, *The Beast and the Sovereign*.[6]

The first part of this chapter shows how his early notion of originary violence is tied to his later analysis of law, a discussion that will also deal with the question of the relationship between justice and law. Doing so will demonstrate that, for Derrida, violence is not distinct from law, but that which underpins it, while justice is that which operates through law, but is always beyond it. Thus, violence subtends law, while law affirms justice without ever fully achieving it.

Having established the relationship between violence and law, I turn to his late seminars on the death penalty[7] where he deals most forcibly with the question of the relationship between justice, law, sovereignty, and violence. As he explains, a 'monopoly on violence is of a piece with the motif of sovereignty. It is also what will always have grounded the death penalty, the right of the [S]tate, the right of the sovereign to punish by death.'[8]

Derrida's seminars on the death penalty took place over two years. The first, occurring between 8 December 1999 and 22 March 2000, covers a diverse range of topics including a critique of abolitionist discourses, discussions of the pardon and cruelty, and detailed readings of, amongst others, Hugo, Kant, and Nietzsche. The second year started on 6 December 2000 and finished on 28 March 2001, covering topics such as the nature of acting, blood, cruelty, calculability, and punishment, and readings of Benjamin, Cortés, Freud, Heidegger, and Kant.

The topics and figures covered are, then, extensive, but I will limit the discussion to Derrida's analysis of (1) the theological-political relationship surrounding the question of the death penalty, (2) the relationship between sovereignty and control inherent in his understanding of the death penalty, and (3) the relationship between the death penalty, the sovereign decision, and life, before (4) turning briefly to his critique of Agamben's notion of biopolitics outlined in the *Beast and the Sovereign*.

From this, I argue that, contrary to Foucault's insistence that juridical conceptions of sovereignty have been replaced by biopolitical ones, or Agamben's claim that juridical sovereignty was always biopolitical, Derrida develops a compatibilist position of the sovereign's relationship to law and life that shows that sovereign violence is not simply orientated to juridical order or the regulation of life through the creation of social norms, but simultaneously expresses itself through two faces – the juridical *and* biopolitical, or law *and* life – wherein the one demands and expresses the other: the juridical expression of sovereignty regulates life, whereas the sovereign's regulation of life (and death), through, for example, symbolic statements regarding the appropriate norms to be adopted, takes a juridical form. Rather than being identified with law *or* life, sovereign violence is bio-juridical, situated *between* both, working on life through its relationship to and control over law, which, in turn, is simultaneously shaped by (the conditions of) life.

VIOLENCE, SIGNIFICATION, AND JURIDICAL SOVEREIGNTY

Derrida's engagement with the meaning and nature of violence goes back to his earliest publications, where he examines the violence that necessarily accompanies the generation of meaning. In *Of Grammatology*, this takes the form of a three-fold hierarchical division that shows that violence conditions the generation of meaning and is therefore a fundamental component of the social world. Far from this world being fundamentally 'peaceful' and 'non-violent', with violence imposing on or disrupting this original state, Derrida suggests that violence is always present at the subterranean level of social existence.

One reason for this is that he does not ground 'things' in a substantial unity, but affirms *différance* as the grounding principle.[9] *Différance* is a neologism combining difference and deferment; the former noting that meaning is generated from the relation between signifiers, with the latter signalling that, because of its relational moment, meaning is always deferred.[10] Because the fundamental structure generating and governing 'things' is relational, there cannot ever be a final meaning: meaning is always becoming and so the perception of identity is based on the attempt to attribute fixed meaning to *différance*.

While this indicates how violence can be imposed on *différance*, it is important to note that Derrida maintains that *différance* 'itself' is intimately tied to violence. To outline this, he introduces a three-fold analytical division. The first level of violence describes the originary violence necessary for signification. This does not entail anything as simple as unifying heterogeneous elements around a homogeneous concept. Rather, because signification results from *différance*, it is always conditioned by the conflicts inherent in the force relations constitutive of *différance*. For this reason, at the root of meaning lies an

> arche-violence, loss of the proper, of absolute proximity, of self-presence, in truth the loss of what has never taken place, of a self-presence which has never been given but only dreamed of and always already split, repeated, incapable of appearing to itself except in its own disappearance.[11]

Meaning is not then *a priori*, but is generated from the arche-violence inherent in *différance*. Rather than being repressive, this arche-violence is fundamentally constructive.

This violence is not, however, left explicit, but is covered or displaced to appear as a nonviolent act. As a consequence, 'out of the arche-violence [comes] a second violence that is reparatory, protective, instituting the "moral", prescribing the concealment of writing and the effacement and obliteration of the so-called proper name which was already dividing the proper'.[12] This second form of violence covers over the arche-violence with a veneer of nonviolent respectability. It is, as Elizabeth Grosz explains, 'a violence that describes and designates itself as the moral counter of violence.

This is the violence that we sometimes name the law, right, or reason.'[13] Law is built on violence, but attempts to foreclose the arche-violence subtending it within a stable system of rules and regulations.

However, from these two forms of violence, 'a third violence can *possibly* emerge or not (an empirical possibility) within what is commonly called evil, war, indiscretion, rape'.[14] This form does not have to emerge but if it does, it does so empirically and is, therefore, the most obvious and directly experienced. For this reason, it is understood as 'the common concept of violence'.[15] While most familiar, however, it is the most complex 'because it refers at the same time to the two inferior levels of arche-violence and of law'.[16] By breaking the law (second form of violence), it reveals the arche-violence that subtends law. But in so doing, it reveals arche-violence to be nothing but a construction from the force relations (= violence) of *différance*.

Thus, the empirical actions of the third form of violence – war, rape, evil, and so on – break through all the significations that condition law, including the fundamental arche-violence that gives rise to the differential system that generates the meaning of law. In so doing, they commit the most obvious infractions against all order and so are often thought to be the cruellest and most senseless forms of violence. But to be understood in that manner, they have to be re-inscribed within the referential system generated from arche-violence and law. Thus, the third form of violence may be the most obvious and empirical form, but it is underpinned by and understood through the far more insidious and subtle form of arche-violence that generates meaning, understanding, and representation.

This three-fold distinction is important, not only because it lays out in schematic fashion the role that violence plays in Derrida's understanding of the process that generates meaning, but also because it subtends his later work on the relationship between sovereignty and law. In the seminal essay 'Force of Law', Derrida returns to the distinction between the first two forms of violence – originary violence and the violence of law – to ask how we can

> distinguish between the force of law [*loi*] of a legitimate power and the allegedly originary violence that must have established this authority and that could not itself have authorised itself by any anterior legitimacy, so that, in this initial moment, it is neither legal nor illegal – as others would quickly say, neither just nor unjust?[17]

In so doing, he interrogates the role that originary violence plays in founding law and sovereignty.

The literature on Derrida's essay is enormous and so I will simply point out, in a rather schematic fashion, some of the main points of the first part of the essay because it is here that Derrida discusses the relationship between violence or force, justice and law, and the sovereign decision that will recur in his analysis of the death penalty.

Starting with the relationship between force and law, Margaret Davies re-enforces the point that 'mainstream legal theory of the past two hundred years or so has been shaped by the modernist desire to ground knowledge about law in some objective or absolute fashion'.[18] In contrast, Derrida claims that, far from being grounded in anything substantial, law is grounded in arche-violence or force. This is because, at the foundation of law, there lies nothing other than the means to create law, which is simply based on its own force. Laws are not then grounded in an external, stable foundation, but in their own authority, which, ultimately, 'rests only on the credit that is granted them. One believes in it; that is their only foundation.'[19]

Furthermore, whereas Benjamin distinguishes between divine and mythic violence, with the latter being distinguished between law-making and law-preserving violence, Derrida suggests that there is a form of violence missing from this schema, one which may be associated with what Benjamin calls law-making violence but which is *mystical* rather than *mythical* because its source cannot be identified. The mystical aspect of law comes both from the perspective of the sovereign whose authority is grounded in an ineffable force granted to him by others and from the perspective of those granting the sovereign authority who do so without being able to ground that decision.

Crucially, with a nod back to his early concept of an ineffable grounding arche-violence, Derrida claims that 'since the origin of authority, the founding or grounding [*la foundation ou le fondemont*], the positing of the law [*loi*] cannot by definition rest on anything but themselves, they are themselves a violence without ground [*sans fondemont*]'.[20] Brian Trainor suggests that this creates and depends upon a troubling 'separation and external relationship between substructure and superstructure',[21] but this seems to misunderstand that, for Derrida, the 'foundation' of law does not refer to a separate external realm, but to the ineffable ground that cannot be identified rationally or logically but which must nevertheless exist for law as such to exist. Without a foundation or ground, law does not rest on anything other than its own force. This does not mean that law is something external to force or a pure effect of force. Rather, there is 'a more internal, more complex relation to what one calls force, power or violence'.[22]

This feeds into Derrida's account of the sovereign decision, an understanding of which requires a brief detour into his analysis of the relationship between justice and law. For Derrida, justice is not synonymous with law, nor does law realise justice. Rather, justice is the term that Derrida uses to describe an 'excess'[23] that is always beyond law. Following Levinas, he explains that it is 'infinite, incalculable, rebellious to rule and foreign to symmetry, heterogeneous and heterotopic'.[24] Law, in contrast, is associated with the application of a predefined rule and is, therefore, based on calculation according to that rule.[25]

That law and justice are different does not, however, mean that they form a binary opposition. In the interview 'Hospitality, Justice, and Responsibility', Derrida explains that while he 'began to use the term justice very late',[26] he did so to determine the limits of law. Because law is constructed from the force of the undecidable decision, it can be deconstructed: we can analyse the structures, norms, values, and so on that give rise to a particular form of law. 'This is an infinite process within the legal space.'[27] What is crucial is that the legal space 'unfolds itself *in the name of justice*'.[28] In other words, Derrida realises that law alone is insufficient; it must be orientated to and grounded in justice. Equally, 'justice requires the law. You can't simply call for justice without trying to embody justice in the law.'[29] Thus, while different to law, 'justice does not end with law'[30] nor is justice 'simply outside the law, it is something which transcends the law, but which, at the same time requires the law'.[31] As that which is different to law and, indeed, that which is not constructed, 'justice' acts as a quasi-transcendental norm – 'quasi' because it is not a 'thing' *per se* but a process constantly sought after – conditioning law. However, as that which generates and exceeds law, justice does not conform to a rule and so is not capable of being deconstructed.[32] Thus, any decision about justice must 'be both regulated and without regulation, it must preserve the law [*loi*] and also destroy or suspend it enough to have [*pour devoir*] to reinvent it in each case, rejustify it, reinvent it at least in the reaffirmation and the new and free confirmation of its principle'.[33]

For Derrida, this means that the just decision is dependent on what he calls 'undecidability',[34] an experience where, at least, two options exist without any norm or rule to determine which to choose:

> The undecidable is not merely the oscillation or the tension between two decisions. Undecidable – this is the experience of that which, though foreign and heterogeneous to the order of the calculable and the rule, must [*doit*] nonetheless ... deliver itself over to the impossible decision while taking account of law and rules.[35]

Derrida considers the condition of undecidability to be so important that he maintains that 'a decision that would not go through the test and ordeal of the undecidable would not be a free decision; it would only be the programmable application or the continuous unfolding of a calculable process. It might perhaps be legal; it would not be just.'[36]

Justice requires therefore an impossible decision where the 'best' option, if there indeed is one, is not apparent and the decision itself cannot be fully justified. For this reason, the operation that amounts to founding, inaugurating, justifying law, to *making law* . . . consist[s] of a *coup de force*, of a performative and therefore interpretative violence that in itself is neither just nor unjust and that no justice and no earlier and previously founding law, no pre-existing foundation, could, by definition, guarantee or contradict or invalidate.[37]

To ground the political decision in one norm rather than another is based on 'a call to faith',[38] wherein one option out of many is chosen and adopted. This is not because it is the 'right' choice, but because it 'feels' like the right one; a mystical epiphany based on and coming from a moment of undecidability; a literal moment of madness[39] that, as Nick Mansfield explains, 'always involves a grasping of the unknowable'.[40]

Crucially, because it is based on the principle of undecidability, the just decision is always a contingent and unstable choice; one that unjustifiably excludes something. This has led to a debate in the literature regarding whether Derrida tries to anchor the just decision in the principle of 'lesser violence'.[41] There is not space to engage with the specifics of this debate, but, needless to say that, even if this criterion is applied, it depends upon notions of 'justice' and 'lesser' that are severely under-determined. It also depends upon a sovereign decision regarding the nature of these terms that returns us to the mystical encounter with undecidability. Given that the just decision is tied to undecidability, it is not clear how it could be calculated or determined in the way that the quantifiable notion 'lesser' demands.

Nevertheless, that the sovereign decision is grounded in undecidability means that any conclusion reached or judgement made in relation to justice is always contingent and unstable: if it tries to overcome this by following a rule, it violates the condition of undecidability and so is not truly just; if it remains a 'true' decision in the encounter with undecidability, it finds that this encounter 'deconstructs from within all assurance of presence, all certainty or all alleged criteriology assuring us of the justice of a decision, in truth of the very event of decision'.[42] Justice is, then, never realised, but always '*to come*'.[43]

From this brief overview, we see that, for Derrida, law and justice are inescapably grounded in force and violence: the former due to its mystical foundations and the latter because the undecidability upon which its decision depends is always 'mystical', insofar as it is a pure decision made without recourse to a prior norm or determining value and so exists simply by its own force. That decision can always be overturned, meaning that the structure of law is inherently fragile; it is grounded in violence and always threatened by its own grounding. This conceptual framework underpins Derrida's analysis of the death penalty, wherein the relationship between justice, violence, and the sovereign decision come explicitly to the fore.

DECONSTRUCTING THE DEATH PENALTY

The first question that arises when we turn to Derrida's seminar on the death penalty is a simple one: why focus on this topic when, at the time he wrote, it had long been abolished in Europe and worldwide abolishment appeared and continues to appear to be gradually gaining the upper hand? Amnesty International, for example, notes that when it started its campaign against the death penalty in 1977, only 16 countries had totally abolished it, whereas, in 2016, 104 countries, representing over half the world's total number, had done so.[44] Given this, was it really a topic that needed to be engaged with, especially over two years?

One possible empirically based response would be to point out that, while the number of States that use the death penalty have decreased, those that use it have increased their dependency on it: 3,117 people were sentenced to death in 55 countries in 2016, constituting a significant increase on the total for 2015 (1,998) and exceeding the previous record high total that the organisation reported in 2014 (2,466).[45] The number of people condemned to death by the State is then substantial, indicating that it is a major political issue that demands analysis.

To do so, Derrida pays particular attention to the United States of America (USA), not only because the seminars were given there, but because he notes that it is the only country in the so-called Western world that continues to employ the death penalty – indeed, it remains one of the biggest executors.[46] This is important for two reasons: first, Derrida claims that the USA 'is the most Christian democracy in the world'.[47] Second, he ties the death penalty to the theologico-political and, indeed, claims that it is 'the hyphen in the theologio-political'.[48] Putting the two together leads Derrida to claim that he is not particularly surprised that the USA is an exception amongst so-called Western countries in continuing to use the death penalty: the dominance of Christianity, or theology more generally, in its culture, in combination with the link between Christianity and the death penalty,[49] leads to an acceptance and even affirmation of the death penalty. Put conversely, that the USA is, on Derrida's telling, culturally defined by its Christian heritage, which, in turn, is closely tied to the affirmation of the death penalty, reveals the intimate relationship between the death penalty and theology and its importance to the theologico-political relation.

In *For what Tomorrow*, Derrida notes, however, that there has never been a properly philosophical argument against the death penalty:

> the most stupefying – also the most stupefied – fact about the history of Western philosophy: never, *to my knowledge*, has any philosopher *as a*

philosopher, in his or her own strictly and systematically philosophical discourse, never has any philosophy *as such* contested the legitimacy of the death penalty.[50]

Historically, those who publicly contested the death penalty 'did so as writers (Voltaire, Hugo, and Camus in France) or as jurists and men of the law (Beccaria ... Robert Badinters ... etc.)'.[51] Therefore, besides the empirical rationale previously given, Derrida's focus on the death penalty is further justified by the lack of *philosophical* attention it has garnered.

He does note, however, that when arguments have been proposed against the death penalty, they have tended to take the following unsatisfactory forms: first, it is objected that the death penalty is cruel,[52] an argument that Derrida rejects because it concerns the application of the death penalty not the death penalty *per se*: 'the principle of the death penalty could be maintained: all it would take would be to make the death penalty insensible, anesthetised, to anesthetise both the condemned and the actors and spectators'.[53] Second, the death penalty is seen to run contrary to 'human dignity',[54] a problematic concept for Derrida because it seems to attribute a single essence to the human that ignores the 'foundational' importance of *différance*.

However, while he is firmly in the abolitionist camp, Derrida resists the temptation to simply propose another, 'better' argument against the death penalty. He insists that it is necessary, before doing so, to understand what the death penalty is and refers to. This requires that the death penalty be deconstructed: the 'scaffolding'[55] supporting it must be identified, before its assumptions are engaged with and questioned; a process that will undermine the premises it is based on and, ultimately, its justification.

To start, he explains that what is unique about the death penalty is that it is fundamentally 'distinct from murder or from putting to death outside the law, from assassination in some sense',[56] because 'it treats the condemned one as a subject of rights, a subject of the law, as human being, with the dignity that this still supposes'.[57] While inherently violent, the death penalty is not outwardly focused, but operates in and through law: it '[i]s a concept of law, the concept of a sanction exercised by law in a [S]tate of law'.[58] Importantly, therefore, the condemned is not excised from law and so is not *homo sacer*; one who is banished from law and can be killed with impunity. The death penalty is a legal concept that condones the killing of a legal citizen by legal means; the condemned never escapes law, he is bound to, exists within, and defined by his legal status.

Beyond a certain relationship between the subject and law, the death penalty is also bound to a particular history linked 'to the Abrahamic and above all the Christian history of sovereignty'.[59] Derrida's point is that Western conceptions of sovereignty are inherently theological in inspiration and intimately tied to violence, in the sense both that violence founds sovereignty and that it is an instrument used by the sovereign to wage wars or maintain his position.

For this reason, the death penalty brings to the fore the constitutive role that violence plays in establishing and maintaining sovereignty. This is obviously not to say that all forms of sovereignty must necessarily employ the death penalty. It *is* to say that even those States that have abolished it 'keep a sovereign right over the life of citizens whom they can send to war to kill or be killed in a space that is radically foreign to the space of internal legality, of the civil law where the death penalty may be either maintained or abolished'.[60]

Sovereign violence is not then simply linked to death. While the sovereign decides on death, his decision has implications for life itself: what counts as life, how is life to be composed, where will resources be distributed to secure life, who qualifies as participating in life and who is excluded, and so on. Through his control over juridical violence, the sovereign uses legal means to determine who will die and who will live;[61] a decision that also conditions life and, indeed, what counts as a legitimate one.

Derrida's deconstruction of the death penalty reveals then that the sovereign does not have to suspend law to control life or wait until this suspension becomes the norm. The regulation of life is achieved through the management of law, in combination with symbolic statements delineating the ethical-social norms that demarcate which forms of life are acceptable. The latter does not, as Agamben claims, require a juridically exceptional situation, but is a condition of the 'internal' operations of law itself; rather than it being divorced from social norms, Derrida – playing on the dual sense of law previously noted, where it refers to both formal statute law and 'informal' social laws/norms – maintains that the regulation of life occurs *within* and through the sovereign's exercise of law. The example of the death penalty reveals therefore that law always regulates life, not by excluding life from law, but simply by virtue of the operation and function of law, with this supported and enforced by the originary violence subtending law.

THE DEATH PENALTY AND THE THEOLOGICO-POLITICAL

Derrida posits that the use of the death penalty is a more complex phenomenon than is usually thought, insofar as it is not only premised on a particular conception of the life–death relationship whereby there is a specific and identifiable moment of transition between the two, but also assumes that the transition can be controlled. This control is, in turn, manifested through the performativity of the death penalty. Even in those countries that do not publicise executions or permit them to be witnessed, sovereign power is still displayed or performed through this ban, insofar as the lack of information regarding it, somewhat paradoxically, demonstrates the sovereign's power over the process.

This reliance on performativity ties the death penalty to theology, which is also understood to be based on a sense of theatrical display of power through rituals, processions, dress, and mannerisms. This commonality is one reason why sovereignty and theology go hand in hand. It is also why Derrida explains that, historically, the death sentence was often passed as a punishment for impiety:

> Socrates, Jesus, Hallaj (922), Joan of Arc (1431). Each time a complaint, an accusation, a religious incrimination aimed at a blaspheming offense against some divine sacredness, a religious incrimination that is invested, taken up, incarnated, incorporated, put into effect, enforced, applied by a sovereign political power, which thereby signals its sovereignty, its sovereign right over souls and bodies, and which in truth defines its sovereign by this right and by this power: over the life and death of subjects.[62]

That all four claimed to hear 'the voice of God'[63] and were put to death for it indicates, to Derrida, that they were executed to silence not only their sovereign claim to speak to God, but also the conception of God they spoke to. Their executions were an attempt to silence a particular conception of theology in defence and affirmation of an alternative conception, one that supported the dominant political structures.

The death penalty has, then, always been tied to the question of which form of theology will underpin sovereignty. This is why both those defending and those seeking to abolish it have often appealed to theology. For example, Derrida produces an extended discussion of Kant's infamous defence of the death penalty to show that it is based on the *lex talionis*, manifested most clearly in the Biblical injunction of an eye for an eye.[64] Similarly, he notes that 'it is in the name of a certain evangelical Christianity that the death penalty is condemned, a death penalty whose history is also linked, in the West, to the history of Christianity and the Christian church'.[65]

While both positions tie the death penalty and, by extension, the sovereign decision to a particular conception of theology, their common appeal to Christian doctrine reveals the tension – between the fundamental injunction against killing (and by extension glorification of life) and the *lex talionis* affirming that the punishment mirror the crime (murder demands death and so killing, for example) – running through it. This tension comes explicitly to the fore in the political activism of certain Christian conservative anti-abortion campaigners in the USA, who, Derrida explains, 'almost always

[wage] violent campaigns against the voluntary interruption of pregnancy and abortion in general',[66] in the name of the absolute defence of life, all the while affirming the death penalty that ends life that is otherwise sanctified.

Derrida suggests that this tension points to a fundamental lesson: the death penalty is always implicitly conditioned by a conception of life. After all,

> it is always in the name of *salut public* that one sentences to death someone who, basically, even if he has killed only one person, in a singular crime, is determined as a public enemy, a threat to society, order, and public security, public safety, *salut public*.[67]

The death penalty's link to life is witnessed further by the way in which a priest traditionally ministers to the condemned and, indeed, accompanies the execution procession. This is not simply to be a comfort to the condemned in his last moments, but aims to get the condemned to admit to the sins that he committed in this life in preparation for his journey to the next life. Through this, Derrida claims that the four axes of sovereignty – law, life, theology, and violence – come together:

> This soteriological function is essential: one must first attempt to amend, save, rehabilitate the soul of the condemned one, and this soteriological mission, this work of saving or salvation is confided, assigned, by statute, to the nocturnal council, to those who alone have visiting rights, in the sophronistery, in the house of correction, in the wising-up institution.[68]

Given the emphasis that the Catholic Church places on confession as a mode of salvation, Derrida claims that it is not surprising, although he does find it highly disturbing, that the Catholic Church has always supported the death penalty: 'From Saint Thomas Aquinas until the first half of the twentieth century, "theologians agree on this point: the State has the right of life and death over its citizens".'[69]

The conclusion offered is that, as witnessed from the 'phantasmatico-theological'[70] basis of sovereignty, the role that the priest plays in the application of the death penalty, and the support and legitimacy provided by the Catholic Church, the death penalty is intimately tied to both the notion of political sovereignty and theological doctrine; specifically that of the Abrahamic and Christian traditions. This link is also demonstrated through the sovereign's capacity to issue a last-minute pardon to the condemned, an action that mirrors God's capacity to offer infinite forgiveness for past sins.

Derrida claims that the death penalty is only given for crimes that are considered 'un-forgivable',[71] 'inexpiable or ... unpardonable'.[72] It is this that makes the sovereign's pardon so difficult and rare. Indeed, this links the pardon to Derrida's notion of justice, which, it will be remembered, always exceeds the law it operates through. A pardon cannot be determined or calculated *through* law, but must always appeal to what exceeds law – justice: 'every pardon worthy of that name, if there ever is any, must be *exceptional*, should be exceptional, that is in short the law of the pardon: it must be lawless and exceptional, above the laws or outside the laws'.[73]

Furthermore, the pardon is a difficult decision, but is possible because the sovereign is both immanent in and transcendent to the legal process that hands down the death penalty. Sovereignty exists within the law by virtue of being that point from and around which the decision of law is located, but is also that which escapes the confines of law by virtue of its mystical-theological grounding, which, as noted, is based on force. This transcendence gives the sovereign the choice of either carrying out the law and fulfilling the death sentence or interceding in law to 'save' the condemned.

That Derrida insists on the relationship between sovereignty and theology returns us to the question of the relationship between divine and legal violence. For Benjamin, the former always transcends the latter. Derrida, however, claims that the death penalty usurps the dichotomy that Benjamin's conclusion is based on: the sovereign mirrors a God *within* the juridical system, meaning that his use of violence in the form of the death penalty brings a form of divine violence into law. Put differently, the sovereign's transcendence to the law is always expressed immanently through the law. So, whereas Benjamin holds that justice results from the expiation of law by divine violence and so links justice to a position transcendent to law, Derrida insists that, rather than impose itself on law, the transcendence of the sovereign passes *through* law.

However, bringing the divine violence of the sovereign into law does not reduce his transcendent relation to law to a purely immanent one. The decision to hand down a death sentence is made '*in the name of* transcendence and *against* transcendence'.[74] Through the sovereign's dual position with regard to law, the sovereign brings transcendence in the form of divine violence into law, all the while remaining transcendent to law; a position that allows the sovereign to intercede to pardon the condemned. If granted, this forgiving is always made in the name of the justice that exceeds and so transcends law.

SOVEREIGNTY AND THE CONTROL OF LIFE AND DEATH

Derrida maintains that the sovereign's quasi-divine status and relation to the condemned are tied to the assumption that the sovereign can control the moment of death of the condemned. In turn, this is based on the notion that the sovereign can control time. The basic premise driving Derrida's analysis is that normally we are aware of our finitude and so know that we will die, but do not know when we will do so: 'even if he is sick, incurable, or even in the throes of death, the mortal that I am does not know the moment, the date, the precise hour that he will die. He does not know, I do not know, and I will never know in advance.'[75]

For Derrida, the lacuna in knowing that we must die but not knowing when we will is a fundamental and inescapable aspect of what it is to live and 'is an essential trait of my relation to death'.[76] The condemned, however, is in a different situation in that he knows 'on which day, at which hour, or even at which instant death will befall him'.[77] He is aware that his life has a fixed endpoint, one that, crucially, has been determined by another. In it being set for him, the sovereign aims to control the moment and method of death. This scheduling, in turn, is premised on the notion 'that the [S]tate, the judges, society, the *bourreaux* and executioners, that is third parties, have mastery over the time of life of the condemned one and thus know how to calculate and produce, in so-called objective time, the deadline to within a second'.[78] On the one hand, this reaffirms the structural affinity between sovereignty and Christian conceptions of God, in which he/He controls time. But, on the other hand, the key difference is that Christian conceptions of God tend to hold that time is not part of God, but that which He controls. In contrast, the sovereign's juncture between immanence and transcendence means that he is both a historical being and that which is portrayed as existing beyond time, capable of mastering and controlling it.

The notion that the death penalty presupposes mastery of time is premised on the responses given to two different, but ultimately related, questions: what is time? And when does death occur?

Regarding the first, Derrida notes that the conception of time underpinning the death penalty is, somewhat paradoxically, firmly tied to life: there is no time in death, which is defined by the absence of time and, thereby, of life. The death penalty severs the time of the condemned prematurely and so makes use of the fundamental and absolute rupture that is thought to exist between the time of life and its absence 'in' death. This rupture is always tied to 'the calculating and exceptional decision of a great other in the figure of the prince, the president, the governor, that is, the sovereign holder of the right to pardon'.[79] If the death penalty removes time from the condemned by seeking to control the moment of the condemned's otherwise certain but indeterminate death, 'the pardon [*la grâce*] gives time, and the only "thing" that can be given graciously is time, that is to say, at once nothing and everything'.[80] By giving more time, the sovereign also gives life.

Derrida's insistence that the death penalty is conditioned by the idea that the sovereign has mastery over time, which is associated with life but absent in death, brings forth the issue of the relationship between life and death, and specifically the question: what form must the life–death relationship take for the sovereign's supposed mastery over time to permit him, through the imposition of the death penalty, to control both?

Derrida approaches the question through the lens of phenomenological accounts of death, namely those of Heidegger and Levinas, to claim that they presuppose 'some pre-comprehension of the meaning of the word "death", a supposed pre-comprehension on the basis of which the question and its elucidation would develop'.[81] This takes different forms, but ensures that 'these refined semantico-ontological analyses must rely, even as they deny it, on so-called common sense, on the alleged objective and familiar knowledge, judged to be indubitable, of what separates a state of death from a state of life'.[82]

Each theory is, then, implicitly based on a binary opposition between life and death, wherein the moment of transition from life to death is singular, clear-cut, and absolute. Based on these assumptions, it is thought possible to not only control the movement across the dividing line, thereby effecting the movement from life to death, but also identify when that moment takes place: 'Without the supposed or supposedly possible knowledge of the clear-cut, sharp limit, there would be no philosophy or thinking of death that could claim to know what it is talking about and [which could] proceed "methodically"'[83] regarding it. The absence of this clear-cut divide would also undermine any juridical-political claim regarding the justice of the sovereign's right to employ the death sentence. After all, if it is not possible to determine the exact moment of death because no such clear-cut division exists, the implicit but fundamental premise – that the sovereign is master of time – underpinning the argument supporting the death penalty would be undermined.

Derrida returns to this issue in the second year of the seminar to explain that

> the work of deconstruction consists in showing that in truth all of these supposedly opposed concepts, which are distinct in their very coupling, touch each other in their coupling; they do not break off contact with each other as they are supposed to. And if I say that these opposed concepts touch each other and that from the moment they touch each other, they are no longer impermeable to one another, they no longer let themselves be closed off.[84]

However, Derrida does not just appeal to his own conceptual critique of the logic of binary oppositions; he also claims that his position has empirical backing. After all, 'it has been known for a long time (these are the ABC's of anthropology) that the criteria of death differ from one society to another, sometimes from one State to another within the same confederation'.[85]

To support this, he provides three empirical examples from spring 1994. First, the case of Teresa Hamilton, who fell

> into a severe diabetic coma and [wa]s diagnosed as brain-dead. Her family refuse[d] to accept this and insist[ed] on taking her body home, on a ventilator. Despite a Florida law that states that people with dead brains are legally dead, and over the protests of doctors, the family g[ot] its wish.[86]

In the second case, two tourists from Japan were shot dead in California and declared brain-dead, with the consequence that hospital staff took them off ventilators 'without consulting their families in Japan where brain death is not recognised. The families [we]re horrified.'[87] Significant debate on the subject ensued.

In the third case, a Hasidic boy was shot on the Brooklyn Bridge in New York and diagnosed as brain-dead, a diagnosis not accepted by his family, who relied on rabbinical advice and a Biblical passage that claims that death occurs not in the brain but in the lungs: 'there is no brain death as long as he is there and can breathe'.[88] A sympathetic doctor refused to declare the patient dead until his heart stopped, making the functioning of the heart, not the lungs or the brain, the criterion for death.

With these examples, Derrida aims to undermine the myth of sovereign omnipotence by showing that the moment of death is not easily definable and hence controllable, but is heterogeneous and contested.

SOVEREIGNTY AND THE QUESTION OF THE CONDEMNED

In the second volume, Derrida continues to undermine the life/death opposition by looking not to the moment of death, but to the act of sentencing and, in particular, the question of *who* can be sentenced to death. Noting that the death penalty is premised on the notion of an age of responsibility – that is, a moment when the individual is thought to be capable of being held legally responsible for his actions – Derrida questions the assumption underpinning this notion by asking what is meant by 'age'.[89]

Whereas we typically respond to being asked our age with a number, Derrida notes that such homogeneous certainty is immediately undermined once we pay attention to the question. To do so, he starts from the empirical example of *Penry v. Lynaugh* from June 1989, where Penry was convicted of rape and murder and sentenced to death. While Penry's 'legal' age was twenty-two, he was found to have a 'mental' age of six and a half, and a 'social' age, that is an age where he could function in the world, of 'nine or ten years old'.[90] As Derrida summarises: 'Here, then, is an accused man, a man sentenced to death who has at least three ages.'[91]

The point of this discussion is not to argue over whether the accused did or did not commit the crime. It is to unearth and bring to light the simplistic assumptions underpinning the trial. Derrida uses this example to remind us that, rather than there being one age that, if above a certain designated number, permits legal sanction, '[t]here is in us simultaneously, in our consciousness and our unconscious, something of the old man and of the child but also of the man of the twenty-first century, of the fifth century BCE, of Cro-Magnon man and the Neanderthal, of the great ape, the tiger, and the squirrel'.[92]

Rather than being a straightforward question, the issue of age and, by extension, legal responsibility is remarkably complicated. It in no way conforms to a binary opposition between those beneath and those above the legal age of responsibility:

> Things are all the more complicated, unsettling, disconcerting, difficult to grasp given that the multiplicity of ages, our ages, of the heterogeneous ages that divide up our lives as mortals, and divide them up simultaneously (synchronically we have more than one age), this dischrony and essential anachrony that divides us, multiplies us, splits us, devours us while leaving remains, leads us to death while leaving vast zones of youthfulness or even embryonic and not yet 'born' virtualities intact in us . . . is not only the ontogenetic multiplicity of ages of an individual, of a conscious or unconscious subject, or even a conscious or unconscious ego; it is not only the multiplicity of ages of each of the agencies of the psychical economy or system . . . but also the irreducible multiplicity, in each of us, of the ages of humanity, of anthropological culture, indeed of the ages of (human or animal) life in general.[93]

Derrida's use of empirical examples to deconstruct the assumptions underpinning the application of the death penalty reveals it to be a fabulously complex issue that traverses cultural, juridical, medical, philosophical, and political discourses. That the meaning of or movement to death is not singular undermines the sovereign's *implicit* claim to control death, thereby opening up the question of what the death penalty really affirms.

For Robert Trumbull, it pushes us to develop 'a notion of life not predicated on its absolute sanctity and infinite dignity, but rather its intrinsic violability, a radical thinking of morality that understands finitude not as something that befalls life but rather as what defines it'.[94] This is no doubt true, but I think that Derrida is also asking us to rethink the nature of sovereignty itself.

Indeed, it is here that we most clearly see the dual nature or two faces of Derrida's analysis of sovereignty, wherein what initially appeared to be a juridical conception of sovereignty, premised on the notion that sovereign violence is used to affirm justice for an unforgivable crime, turns into what starts to look like an example of biopolitical sovereignty, wherein sovereign violence is tied not to the search for justice through law, but to the management and regulation of life.

Life has been a constant, if somewhat implicit, companion in Derrida's analysis of the death penalty, which delineates the ethical and social norms of the community and so outlines what is unforgivable for the society, is handed down for the good health of the living community, is administered by priests to save the soul of the condemned for the next life, and is a theatrical spectacle designed to showcase the sovereign's mastery over time (= life) and death. By tying the death penalty to questions of life, rather than to a juridical-theological search for justice, Derrida subtly, but definitively, moves the debate regarding sovereign violence away from the question of law to that of life.

DERRIDA ON BIOPOLITICS

However, while Derrida starts to tie sovereign violence to the regulation and management of life, this does not mean, as Thomas Dutoit claims, that, for Derrida, 'the *real* sovereign ... is life, [with] its majesty consist[ing] in its immasterability'.[95] This conclusion is premised on the idea that sovereignty is concerned with mastery. That which sovereignty cannot master – life – must, then, be master over sovereignty. As we have seen, however, Derrida's deconstruction of the death penalty shows that only *one* conception of sovereignty – namely, the classic-juridical conception of sovereignty advocated, on Derrida's telling, by proponents of the death penalty – aims for absolute mastery; it does not describe all forms of sovereignty.

Furthermore, Dutoit's argument is underpinned by a binary opposition between a juridical conception of sovereignty that tries to control life through law and a notion of sovereignty that is controlled by life (without law). From this assumption, Dutoit holds that Derrida rejects the juridical conception of sovereignty and so concludes that the sovereign is an effect of life. However, as Derrida points out, simply reversing the privileged term in a binary opposition does not go far enough because it leaves intact the logic governing the opposition. Rather than turning from a notion of sovereignty that controls life through law to one that is controlled by life, Derrida demonstrates the complexity of the sovereign's relation to law *and* life. With this, he undermines the juridical and biopolitical approaches, claiming that both are one-dimensional and underpinned by an implicit and simplistic binary logic. He further distances himself from *biopolitical* conceptions of sovereignty by calling into question the notion of life that they depend upon. His most condensed statements on this issue are found in the following year's seminar on *The Beast and the Sovereign*, where he criticises Agamben's conception of life.

Derrida starts by outlining the fundamental premise of Agambian biopolitics: 'Agamben wants absolutely to define th[e] specificity [of biopolitical sovereignty] by putting his money on the concept of "bare life", which he identifies with *zoē*, in opposition to *bios*.'[96] To do so, Agamben must 'demonstrate that the difference between *zoē* and *bios* is absolutely rigorous, already in Aristotle'.[97]

Not surprisingly, Derrida rejects this: 'I don't believe . . . that the distinction between *zoē* and *bios* is a reliable and effective instrument, sufficiently sharp and, to use Agamben's language, which is not mine here, sufficiently deep to get to the depth of this "[so-called] founding event".'[98] Not only does the absolute distinction between *zoē* and *bios* not hold, but Derrida rejects any notion of a founding moment or event governing that which emanates from it. He also dismisses the idea that biopolitics is originary; that is, that it offers an innovative or original perspective: 'I am not saying that there is no "new biopower", I am suggesting that "bio-power" itself is not new. There are incredible novelties in bio-power, but bio-power or zoo-power are not new.'[99] With this, Derrida criticises the notion that there was ever a form of sovereignty that was not biopolitical. By structuring the norms, rules, and processes defining society, all forms of sovereignty are ultimately concerned with and shape life and are, therefore, biopolitical.

Indeed, Derrida thinks that Agamben recognises this:

> What surprises me most, incidentally, and constantly disconcerts me in Agamben's argumentation and rhetoric, is that he clearly recognises what I have just said, namely that biopolitics is an arch-ancient thing and bound up with the very idea of sovereignty. But, then, if one recognises this, why all the effort to pretend to wake politics up to something that is supposedly, I quote, 'the decisive event of modernity'?[100]

In other words, Derrida charges that there is a contradiction between Agamben's historical and conceptual analyses: *historically*, Agamben claims that sovereignty has always been concerned with life, but, *conceptually*, he insists that biopolitics is fundamentally different to other non-biopolitical forms of sovereignty.

Agamben might defend himself by pointing out that he does not claim that *all* forms of sovereignty are biopolitical; it is only since Aristotle that biopolitics has defined Western political thought. Agamben's analysis is, then, purposefully limited to a particular temporal and geographical location: post-

Aristotelian Western political thought. In response, however, Derrida would be likely to counter by returning to his deconstruction of the *zoē/bios* binary opposition underpinning Agamben's analysis to show that Aristotle does not adhere to this opposition, which would allow Derrida to conclude that Agamben is simply mistaken to claim that it conditions all subsequent Western political thinking.

In any case, Derrida's third argument depends upon the first two: if sovereignty is always concerned with life and Aristotle does not affirm the binary opposition between *zoē* and *bios* that Agamben depends upon to develop his notion of biopolitics, then Agamben's claim that biopolitics is grounded in a particular historical moment or foundation is also incorrect.

Derrida is not here simply doing to Agamben what Agamben does to Foucault; namely, claiming that he misunderstands the moment where biopolitics enters history. Derrida is going beyond that by questioning the logic of origins underpinning biopolitical theory to 'give up . . . the idea of a decisive and founding event'.[101] This is not simply to adopt an anti-foundationalist stance that claims that sovereignty is a free-floating construction that is concerned with everything or nothing. It is to question the dichotomy between diachronic and synchronic – that is, between becoming and being, change and order – that Derrida claims implicitly underpins Agamben's argument regarding the existence of a definitive founding moment for biopolitics. Once we do so, we will find, according to Derrida, that sovereignty 'has neither a solid foundation nor . . . a founding decision . . . The abyss, if there is an abyss, is that there is *more than one ground* [*sol*], more than one solid, and more than one single threshold [*plus d'un seul seuil*].'[102]

Contrary to juridical or biopolitical conceptions, sovereignty cannot be thought in terms of a unitary and homogeneous principle or concern for law or life. It is always expressed through both; a heterogeneity that changes configuration historically. We must, then, reconfigure our understanding of sovereignty to accord with its heterogeneity, both conceptually and historically; a rethinking that will also require a reconceptualisation of the concepts – law and life – that are intimately connected to it.

Rather than a general orientation to something called 'Life', Derrida suggests that sovereignty is always tied to and set 'out from and within a life, "my life"'.[103] Similarly, death never refers to a universal, but always to a single event:

> one cannot share the death penalty, even supposing, which is very improbable, that one could share a death, die together, desire to die together . . . people are condemned to death always one by one [*un par un, une par une*], even if an entire group is executed by the same firing squad.[104]

The death penalty and, by extension, death always refer to unique cases; they cannot be orientated around or understood from a universal principle. When this is linked back to his earlier claim that the death penalty reveals the sovereign's attempt to master life, we find that, for Derrida, the sovereign always aims to control a particular form of life. It is this that ties the death penalty to politics: it determines what form of life is acceptable and re-enforces it over other forms.

Derrida's abolitionist stance is not then due to the perceived injustice of the death penalty *per se*, but is based on his rejection of the theological premises subtending it, whereby the sovereign is implicitly understood to be able to control life and death by calculating, determining, and controlling the moment of *a* death:

> The insult, the injury, the fundamental injustice done to the life in me, to the principle of life in me, is not death itself, from this point of view, it is rather the interruption of the principle of indetermination, the ending imposed on the incalculable chance whereby a living being has a relation to what comes, to the to-come and thus to some other event, as guest, as *arrivant*.[105]

By trying to control the indeterminacy of the future, the death penalty violates the fundamental condition of human life, all the while depending upon and affirming a worrying conception of an all-powerful sovereign wherein the sovereign threatens those non-sanctioned forms of life.

It might be objected, however, that Derrida has already pointed out that the indeterminateness of the transition from life to death and the moment of death itself always undermines the sovereign's *implicit* claim to control it. Therefore, if the death penalty is always based on a failing – namely, because the heterogeneity of the life–death relationship always undermines the sovereign's attempt to master or control it – why do we have to fight to abolish it? And if the sovereign's attempt always fails, why does the death penalty continue to exist? If it does not realise justice and does not control time, where does its power or usefulness to the sovereign and, indeed, the populace come from?

CONCLUDING REMARKS

The answer, Derrida thinks, lies in realising that the death penalty is not premised on or orientated towards the realisation of justice; it is designed to make the sovereign *appear* as an absolute power. The projection of a phantasmic power is fundamental because, in reality, it is all that sovereignty entails.

Gwynne Fulton explains that this results from the sovereign's supposed ability to 'master an objective instant of death clearly divided against life in the clearcut conceptual opposition of Life/Death'.[106] This is, as noted, one aspect of it, insofar as, by condemning another to death, the sovereign aims to demonstrate his mastery over life and death. Even if this fails or we 'know' that the sovereign does not have this mastery, the death penalty shows us that he '*seems to*'[107] possess this capacity and so allows us to believe in his phantasmic power.

Derrida goes on to point out that, through the spectacular demonstration of his power over life and death, the sovereign's phantasmatic structure also permits him to appear to be 'one with God, with, if you prefer, the belief in God, the experience of God, the relation to God, faith or religion'.[108] The power and authority of the sovereign God are a phantasmic mirage that exists only so long as it is believed to exist; and it is only believed to exist because we see it operating *as if* it were all-powerful. The death penalty acts as the most explicit manifestation of this phantasmic power. For this reason,

> it will always be in vain to conclude that universal abolition of the death penalty, if it comes one day, means the effective end of any death penalty ... even when the death penalty will have been abolished, when it will have been purely and simply, absolutely and unconditionally, abolished on earth, it will survive; other figures will be invented for it, other turns, in the condemnation to death.[109]

Sovereign violence – as a consequence of both its underlying originary violence and its need to express itself violently to appear to master life and death – is ubiquitous, insidious, and necessary. Any critical analysis worthy of its name must then recognise that, far from being one-dimensional or substantial, sovereignty is a complicated, multi-dimensional, and heterogeneous phantasmic structure caught between its founding violence and, through its relationship to law, an unrealisable justice. As such, every sovereign (juridical) decision will necessarily employ violence to affirm one (form of) life over another and so be both inclusionary and exclusionary.

Derrida's pessimistic conclusion is then that the abolition of the death penalty will not abolish sovereign violence *per se*. It will necessarily have to find other forms. Elizabeth Rottenburg[110] suggests that this will mean that sovereign violence will morph from a physical orientation to a psychic one. This might be so, but psychic violence does not contain the same spectacular aspect as physical violence. Sovereignty will also have to find and/or invent new ways, figures, and villains to judge, condemn, and be seen to inflict spectacular displays of physical violence on.[111] As such, sovereignty will necessarily have to continue to inflict juridically sanctioned violence and, by extension, death on some to both demonstrate its power over life and regulate those left living.

NOTES

1. Michel Foucault, *A History of Sexuality, vol. 1*, trans. Robert Hurley (New York: Vintage, 1990), p. 144.
2. Jacques Derrida, *Of Grammatology*, trans. Gayatri Chakravorty Spivak (Baltimore: Johns Hopkins University Press, 1997), p. 112.
3. Jacques Derrida, 'Before the Law', in *Acts of Literature*, ed. Derek Attridge (Abingdon: Routledge, 1992), pp. 183–220.
4. Jacques Derrida, 'Force of Law: The "Mystical Foundation of Authority"', trans. Mary Quaintance, in *Acts of Religion*, ed. Gil Andjar (Abingdon: Routledge, 2002), pp. 230–98.
5. Jacques Derrida, *Rogues: Two Essays on Reason*, trans. Pascale-Anne Brault and Michael Naas (Stanford: Stanford University Press, 2005).
6. Jacques Derrida, *The Beast and the Sovereign, vol. 1*, ed. Michel Lisse, Marie-Louise Mallet, and Ginette Michaud, trans. Geoffrey Bennington (Chicago: University of Chicago Press, 2009); and Jacques Derrida, *The Beast and the Sovereign, vol. 2*, ed. Michel Lisse, Marie-Louise Mallet, and Ginette Michaud, trans. Geoffrey Bennington (Chicago: University of Chicago Press, 2011). For a discussion of this seminar, see Gavin Rae, 'The Wolves of the World: Derrida on the Political Symbolism of the Beast and the Sovereign', in *Seeing Animals after Derrida*, ed. Sarah Bezan and James Tink (Lanham: Lexington, 2018), pp. 3–19.
7. Jacques Derrida, *The Death Penalty, vol. 1*, ed. Geoffrey Bennington, Marc Crépon, and Thomas Dutoit, trans. Peggy Kamuf (Chicago: University of Chicago Press, 2014); and Jacques Derrida, *The Death Penalty, vol. 2*, ed. Geoffrey Bennington and Marc Crépon, trans. Elizabeth Rottenburg (Chicago: University of Chicago Press, 2017).
8. Jacques Derrida, 'Psychoanalysis Searches the States of its Soul: The Impossible Beyond of a Sovereign Cruelty', p. 268, in *Without Alibi*, ed. and trans. Peggy Kamuf (Stanford: Stanford University Press, 2002), pp. 238–80.
9. For Derrida's analysis of *différance*, see Jacques Derrida, 'Différance', in *Margins of Philosophy*, trans. Alan Bass (Chicago: University of Chicago Press, 1982), pp. 3–27.
10. For a more extensive discussion of this concept, see Gavin Rae, 'Disharmonious Continuity: Critiquing Presence with Sartre and Derrida', *Sartre Studies International*, 23:2, 2017, pp. 58-81.
11. Derrida, *Of Grammatology*, p. 112.
12. Ibid. p. 112.
13. Elizabeth Grosz, 'The Time of Violence: Deconstruction and Value', *Cultural Values*, 2:2–3, 1998, pp. 190–205 (p. 193).
14. Derrida, *Of Grammatology*, p. 112.
15. Ibid. p. 112.
16. Ibid. p. 112.
17. Derrida, 'Force of Law', p. 234. It is important to note that Derrida talks here of *loi*, meaning the form of law that includes but also goes beyond *droit*, or statue law. His point is that *all* forms of law are grounded in force.
18. Margaret Davies, 'Derrida and Law: Legitimate Fiction', p. 215, in *Jacques Derrida and the Humanities: A Critical Reader*, ed. Tom Cohen (Cambridge: Cambridge University Press, 2002), pp. 213–37.
19. Derrida, 'Force of Law', p. 240.

20. Ibid. p. 242.
21. Brian Trainor, 'The State as the Mystical Foundation of Authority', *Philosophy and Social Criticism*, 32:6, 2006, pp. 767–79 (p. 771).
22. Derrida, 'Force of Law', p. 241.
23. Ibid. p. 257.
24. Ibid. p. 250. For a discussion of Levinas's notion of justice, see Gavin Rae, 'The Politics of Justice: Levinas, Violence, and the Ethical-Political Relationship', *Contemporary Political Theory*, 17:1, 2018, pp. 49–68.
25. In the second volume of the death penalty seminars, Derrida returns to the issue of calculability to distinguish between that which is (1) 'calculable'; (2) 'incalculable', which refers to that which is theoretically calculable but practically beyond the finite limits of (a) human consciousness; and (3) 'non-calculable', which refers to that which is not theoretically or practically calculable (*The Death Penalty, vol. 2*, p. 140).
26. Jacques Derrida, 'Hospitality, Justice and Responsibility: A Dialogue with Jacques Derrida', p. 72, in *Questioning Ethics: Contemporary Debates in Continental Philosophy*, ed. Mark Dooley and Richard Kearney (Abingdon: Routledge, 1999), pp. 65–83.
27. Ibid. p. 72.
28. Ibid. p. 72.
29. Ibid. p. 72.
30. Jacques Derrida, 'Autoimmunity: Real and Symbolic Suicides', p. 133, in *Philosophy in a Time of Terror*, ed. Giovanna Borradori (Chicago: University of Chicago Press, 2003), pp. 85–136.
31. Ibid. pp. 72–3.
32. Derrida, 'Force of Law', p. 243. It is in this context that Derrida makes his infamous claim that '*Deconstruction is justice*.' For a brief discussion of this notion, see Elisabeth Webber, 'Deconstructionism is Justice', *SubStance*, 34:1, 2005, pp. 38–43.
33. Derrida, 'Force of Law', p. 251.
34. Ibid. p. 252.
35. Ibid. p. 252.
36. Ibid. p. 252.
37. Ibid. p. 241.
38. Ibid. p. 241.
39. 'The instant of decision is a madness.' (Ibid. p. 255.)
40. Nick Mansfield, 'Derrida, Democracy, and Violence', *Studies in Social Justice*, 5:2, 2011, pp. 231–40 (p. 234).
41. For a defence of this position, see Richard Beardsworth, *Derrida and the Political* (Abingdon: Routledge, 1996), and Martin Hägglund, 'The Necessity of Discrimination: Disjoining Derrida and Levinas', *Diacritics*, 34:1, 2004, pp. 40–71. For a critique, see Samir Haddad, 'A Genealogy of Violence, from Light to the Autoimmune', *Diacritics*, 38:1–2, 2008, pp. 121–42.
42. Derrida, 'Force of Law', p. 253.
43. Ibid. p. 256.
44. Amnesty International, 'Death Penalty': https://www.amnesty.org/en/what-we-do/death-penalty.
45. Amnesty International, 'Global Report 2016: Death Sentences and Executions', p. 5, in Amnesty International, 'Death Penalty'.
46. In 2016, the USA executed twenty individuals, the seventh largest number in the world. This was the first time since 2006 that it featured outside the top five (ibid. p. 5).
47. Derrida, *The Death Penalty, vol. 1*, p. 192.

48. Ibid. p. 23.
49. Derrida explains that 'the death penalty is at the centre of the Christian experience or interpretation of Christianity, of the Gospels, and Christianity, with all the differences that can be situated within Christianity, between Catholicism, Protestantism, the Orthodox Church, and other variations of Christianity'. (*The Death Penalty, vol. 2*, p. 246.)
50. Jacques Derrida and Elisabeth Roudinesco, *For what Tomorrow... A Dialogue*, trans. Jeff Fort (Stanford: Stanford University Press, 2004), p. 146.
51. Ibid. p. 147.
52. Derrida, *The Death Penalty, vol. 1*, p. 48.
53. Ibid. pp. 48–9.
54. Ibid. pp. 192–3.
55. Ibid. p. 23.
56. Ibid. p. 8.
57. Ibid. p. 8.
58. Ibid. p. 40.
59. Ibid. p. 23.
60. Ibid. p. 5.
61. Derrida also reports a case from France where the parents of a severely handicapped young man 'sued the medical establishment for its diagnostic failure and for not having informed them or advised them in due time of the possibility or necessity of preventing the impending birth', to suggest that the sovereign decision is no longer simply about who lives and dies, but also about 'the right not to be born'. (*The Death Penalty, vol. 2*, p. 15.)
62. Derrida *The Death Penalty, vol. 1*, p. 22.
63. Ibid. p. 24.
64. Ibid. pp. 126–8. Derrida returns to this issue in the second year of the seminar: *The Death Penalty, vol. 2*, pp. 37–47, 84–102, 128–35, 138–9. Kant's analysis is found in *The Metaphysics of Morals*, trans. Mary Gregor (Cambridge: Cambridge University Press, 1996), 6:331–6:337.
65. Derrida, *The Death Penalty, vol. 1*, p. 129.
66. Ibid. p. 121.
67. Ibid. p. 85.
68. Ibid. p. 8.
69. Ibid. pp. 181–2.
70. Ibid. p. 5.
71. Ibid. p. 45.
72. Ibid. p. 46.
73. Ibid. p. 47.
74. Ibid. p. 26.
75. Ibid. p. 219.
76. Ibid. p. 219.
77. Ibid. p. 220.
78. Ibid. p. 220.
79. Ibid. p. 220.
80. Ibid. p. 220.
81. Ibid. p. 237.
82. Ibid. p. 238.
83. Ibid. p. 238.

84. Derrida, *The Death Penalty*, vol. 2, p. 218.
85. Derrida, *The Death Penalty*, vol. 1, p. 239.
86. Ibid. p. 242.
87. Ibid. p. 242.
88. Ibid. p. 242.
89. Derrida, *The Death Penalty*, vol. 2, p. 11.
90. Ibid. p. 11.
91. Ibid. p. 11.
92. Ibid. pp. 12–13.
93. Ibid. p. 12.
94. Robert Trumbull, 'Derrida and the Death Penalty: The Question of Cruelty', *Philosophy Today*, 59:2, 2015, pp. 317–36 (p. 331).
95. Thomas Dutoit, 'Kant's Retreat, Hugo's Advance, Freud's Erection: Or, Derrida's Displacements in his Death Penalty Lectures', *The Southern Journal of Philosophy*, 50, Supplement, 2012, pp. 107–35 (p. 134).
96. Derrida, *The Beast and the Sovereign*, vol. 1, p. 325.
97. Ibid. p. 326.
98. Ibid. p. 326.
99. Ibid. p. 330.
100. Ibid. p. 330.
101. Ibid. p. 333.
102. Ibid. pp. 333–4.
103. Ibid. p. 255.
104. Derrida, *The Death Penalty*, vol. 1, p. 247.
105. Ibid. p. 256.
106. Gwynne Fulton, '*Phantasmatics*: Sovereignty and the Image of Death in Derrida's First Death Penalty Seminar', *Mosaic*, 48:3, 2015, pp. 75–94 (p. 76).
107. Derrida, *The Death Penalty*, vol. 1, p. 258.
108. Ibid. p. 259.
109. Ibid. p. 282.
110. Elizabeth Rottenburg, 'Cruelty and its Vicissitudes: Jacques Derrida and the Future of Psychoanalysis', *The Southern Journal of Philosophy*, 50, Supplement, 2012, pp. 147–59 (p. 153).
111. For a discussion of the relationship between invention and the notion of the death-penalty-to-come, see Ronald Mendoza-de Jesús, 'Invention of the Death Penalty: Abolitionism at its Limits', *Oxford Literary Review*, 35:2, 2013, pp. 221–40.

Conclusion

In the preceding pages, I have sought to show that the question of sovereign violence has been a major concern for Western philosophical and political thought for over a millennium. This initially gave rise to the classical-juridical model wherein sovereign violence is defined from and around a singular sovereign figure who uses violence instrumentally to establish and preserve the juridical order. While dominant for the overwhelming majority of Western thinking on the topic, this understanding came under sustained attack in the twentieth century, where proponents of, amongst others, biopolitical theory, critical theory, deconstruction, and post-structuralism questioned the assumptions it is premised on to undertake a renewed and sustained engagement with the topic.

Whereas the need for this questioning was perhaps not surprising given the historical period within and from which it took place – marked as it was by major cultural, economic, political, and technological alterations that called into question long-held assumptions about the nature and structure of the juridical-political – it did not lead to agreement on what sovereignty entails or the role that violence plays in relation to it. Instead, I have argued that three fundamental models and logics, termed the radical-juridical, the biopolitical, and the bio-juridical, can be discerned from the debate.

The logic of the radical-juridical model – manifested here through the works of Hannah Arendt, Walter Benjamin, Gilles Deleuze and Felix Guattari, and Carl Schmitt – criticises the classic-juridical model of sovereignty by questioning its conception of either 'sovereignty' or 'violence'. The basic premise is that 'sovereignty' is divisible (not indivisible as the classical-juridical model holds), while 'violence' is problematised and no longer simply held to be an instrument of the sovereign figure. As a consequence, the relationship between sovereignty and violence is understood to be far more heterogeneous than conceived in the classical-juridical model.

However, while the specifics differ depending on the thinker in question, the logic underpinning the radical-juridical model remains tied to the classical-juridical one by virtue of its claim that sovereignty is orientated or intimately linked to the establishment, preservation, or disruption of juridical order. For this reason, the radical-juridical model entails a radicalisation of the premises of the classic-juridical model, without departing from the latter's fundamental claim that sovereign violence is tied to law.

The second model, manifested through the biopolitical theories of Michel Foucault and Giorgio Agamben, goes further in its critique of the classical-juridical model, while also, in so doing, implicitly criticising the fundamental tenets of the radical-juridical model. Again, despite subtle differences between the theorists included within this model, their shared fundamental premise is that sovereign violence is not – because it no longer is (Foucault) or never was (Agamben) – linked primarily to the establishment and maintenance of juridical order. Sovereignty is defined by the attempt to regulate *life*, which is both the condition of sovereignty and the politicalised object that it violently works on. This is not, however, to say that biopolitical theories simply abandon law, but that the configuration of law underpinning them is different to the one that dominates juridical models because it emphasises the way in which sovereign violence operates through social norms and juridical exclusion, rather than through formal statute law and imposition.

One of the key differences between the radical-juridical and biopolitical models refers then to the way(s) in which sovereign violence is related to law and, indeed, what law means: radical-juridical theories continue to insist that sovereign violence is tied to the establishment and maintenance of a juridical order, which influences and impacts on the life of the populace by controlling it from 'above'. Biopolitical theories, in contrast, insist that sovereign violence is orientated primarily towards not the juridical order, but the regulation of life, which occurs mainly, though not exclusively, through juridical exclusion and the management of social norms rather than the imposition of formal law. In opposition to the radical-juridical logic that controls life by focusing on formal laws to create and maintain juridical order, the biopolitical one creates order by regulating life through the management of social norms (and to a lesser extent formal laws). While both logics create order, they do so in diametrically opposed fashion: the radical–juridical model aims to impose law on life, the biopolitical model regulates life by excluding it from law.

From this, it appears that we are faced with an antinomy, wherein we tie sovereign violence primarily either to the juridical order or to life. However, as I have argued, such a conclusion is not warranted once we note that biopolitical theories themselves recognise that their conception of sovereignty is grounded in a particular historically contingent logic. For Foucault, this was the logic of late modernity; for Agamben, the logic of Western thinking since the ancient Greeks. Both hold that, as a historical construction, the biopolitical version of sovereign violence is not the final word on the topic, but should be altered, with this leading Foucault to the notion of 'governmentality' and Agamben to what he calls the coming politics. Therefore, for all its innovation and conceptual insights, biopolitical theory itself affirms the need to go beyond its analysis and, indeed, that provided by juridical models. As such, it is not the case that, when thinking about sovereign violence, we are simply locked in a binary opposition between accounts that privilege the sovereign's relation to law and those that privilege its relation to life. We need to go beyond juridical and biopolitical theories to explore alternatives.

This does, however, give rise to the question of what these entail and, by extension, how the notion 'sovereign violence' should be understood. At least two options present themselves, insofar as we can (1) follow Foucault or Agamben in affirming governmentality or the notion of the coming politics, or (2) develop an alternative that rejects the premises of and binary logic inherent in the juridical and biopolitics models.

I have argued for the latter position and outlined what it might look like by turning to Derrida's bio-juridical analysis of the sovereign violence involved in the death penalty. To develop this bio-juridical model, Derrida calls into question the claim that biopolitical theory entails a departure from juridical models by showing that both are premised on a fundamental binary opposition that pitches law over life (classical- and radical-juridical models) or life over law (biopolitical theory). Derrida's problem with this is both *logical*, insofar as simply inverting the privileged term in this dichotomy leaves us trapped within a logic of *versus* that is unable to coherently take into consideration the fluidity and impurity of the categories used to describe actual existence or indeed actual existence itself,[1] and *conceptual*, insofar as he holds that sovereign violence is not simply orientated to one thing – law or life – but is far more sophisticated, fluid, and multi-dimensional.

From this, Derrida's bio-juridical model tentatively proposes an alternative conception of the law–life/sovereignty–violence relationship that combines the claims derived from the juridical and biopolitical models regarding the sovereign's relationship to law and life, but breaks with the binary logic that constitutes each one individually and, indeed, the relation between them. Rather than this simply entailing a synthesis of the juridical and biopolitical approaches through a moment of Hegelian determinate negation,[2] wherein the partial 'truths' inherent in both are recuperated into a more advanced understanding, Derrida intends to incorporate (rethought) aspects of the juridical and biopolitical models, but depart substantially from the conclusions reached by them. As such, his thinking is not grounded in the juridical or biopolitical models, but mirrors aspects of them, all the while taking off in a different direction from them to provide a distinct understanding of sovereign violence.

To do so, sovereignty is reconceptualised away from the notions of substance, unity, or nexus, and understood as an imaginary and imagined phantasmatic that is grounded in a pre-personal originary violence that constructs the meaning of the sovereign. Thus, sovereignty is not founded on agreement or divine authority; it is created through the force that generates meaning and continues to exist because those whom it is exercised on and through believe in its merits, power, and justification. In turn, this is supported by and given a sense of objectivity, permanence, and omnipotence through the creation of a juridical order headed by the sovereign *and* the expression of sovereign symbolic significations that regulate social norms.

By operating juridically *and* non-juridically, sovereign violence influences, directs, and regulates all aspects of life, a process that (1) requires violent acts to display to the populace the sovereign's omnipotent power over life and death, with these supported by and passing through the juridical system, itself headed by the sovereign and so re-enforcing the appearance of and belief in 'his' omnipotent power; and (2) depends upon the sovereign creating outsider groups or forms of life that are considered to be unacceptable. If the sovereign cannot (violently) exert itself on outsider groups or display its sovereign power, the risk is that the populace will stop believing in its omnipotent power and, if that were to occur, the sovereign may appear for what it is: an imaginary phantasm.

Derrida's bio-juridical model offers then a far more sophisticated account of sovereign violence than the classical-/radical-juridical and biopolitical models because it shows that sovereign violence is not tied simply to a unitary end, whether in the form of the regulation of life or the creation and maintenance of the juridical order, but is bound to both by virtue of being Janus-faced, insofar as it operates through and is defined by a complex and fluid relationship to law and life simultaneously.

Furthermore, whereas radical-juridical models speak little of life and tend to reduce 'law' to formal, positive conceptions, and biopolitical models (implicitly) distinguish between the law of social norms and formal juridical law, but implicitly start from a unitary conception of life that is subsequently divided into different forms of life, Derrida's bio-juridical model not only explicitly distinguishes between two forms of law – social norms and formal law – to suggest that sovereign violence works through both simultaneously, but also explicitly rejects the biopolitical premise of a unitary foundational notion of 'life' *per se*, to argue that sovereign violence is always exercised on one particular concrete life; an exercise that depends upon the creation of norms to distinguish between those forms of life considered acceptable and those which are held to be unacceptable. In turn, the latter are subject to sanction, both legally and socially, for being unacceptable, which reaffirms the desired social norm and mode of life and demonstrates and re-enforces (the perception of) sovereign power.

With this, Derrida's bio-juridical model points to a non-substantial, phantasmatic conception of sovereignty that is orientated to and expresses itself simultaneously through different forms of law and the regulation of different forms of life. Therefore, unlike the juridical and biopolitical models, it cannot be reduced to a single goal, object, or end. Rather, sovereign violence is expressed and expresses itself through different forms of law to discriminate between and regulate different modes of life, with that regulation of life, in turn, feeding the belief in and the need for the laws and regulations supporting it and ultimately the omnipotence of the sovereign power.

This does, of course, make 'proper' concrete analyses of it increasingly difficult and complex, but this also re-enforces its (appearance of) phantasmatic omnipotence: its insidious ineffability gives off the impression that it is both everywhere and capable of everything. However, it must be remembered that, far from being omnipotent, sovereign violence is actually constituted by and an effect of the violence inherent in the contingent and contestable configuration of forces that 'ground' it. Because instability would result if that ground were left explicit – individuals would be left in constant battle for sovereign supremacy – sovereignty must continuously cover over its phantasmatic structure with violent, spectacular displays that affirm its power over life and death. There is, however, always the possibility that such action will fail and so reveal that far from being immutable, sovereignty is, in actuality, grounded in nothing other than the *appearance* of omnipotence.

From this, Derrida's bio-juridical model reveals that sovereignty is caught in an inescapable double-bind, insofar as, to exist, it must project, through violent displays of its power over life and death, the phantasm of omnipotence, despite (its dependence on) that projection always threatening to reveal that it is simply a phantasmatic figure grounded in nothing other than contingent force-relations and *belief* in its omnipotence. The important abiding lesson of Derrida's bio-juridical model is then that, despite intended appearances, sovereign violence is structured from an unavoidable and potentially terminal paradox, wherein its necessary projection of an aura of overwhelming omnipotent power depends upon and is always accompanied by a fragile 'ground' that constantly threatens to give way to undermine it.

NOTES

1. For a discussion of the '[c]risis of *versus*', see Jacques Derrida, *Dissemination*, trans. Barbara Johnson (London: Continuum, 1981), pp. 20–1.
2. For an extended analysis of Hegel's notion of determinate negation, see Gavin Rae, *Realizing Freedom: Hegel, Sartre, and the Alienation of Human Being* (Basingstoke: Palgrave Macmillan, 2011), pp. 113–22.

Bibliography

Adkins, Brent, *Deleuze and Guattari's A Thousand Plateaus: A Critical Introduction and Guide* (Edinburgh: Edinburgh University Press, 2015).
Agamben, Giorgio, *Language and Death: The Place of Negativity*, trans. Karen E. Pinkus and Michael Hardt (Minneapolis: University of Minnesota Press, 1991).
— *The Coming Community*, trans. Michael Hardt (Minneapolis: University of Minnesota Press, 1993).
— *Homo Sacer: Sovereign Power and Bare Life*, trans. Daniel Heller-Roazen (Stanford: Stanford University Press, 1998).
— 'On Potentiality', in *Potentialities: Collected Essays in Philosophy*, ed. and trans. Daniel Heller-Rozen (Stanford: Stanford University Press, 1999), pp. 177–85.
— 'Bartleby, or on Contingency', in *Potentialities: Collected Essays in Philosophy*, ed. and trans. Daniel Heller-Rozen (Stanford: Stanford University Press, 1999), pp. 243–71.
— *Means without Ends: Notes on Politics*, trans. Vincenzo Binetti and Cesare Casarino (Minneapolis: University of Minnesota Press, 2000).
— *State of Exception*, trans. Kevin Attell (Chicago: University of Chicago Press, 2005).
— 'On the Limits of Violence', trans. Elisabeth Fay, *Diacritics*, 39:4, 2009, pp. 103–11.
— *Remnants of Auschwitz: The Witness and the Archive*, trans. Daniel Heller-Roazen (New York: Zone Books, 2012).
— *Stasis: Civil War as a Political Paradigm*, trans. Nicholas Heron (Edinburgh: Edinburgh University Press, 2015).
— *The Use of Bodies*, trans. Adam Kotsko (Stanford: Stanford University Press, 2016).
Ahmadi, Amir, 'Benjamin's Niobe', in *Toward a Critique of Violence: Walter Benjamin and Giorgio Agamben*, ed. Brendan Moran and Carlo Satzani (London: Bloomsbury, 2015), pp. 57–71.
Allen, Ansgar, and Roy Goddard, 'The Domestication of Foucault: Government, Critique, War', *History of the Human Sciences*, 27:5, 2004, pp. 26–53.
Amnesty International, 'Death Penalty': https://www.amnesty.org/en/what-we-do/death-penalty.
Arendt, Hannah, *The Origins of Totalitarianism* (New York: Harcourt, 1951).
— *On Revolution* (London: Penguin, 1963).

— *On Violence* (New York: Harcourt, 1970).
— 'On the Nature of Totalitarianism', in *Essays in Understanding, 1930–1954*, ed. Jerome Kohn (New York: Schocken Books, 1994), pp. 328–60.
— *Love and Saint Augustine*, ed. Joanna Vecchairelli Scott and Judith Chelius Stark (Chicago: University of Chicago Press, 1996).
— *The Human Condition*, 2nd edn (Chicago: University of Chicago Press, 1998).
— *Between Past and Future* (London: Penguin, 2006).
— 'The Jewish Army: The Beginning of Jewish Politics?', in *The Jewish Writings*, ed. Jerome Kohn and Ron H. Feldman (New York: Schocken Books, 2007), pp. 136–8.
Arendt, Hannah, and Karl Jaspers, *Correspondence: 1932–1969*, ed. Lotte Kohler and Hans Sander (New York: Harcourt, 1992).
Armitage, David, *Civil Wars: A History in Ideas* (New Haven: Yale University Press, 2017).
Attell, Kevin, *Giorgio Agamben: Beyond the Threshold of Deconstruction* (New York: Fordham University Press, 2015).
Balakrishnan, Gopal, *The Enemy: An Intellectual Portrait of Carl Schmitt* (London: Verso, 2000).
Barder, Alexander, and François Debrix, 'Agonal Sovereignty: Rethinking War and Politics with Schmitt, Arendt, and Foucault', *Philosophy and Social Criticism*, 37:7, 2011, pp. 775–93.
Bartelson, Jens, *A Genealogy of Sovereignty* (Cambridge: Cambridge University Press, 1995).
Bates, David W., *States of War: Enlightenment Origins of the Political* (New York: Columbia University Press, 2012).
Beardsworth, Richard, *Derrida and the Political* (Abingdon: Routledge, 1996).
Benhabib, Seyla, 'Carl Schmitt's Critique of Kant: Sovereignty and International Law', *Political Theory*, 40:6, 2012, pp. 688–713.
Benjamin, Walter, 'On Language as Such and on the Language of Man', trans. Edmund Jephcott, in *Selected Writings, vol. 1, 1913–1926*, ed. Marcus Bullock and Michael W. Jennings (Cambridge, MA: Harvard University Press, 1996), pp. 62–74.
— 'Critique of Violence', trans. Edmund Jephcott, in *Selected Writings, vol. 1, 1913–1926*, ed. Marcus Bullock and Michael W. Jennings (Cambridge, MA: Harvard University Press, 1996), pp. 236–52.
— *Gesammelte Briefe* (Frankfurt-am-Main: Suhrkamp, 1997).
Bernasconi, Robert, 'The Policing of Race Mixing: The Place of Biopower within the History of Racisms', *Journal of Bioethical Inquiry*, 7:2, 2010, pp. 205–16.
Bernstein, Richard, 'The Aporias of Carl Schmitt', *Constellations*, 18:3, 2011, pp. 403–30.
— *Violence: Thinking without Bannisters* (Cambridge: Polity, 2013).
Blumenthal-Barby, Martin, 'Pernicious Bastardisation: Benjamin's Ethics of Pure Violence', *Modern Language Notes*, 124:3, 2009, pp. 728–51.
Böckenförde, Ernst W., 'The Concept of the Political: A Key to Understanding Carl Schmitt's Constitutional Theory', *Canadian Journal of Law and Jurisprudence*, 10:1, 1997, pp. 5–19.
Bodin, Jean, *On Sovereignty*, ed. and trans. Julian H. Franklin (Cambridge: Cambridge University Press, 1992).
Bredekamp, Horst, 'Walter Benjamin to Carl Schmitt, via Thomas Hobbes', trans. Melissa Thorson Hause and Jackson Bond, *Critical Inquiry*, 25:2, 1999, pp. 247–66.
Breen, Keith, 'Violence and Power: A Critique of Hannah Arendt on the "Political"', *Philosophy and Social Criticism*, 33:3, 2007, pp. 343–72.
Buckler, Steve, *Hannah Arendt and Political Theory: Challenging the Tradition* (Edinburgh: Edinburgh University Press, 2011).
Butler, Judith, 'Critique, Coercion and Sacred Life in Benjamin's "Critique of Violence"', in

Political Theologies: Public Relations in a Post-Secular World, ed. Hent de Vries and Lawrence E. Sullivan (New York: Fordham University Press, 2006), pp. 201–19.

Canovan, Margaret, 'Arendt, Rousseau, and Human Plurality in Politics', *Journal of Politics*, 45:2, 1983, pp. 286–302.

Champlin, Jeffrey, 'Born Again: Arendt's "Natality" as Figure and Concept', *The Germanic Review*, 88:2, 2013, pp. 150–64.

Clausewitz, Carl von, *On War*, ed. and trans. Michael Howard and Peter Paret (Princeton: Princeton University Press, 1984).

Cohen, Einat Bar-on, 'Events of Organicity: The State Abducts the War Machine', *Anthropological Theory*, 11:3, 2011, pp. 259–82.

Connolly, William E., 'The Complexities of Sovereignty', in *Giorgio Agamben: Sovereignty and Life*, ed. Mathew Calarco and Steven DeCaroli (Stanford: Stanford University Press, 2007), pp. 23–42.

Critchley, Simon, *The Faith of the Faithless: Experiments in Political Theology* (London: Verso, 2012).

Davies, Margaret, 'Derrida and Law: Legitimate Fiction', in *Jacques Derrida and the Humanities: A Critical Reader*, ed. Tom Cohen (Cambridge: Cambridge University Press, 2002), pp. 213–37.

DeCaroli, Steven, 'Political Life: Giorgio Agamben and the Idea of Authority', *Research in Phenomenology*, 43:2, 2013, pp. 220–42.

Degryse, Annelies, 'The Sovereign and the Social: Arendt's Understanding of Hobbes', *Ethical Perspectives*, 15:2, 2008, pp. 239–58.

Deleuze, Gilles, *Difference and Repetition*, trans. Paul Patton (New York: Columbia University Press, 1994).

— 'Three Group-Related Problems', in *Desert Islands and Other Texts, 1953–1974*, ed. David Lapoujade, trans. Michael Taomini (New York: Semiotext, 2004), pp. 193–203.

— 'Nomadic Thought', in *Desert Islands and Other Texts, 1953–1974*, ed. David Lapoujade, trans. Michael Taomini (New York: Semiotext, 2004), pp. 252–61.

— 'On Capitalism and Desire', in *Desert Islands and Other Texts, 1953–1974*, ed. David Lapoujade, trans. Michael Taomini (New York: Semiotext, 2004), pp. 262–73.

— 'Five Propositions in Psychoanalysis', in *Desert Islands and Other Texts, 1953–1974*, ed. David Lapoujade, trans. Michael Taomini (New York: Semiotext, 2004), pp. 274–80.

— 'Desire and Pleasure', in *Two Regimes of Madness: Texts and Interviews, 1975–1995*, ed. David Lapoujade, trans. Ames Hodges and Mike Taormina (New York: Semiotext, 2007), pp. 122–34.

Deleuze, Gilles, and Felix Guattari, *Anti-Oedipus: Capitalism and Schizophrenia*, trans. Robert Hurley, Mark Seem, and Helen R. Lane (London: Continuum, 2004).

— *A Thousand Plateaus*, trans. Brian Massumi (London: Continuum, 2004).

Deleuze, Gilles, and Claire Parnet, *Dialogues II*, trans. Hugh Tomlinson and Barbara Habberjam (London: Continuum, 2006).

Depoortere, Frederiek, 'Reading Giorgio Agamben's *Homo Sacer* with René Girard', *Philosophy Today*, 56:2, 2012, pp. 154–63.

Derrida, Jacques, *Dissemination*, trans. Barbara Johnson (London: Continuum, 1981).

— 'Différance', in *Margins of Philosophy*, trans. Alan Bass (Chicago: University of Chicago Press, 1982), pp. 3–27.

— 'Before the Law', in *Acts of Literature*, ed. Derek Attridge (Abingdon: Routledge, 1992), pp. 183–220.

— *Of Grammatology*, trans. Gayatri Chakravorty Spivak (Baltimore: Johns Hopkins University Press, 1997).

— 'Hospitality, Justice and Responsibility: A Dialogue with Jacques Derrida', in *Questioning Ethics: Contemporary Debates in Continental Philosophy*, ed. Mark Dooley and Richard Kearney (Abingdon: Routledge, 1999), pp. 65–83.
— 'Force of Law: The "Mystical Foundation of Authority"', trans. Mary Quaintance, in *Acts of Religion*, ed. Gil Andjar (Abingdon: Routledge, 2002), pp. 230–98.
— 'Psychoanalysis Searches the States of its Soul: The Impossible Beyond of a Sovereign Cruelty', in *Without Alibi*, ed. and trans. Peggy Kamuf (Stanford: Stanford University Press, 2002), pp. 238–80.
— 'Autoimmunity: Real and Symbolic Suicides', in *Philosophy in a Time of Terror*, ed. Giovanna Borradori (Chicago: University of Chicago Press, 2003), pp. 85–136.
— *Rogues: Two Essays on Reason*, trans. Pascale-Anne Brault and Michael Naas (Stanford: Stanford University Press, 2005).
— *The Politics of Friendship*, trans. George Collins (London: Verso, 2005).
— *The Beast and the Sovereign*, vol. *1*, ed. Michel Lisse, Marie-Louise Mallet, and Ginette Michaud, trans. Geoffrey Bennington (Chicago: University of Chicago Press, 2009).
— *The Beast and the Sovereign*, vol. *2*, ed. Michel Lisse, Marie-Louise Mallet, and Ginette Michaud, trans. Geoffrey Bennington (Chicago: University of Chicago Press, 2011).
— *The Death Penalty*, vol. *1*, ed. Geoffrey Bennington, Marc Crépon, and Thomas Dutoit, trans. Peggy Kamuf (Chicago: University of Chicago Press, 2014).
— *The Death Penalty*, vol. *2*, ed. Geoffrey Bennington and Marc Crépon, trans. Elizabeth Rottenburg (Chicago: University of Chicago Press, 2017).
Derrida, Jacques, and Elisabeth Roudinesco, *For what Tomorrow ... A Dialogue*, trans. Jeff Fort (Stanford: Stanford University Press, 2004).
Durantaye, Leland de la, *Giorgio Agamben: A Critical Introduction* (Stanford: Stanford University Press, 2009).
Dutoit, Thomas, 'Kant's Retreat, Hugo's Advance, Freud's Erection: Or, Derrida's Displacements in his Death Penalty Lectures', *The Southern Journal of Philosophy*, 50, Supplement, 2012, pp. 107–35.
Dyzenhaus, David, 'Putting the State Back in Credit', in *The Challenge of Carl Schmitt*, ed. Chantel Mouffe (London: Verso, 1999), pp. 75–91.
Elden, Stuart, *Foucault's Last Decade* (Cambridge: Polity, 2016).
Esposito, Roberto, *Two: The Machine of Political Theology and the Place of Thought*, trans. Zakiya Hanafi (New York: Fordham University Press, 2015).
Evans, Brad, and Julian Reid, eds, *Deleuze and Fascism: Security, War, Aesthetics* (Abingdon: Routledge, 2015).
Finlay, Christopher, 'Hannah Arendt's Critique of Violence', *Thesis Eleven*, 97, May, 2009, pp. 26–45.
Foucault, Michel, *A History of Sexuality*, vol. *1*, trans. Robert Hurley (New York: Vintage, 1990).
— *Discipline and Punish: Birth of the Prison*, trans. Alan Sheridan (New York: Vintage, 1995).
— 'Truth and Power', in *Power: Essential Works of Foucault, 1954–1984*, vol. *3*, ed. James D. Faubion, trans. Robert Burchell and others (London: Penguin, 2000), pp. 111–33.
— *Abnormal: Lectures at the Collège de France, 1974–1975*, ed. Valerio Marchetti and Antonella Salomoni, trans. Graham Burchell (New York: Picador, 2003).
— *Society Must Be Defended*, ed. Mauro Bertani and Alessandro Fontana, trans. David Macey (London: Penguin, 2003).
— *The Birth of Biopolitics: Lectures at the Collège de France, 1978–1979*, ed. Michel Senellart, trans. Graham Burchell (Basingstoke: Palgrave Macmillan, 2008).

— *Psychiatric Power: Lectures at the Collège de France, 1973–1974*, ed. Jacques Lagrange, trans. Graham Burchell (Basingstoke: Palgrave Macmillan, 2008).
— 'Nietzsche, Genealogy, History', in *The Foucault Reader*, ed. Paul Rabinow (New York: Vintage, 2010), pp. 76–100.
Franklin, Julian H., *Jean Bodin and the Rise of Absolutist Theory* (Cambridge: Cambridge University Press, 2009).
Frazer, Elizabeth, and Kimberly Hutchings, 'On Politics and Violence: Arendt contra Fanon', *Contemporary Political Theory*, 7:1, 2008, pp. 90–108.
— 'Avowing Violence: Foucault and Derrida on Politics, Discourse, and Meaning', *Philosophy and Social Criticism*, 37:1, 2011, pp. 3–23.
Fulton, Gwynne, '*Phantasmatics*: Sovereignty and the Image of Death in Derrida's First *Death Penalty* Seminar', *Mosaic*, 48:3, 2015, pp. 75–94.
Grosz, Elizabeth, 'The Time of Violence: Deconstruction and Value', *Cultural Values*, 2:2–3, 1998, pp. 190–205.
Guattari, Felix, 'Causality, Subjectivity and History', in *Psychoanalysis and Transversality*, trans. Ames Hodges (Cambridge, MA: MIT Press, 2015), pp. 235–80.
— 'Machine and Structure', in *Psychoanalysis and Transversality*, trans. Ames Hodges (Cambridge, MA: MIT Press, 2015), pp. 318–30.
Habermas, Jürgen, 'Hannah Arendt's Communications Concept of Power', trans. Thomas McCarthy, *Social Research*, 44:1, 1977, pp. 3–24.
— 'Walter Benjamin: Consciousness-Raising or Rescuing Critique', in *On Walter Benjamin: Critical Essays and Recollections*, ed. Gary Smith (Stanford: Stanford University Press, 1992), pp. 90–128.
Haddad, Samir, 'A Genealogy of Violence, from Light to the Autoimmune', *Diacritics*, 38:1–2, 2008, pp. 121–42.
Hägglund, Martin, 'The Necessity of Discrimination: Disjoining Derrida and Levinas', *Diacritics*, 34:1, 2004, pp. 40–71.
Hamacher, Werner, 'Afformative, Strike: Benjamin's "Critique of Violence"', trans. Dana Hollander, in *Walter Benjamin's Philosophy: Destruction and Experience*, ed. Andrew Benjamin and Peter Osborne (Abingdon: Routledge, 2000), pp. 110–38.
Hanssen, Beatrice, *Critique of Violence: Between Poststructuralism and Critical Theory* (Abingdon: Routledge, 2000).
Heil, Susanne, *Gefährliche Beziehungen: Walter Benjamin und Carl Schmitt* (Stuttgart: J. B. Metzler, 1996).
Hirvonen, Ari, 'The Politics of Revolt: On Benjamin and Critique of Law', *Law Critique*, 22:2, 2011, pp. 101–18.
— 'Marx and God with Anarchism: On Walter Benjamin's Concepts of History and Violence', *Continental Philosophy Review*, 45:5, 2012, pp. 519–43.
Hobbes, Thomas, *Leviathan*, ed. J. C. A. Gaskin (Oxford: Oxford University Press, 1996).
Holland, Eugene W., 'Schizoanalysis, Nomadology, Fascism', in *Deleuze and Politics*, ed. Ian Buchanan and Nicholas Thorburn (Edinburgh: Edinburgh University Press, 2008), pp. 74–97.
— *Deleuze and Guattari's A Thousand Plateaus* (London: Bloomsbury, 2013).
Kahn, Paul, *Political Theology: Four New Chapters on the Concept of Sovereignty* (New York: Columbia University Press, 2012).
Kalyvas, Andreas, *Democracy and the Politics of the Extraordinary: Max Weber, Carl Schmitt, and Hannah Arendt* (Cambridge: Cambridge University Press, 2008).
Kant, Immanuel, *The Metaphysics of Morals*, trans. Mary Gregor (Cambridge: Cambridge University Press, 1996).

Kaplan, Caren, *Questions of Travel: Postmodern Discourses of Displacement* (Durham: Duke University Press, 1996).
Kellog, Catherine, 'Walter Benjamin and the Ethics of Violence', *Law, Culture, and the Humanities*, 9:1, 2011, pp. 71–90.
Kolozova, Katerina, 'Violence: The Indispensable Condition of Law (and the Political)', *Angelaki: Journal of the Theoretical Humanities*, 19:2, 2014, pp. 99–111.
Lambert, Gregg, 'The War-Machine and "a people who revolt"', *Theory and Event*, 13:3, 2010: https://muse.jhu.edu/article/396506.
Levine, Andrew, *The General Will: Rousseau, Marx, Communism* (Cambridge: Cambridge University Press, 2008).
Lievens, Mathias, 'Carl Schmitt's Metapolitics', *Constellations*, 20:1, 2013, pp. 121–37.
Lincoln, Abraham, 'The Gettysburg Address', in *Political Writings and Speeches*, ed. Terence Ball (Cambridge: Cambridge University Press, 2012), pp. 191–2.
Loraux, Nicole, *The Divided City: On Memory and Forgetting in Ancient Athens*, trans. Corinne Pache and Jeff Fort (New York: Zone Books, 2006).
Luchese, Filippo del, *The Political Philosophy of Niccolò Machiavelli* (Edinburgh: Edinburgh University Press, 2015).
McLoughlin, Daniel, 'The Fiction of Sovereignty and the Real State of Exception: Giorgio Agamben's Critique of Carl Schmitt', *Law, Culture and the Humanities*, 12:3, 2016, pp. 509–28.
McNulty, Tracy, 'The Commandment against the Law: Writing and Divine Justice in Walter Benjamin's "Critique of Violence"', *Diacritics*, 37:2–3, 2007, pp. 34–60.
Mansfield, Nick, 'Derrida, Democracy, and Violence', *Studies in Social Justice*, 5:2, 2011, pp. 231–40.
Marcuse, Herbert, 'Nachwort', in Walter Benjamin, *Walter Benjamin, zur Kritik der Gewalt und andere Aufsätze* (Frankfurt-am-Main: Suhrkamp, 1965), pp. 98–107.
Marks, John, 'Michel Foucault: Biopolitics and Biology', in *Foucault in an Age of Terror: Essays on Biopolitics and the Defence of Society*, ed. Stephen Morton and Stephen Bygrave (Basingstoke: Palgrave Macmillan, 2008), pp. 88–105.
Martel, James R., *Divine Violence: Walter Benjamin and the Eschatology of Sovereignty* (Abingdon: Routledge, 2012).
— 'The Anarchist Life We Are Already Living: Benjamin and Agamben on Bare Life and the Resistance to Sovereignty', in *Toward a Critique of Violence: Walter Benjamin and Giorgio Agamben*, ed. Brendan Moran and Carlo Satzani (London: Bloomsbury, 2015), pp. 125–38.
— 'Walter Benjamin and the General Strike: Non-Violence and the Archeon', in *The Meanings of Violence: From Critical Theory to Biopolitics*, ed. Gavin Rae and Emma Ingala (Abingdon: Routledge, 2019), pp. 13–30.
Martinich, A. P., *The Two Gods of Leviathan: Thomas Hobbes on Religion and Politics* (Cambridge: Cambridge University Press, 2003).
Mendoza-de Jesús, Ronald, 'Invention of the Death Penalty: Abolitionism at its Limits', *Oxford Literary Review*, 35:2, 2013, pp. 221–40.
Miller, Christopher L., 'Beyond Identity: The Postidentarian Predicament of *A Thousand Plateaus*', in *Nationalists and Nomads: Essays on Francophone African Literature and Culture* (Chicago: University of Chicago Press, 1998), pp. 171–244.
Moran, Brendan, 'Exception, Division and Philosophical Politics: Benjamin and the Extreme', *Philosophy and Social Criticism*, 40:2, 2014, pp. 145–70.
Nguyen, Duy Lap, 'On the Suspension of Law and the Total Transformation of Labour: Reflections on the Philosophy of History in Walter Benjamin's "Critique of Violence"', *Thesis Eleven*, 130:1, 2015, pp. 96–116.

Nishiyami, Hidefumi, 'Towards a Global Genealogy of Biopolitics: Race, Colonialisation, and Biometrics beyond Europe', *Environment and Planning D: Society and Space*, 33:2, 2015, pp. 331–46.
Oksala, Johanna, 'From Biopolitics to Governmentality', in *A Companion to Foucault*, ed. Christopher Falzon, Timothy O'Leary and Jana Sawicki (London: Wiley-Blackwell, 2013), pp. 320–36.
Ott, Paul, 'World and Earth: Hannah Arendt and the Human Relationship to Nature', *Ethics, Place and Environment: A Journal of Philosophy and Geography*, 12:1, 2009, pp. 1–16.
Pan, David, 'Carl Schmitt on Culture and Violence in the Political Decision', *Telos*, 142, Spring, 2008, pp. 49–72.
— 'Against Biopolitics: Walter Benjamin, Carl Schmitt, and Giorgio Agamben on Political Sovereignty and Symbolic Order', *The German Quarterly*, 82:1, 2009, pp. 42–62.
Passerin d'Entrèves, Maurizio, *The Political Philosophy of Hannah Arendt* (Abingdon: Routledge, 1994).
Patton, Paul, *Deleuze and the Political* (Abingdon: Routledge, 2000).
— *Deleuzian Concepts: Philosophy, Colonisation, Politics* (Stanford: Stanford University Press, 2010).
— 'From Resistance to Government: Foucault's Lectures 1976–1979', in *A Companion to Foucault*, ed. Christopher Falzon, Timothy O'Leary, and Jana Sawicki (London: Wiley-Blackwell, 2013), pp. 172–88.
Prozorov, Sergei, 'Foucault and Soviet Biopolitics', *History of the Human Sciences*, 27:5, 2014, pp. 6–25.
Rae, Gavin, *Realizing Freedom: Hegel, Sartre, and the Alienation of Human Being* (Basingstoke: Palgrave Macmillan, 2011).
— 'Violence, Territorialisation, and Signification: The Political from Carl Schmitt and Gilles Deleuze', *Theoria and Praxis: International Journal of Interdisciplinary Thought*, 1:1, 2013, pp. 1–17.
— *Ontology in Heidegger and Deleuze* (Basingstoke: Palgrave Macmillan, 2014).
— *The Problem of Political Foundations in Carl Schmitt and Emmanuel Levinas* (Basingstoke: Palgrave Macmillan, 2016).
— 'Disharmonious Continuity: Critiquing Presence with Sartre and Derrida', *Sartre Studies International*, 23:2, 2017, pp. 58–81.
— 'The Wolves of the World: Derrida on the Political Symbolism of the Beast and the Sovereign', in *Seeing Animals after Derrida*, ed. Sarah Bezan and James Tink (Lanham: Lexington, 2018), pp. 3–19.
— 'The Politics of Justice: Levinas, Violence, and the Ethical-Political Relationship', *Contemporary Political Theory*, 17:1, 2018, pp. 49–68.
— *Evil in the Western Philosophical Tradition* (Edinburgh: Edinburgh University Press, 2019).
— 'Agency and Will in Agamben's Coming Politics', *Philosophy and Social Criticism*, vol. 44, n. 9, 2018, pp. 978–96.
— 'Hannah Arendt, Evil, and Political Resistance,' forthcoming in *History of the Human Sciences*.
Rasmussen, Kim Su, 'Foucault's Genealogy of Racism', *Theory, Culture, and Society*, 28:5, 2011, pp. 34–51.
Reid, Julian, 'Deleuze's War Machine: Nomadism against the State', *Millennium: Journal of International Studies*, 32:1, 2003, pp. 57–85.
Ross, Alison, 'The Distinction between Mythic and Divine Violence: Walter Benjamin's "Critique of Violence" from the Perspective of "Goethe's Elective Affinities"', *New German Critique*, 41:1, 2014, pp. 93–128.

— 'The Ambiguity of Ambiguity in Benjamin's "Critique of Violence"', in *Towards the Critique of Violence: Walter Benjamin and Giorgio Agamben*, ed. Brendan Moran and Carlo Salzani (London: Bloomsbury, 2015), pp. 39–56.
Rottenburg, Elizabeth, 'Cruelty and its Vicissitudes: Jacques Derrida and the Future of Psychoanalysis', *The Southern Journal of Philosophy*, 50, Supplement, 2012, pp. 147–59.
Rousseau, Jean-Jacques, *The Social Contract*, trans. Christopher Betts (Oxford: Oxford University Press, 1994).
Sartori, Giovanni, 'The Essence of the Political in Carl Schmitt', *Journal of Theoretical Politics*, 1:1, 1989, pp. 63–75.
Schmitt, Carl, *The Crisis of Parliamentary Democracy*, trans. Ellen Kennedy (Cambridge, MA: MIT Press, 1988).
— *The Concept of the Political*, trans. Georg Schwab (Chicago: University of Chicago Press, 1996).
— 'The Age of Neutralisations and Depoliticisations', trans. Mathias Konzeit and John P. McCormick, in *The Concept of the Political*, trans. Georg Schwab (Chicago: University of Chicago Press, 1996), pp. 80–96.
— *Legality and Legitimacy*, trans. Jeffrey Seitzer (Durham: Duke University Press, 2004).
— *Political Theology: Four Chapters on the Concept of Sovereignty*, trans. George Schwab (Chicago: University of Chicago Press, 2005).
— *Hamlet or Hecuba: The Interruption of Time in the Play*, trans. Simona Draghici (Oregon: Plutarch Press, 2006).
— *The Nomos of the Earth in the International Law of the Jus Publicum Europaeum*, trans. G. L. Ulmen (New York: Telos, 2006).
— *Theory of the Partisan: Intermediate Commentary on the Concept of the Political*, trans. G. L. Ulmen (New York: Telos, 2007).
— *Constitutional Theory*, trans. Jeffrey Seitzer (Durham: Duke University Press, 2008).
— 'The Turn to the Discriminating Concept of War', in *Writings on War*, ed. and trans. Timothy Nunan (Cambridge: Polity, 2011), pp. 30–74.
— *Dictatorship*, trans. Michael Hoelzl and Graham Ward (Cambridge: Polity, 2014).
Schwab, George, *The Challenge of the Exception: An Introduction to the Political Ideas of Carl Schmitt between 1921 and 1936* (Berlin: Duncker and Humblot, 1970).
Shapiro, Kam, *Carl Schmitt and the Intensification of the Political* (New York: Rowman & Littlefield, 2008).
Shelton, George, *Morality and Sovereignty in the Philosophy of Hobbes* (Basingstoke: Palgrave Macmillan, 2014).
Sibertin-Blanc, Guillaume, 'The War-Machine, the Formula, and the Hypothesis: Deleuze and Guattari as Readers of Clausewitz', *Theory and Event*, 13:3, 2010: https://muse.jhu.edu/article/396505.
— *State and Politics: Deleuze and Guattari on Marx*, trans. Ames Hodges (New York: Semiotext, 2016).
Sinnerbrink, Robert, 'Deconstructive Justice and the "Critique of Violence": On Derrida and Benjamin', *Social Semiotics*, 11:3, 2006, pp. 485–97.
Skinner, Quentin, 'The Sovereign State: A Genealogy', in *Sovereignty in Fragments: The Past, Present and Future of a Contested Concept*, ed. Hent Kalmo and Quentin Skinner (Cambridge: Cambridge University Press, 2010), pp. 26–46.
Slomp, Gabriella, *Carl Schmitt and the Politics of Hostility, Violence and Terror* (Basingstoke: Palgrave Macmillan, 2009).
Sorel, Georg, *Reflections on Violence*, ed. Jeremy Jennings (Cambridge: Cambridge University Press, 1999).

Tanke, Joseph, 'Michel Foucault at the Collège de France, 1974–1976', *Philosophy and Social Criticism*, 31:5–6, 2005, pp. 687–96.
Taubes, Jacob, *The Political Theology of Paul*, trans. Dana Hollander (Stanford: Stanford University Press, 2004).
Taylor, Alan, *American Colonies: The Settling of North America* (London: Penguin, 2002).
Tomba, Massimiliano, 'Another Kind of *Gewalt*: Beyond Law Re-Reading Walter Benjamin', *Historical Materialism*, 17:1, 2009, pp. 126–44.
Trainor, Brian, 'The State as the Mystical Foundation of Authority', *Philosophy and Social Criticism*, 32:6, 2006, pp. 767–79.
Trumbull, Robert, 'Derrida and the Death Penalty: The Question of Cruelty', *Philosophy Today*, 59:2, 2015, pp. 317–36.
Vardoulakis, Dimitris, *Sovereignty and its Other: Toward the Dejustification of Violence* (New York: Fordham University Press, 2013).
Vatter, Miguel, *The Republic of the Living: Biopolitics and the Critique of Civil Society* (New York: Fordham University Press, 2014).
Viesel, Hansjörg, *Jawohl, der Schmitt: Zehn Briefe aus Plettenberg* (Berlin: Support, 1988).
Virilio, Paul, *Speed and Politics*, trans. Mark Polizzoti (New York: Semiotext, 1986).
Voice, Paul, 'Consuming the World: Hannah Arendt on Politics and the Environment', *Journal of International Political Theory*, 9:2, 2013, pp. 178–93.
Volk, Christian, 'Towards a Critical Theory of the Political: Hannah Arendt on Power and Critique', *Philosophy and Social Criticism*, 42:6, 2015, pp. 549–75.
Webber, Elisabeth, 'Deconstructionism is Justice', *SubStance*, 34:1, 2005, pp. 38–43.
Weigel, Sigrid, *Walter Benjamin: Images, the Creaturely, and the Holy*, trans. Chadwick Truscott Smith (Stanford: Stanford University Press, 2013).
Widder, Nathan, *Political Theory after Deleuze* (London: Continuum, 2012).
— 'State Philosophy and the War Machine', in *At the Edges of Thought: Deleuze and Post-Kantian Philosophy*, ed. Craig Lundy and Danielle Voss (Edinburgh: Edinburgh University Press, 2015), pp. 190–211.
Wilde, Marc de, 'Meeting Opposites: The Political Theologies of Walter Benjamin and Carl Schmitt', *Philosophy and Rhetoric*, 44:4, 2011, pp. 363–81.
Young-Bruehl, Elisabeth, *Hannah Arendt: For Love of the World*, 2nd edn (New Haven: Yale University Press, 2004).
Žižek, Slavoj, *Violence* (London: Profile Books, 2009).
Zuckert, Catherine, *Machiavelli's Politics* (Chicago: University of Chicago Press, 2017).

Index

Agamben, Giorgio, 47, 147, 201
agreement, 1, 3, 17, 23, 30–1, 50, 81, 85, 131–2, 200, 203
annihilation, 36, 49, 51, 56, 62, 107, 109–11
Arendt, Hannah, 11, 15, 63, 147, 200
Aristotle, 3, 152, 192–3
assemblage, 93, 104–5, 112–13
auctoritas, 82, 151, 162
Augustine, 3–4, 17, 69
authority, 2–6, 8, 10, 23, 34, 39, 41, 68, 82–3, 177–8, 195–7
  legal, 10, 25

ban, 154–5, 160–2, 174, 184
Bartelson, Jens, 1–3, 5, 17
Benjamin, Walter, 11, 14, 23, 200
Bernstein, Richard, 37–8, 62
binary
  logic, 149, 163, 165, 191, 202
  opposition, 11–12, 16, 142, 160–2, 165, 179, 188, 190–1, 193, 202
bio-juridical, 11–13, 17, 166, 175, 200, 202
biopolitical, 11, 13, 16–17, 147–8, 152, 155, 166, 174–5, 192, 200–1
  machine, 163–4
biopolitics, 13, 136–43, 147–8, 152–4, 160, 164–6, 173, 175, 191–3
  contemporary, 157
  logic of, 165–6
  modern, 152, 156
biopower, 121, 135, 139–40, 153, 192
bodies, 2–3, 6–7, 9–10, 101, 104, 124, 127–8, 131–2, 134, 136, 138, 148, 153, 164

Bodin, Jean, 5
Butler, Judith, 37

capitalism, 9, 96, 109–10
Christianity, 181, 184
Church, 1–4, 82
citizens, 29–30, 67, 138, 160–1, 183, 185
city, 16, 38, 95, 107, 142, 155, 158–63
Clausewitz, Carl von, 109, 127, 130
Collège de France, 121, 123
commonwealth, 6–8, 68
communication, 31–2, 102
community, 2, 39, 50, 53–4, 61, 153, 191
  political, 50, 54, 58, 60, 85
concentration camps, 67, 77, 152, 155
consent, 6–7, 50–1, 80–1, 84
constitution, 14, 48–52, 70, 79–80, 131
contract, 30, 126–8
critical theory, 11, 24, 200
critique, 7, 11, 15, 23–4, 26, 40–1, 57, 68, 175, 201
  radical, 9, 11, 17
cruelty, 175
culture, 181

death, 29, 34, 40, 123, 136–40, 148, 151, 153–4, 175, 181–91, 193–5, 203–4
  brain, 189
  penalty, 11–13, 16–17, 29, 174–5, 178, 180–91, 193–9, 202
decision, 12, 14–15, 40, 46, 49–51, 63, 73, 80, 87, 156, 178–80, 183, 186, 195
  individual, 40–1
  normless, 14, 48

Deleuze, Gilles, 11, 15, 87, 93, 96, 100, 104–6, 110, 200
depoliticisation, 52, 57, 59, 61–3, 161–2
Derrida, Jacques, 11, 23, 27, 39, 47
différance, 176–7, 182
divinity, 46–7, 49, 51, 53, 55, 57, 59, 61, 63
domination, 23, 76, 85–6, 98, 107, 124, 128–30, 135

earth, 5–6, 68, 70–1, 73–4, 77, 96, 102, 195
economy, 28, 32–3, 110, 113, 126
enemy, 8, 14, 49, 53–63, 86, 107, 111, 131, 138, 155, 157, 160
  absolute, 57–63
  classical, 55, 58–60
  real, 53, 58–63
evil, 77, 87, 177
exception, 12, 33, 49, 110, 148–50, 155–6, 161–2, 165, 181
  state of, 12, 147–54, 156, 158, 162–3, 174
exclusion, 11–12, 33, 47, 68, 124, 134–5, 148–9, 153, 155, 157, 160, 163–4, 174
existence, 4, 27, 29, 40, 48, 50, 63–4, 68, 80, 82, 107, 111, 129, 134, 202
  human, 71–2, 74
  political, 49, 51, 157
expiation, 36–7, 186

fabrication, 15, 69–70, 72–6, 87
  act of, 69, 73–5
family, 158–62, 189
fascism, 70, 110
force, 10, 15, 23, 79, 82–3, 98, 107, 112, 133, 138, 151, 178–80, 186, 203–4
  -of-law, 150
Foucault, Michel, 11, 16, 121, 201
foundation, 11, 33, 36, 49, 68, 80–1, 96, 147, 151, 160, 163, 178, 180, 192–3
freedom, 50, 69, 72, 77
friend, 14, 53, 60, 130, 154–5, 157
  /enemy distinction, 48, 53–4, 62, 155

genealogy, 121–2, 124–5
Gewalt, 23
God, 2–3, 5–6, 34–5, 37, 80, 85, 99, 152–3, 184–7, 195
government, 3, 7, 9, 79–80, 83–6, 122
great criminals, 27–8
ground, 14, 35, 70, 98, 141, 176, 178, 180, 193, 204
groups, 11, 57, 77–8, 80–3, 85, 94, 105, 128, 131, 133–4, 142, 152, 193
Guattari, Felix, 11, 87, 200

Habermas, Jürgen, 23
Heidegger, Martin, 175, 188
hierarchy, 60, 105, 124, 139
history, 17, 95, 121, 123–4, 173, 181, 184, 193
Hobbes, Thomas, 7, 15, 47, 67–8, 129
Holocaust, 39, 67
homo
  faber, 72–3, 75–7
  sacer, 12, 17, 147, 153–5, 160, 174, 182
homogeneity, 68, 80–1, 87, 107, 131
household, 16, 73, 142, 158, 160
humanity, 34–5, 37, 190
hygiene function, 134, 140–1
hypothesis
  Nietzsche's, 126–7, 129
  Reich's, 126–8

image of thought, 105–6
inoperativity, 163–5
institutions, 29–30, 49, 80, 99, 123, 125, 127, 129, 131–2, 134–5, 173, 185
  military, 100, 107–8
intensity, 53, 58–62, 80, 101

judgement, 7, 39–40, 59, 180
juridical, 12, 17, 48–9, 147, 151, 154, 162–4, 166, 173, 175, 190–1, 193, 195, 202, 204
  order, 11–13, 15–17, 49, 52, 68, 94, 113, 123, 131, 148–9, 163, 174–5, 200–1, 203
jus publicum Europaeum, 55–60
justice, 16–17, 24–5, 29, 34, 36, 86–7, 173–5, 178–80, 186, 188, 191, 194

Kant, Immanuel, 175, 184
King, 2–3, 6, 56, 128

labour, 27, 70–2, 74–5, 96
language, 31–3, 104, 127, 133, 150, 153, 157
law, 6, 10–17, 23–31, 33–9, 46–53, 79–81, 129–33, 147–57, 173–5, 177–83, 185–7, 191, 195–7, 201–4
  constitutional, 46, 48
  natural, 25–6
  outside of, 36, 47, 49, 148, 153, 156
  positive, 25–6
  suspension of, 148, 150, 154
legal
  system, 25–9, 37–8, 46, 49, 174
  violence, 14, 24, 26–7, 33, 36–7, 39, 46–7, 83, 186
Levinas, Emmanuel, 178, 188

life
  bare, 152–3, 155, 157, 163, 165–6, 192
  biological, 16, 152
  form-of-, 164–6
  human, 53, 72, 194
  political, 71, 154, 162
  regulation of, 11, 13, 16–17, 139, 173, 175, 183, 191, 201, 203–4
  sacred, 41, 156
logic, 11, 15–16, 31–3, 35–6, 69–70, 76, 96, 99, 106, 134–5, 163–6, 188, 191, 193, 200–2
  instrumental, 70, 77, 164

machine, 100, 108, 111, 164
  territorial, 96, 98
Marx, Karl, 9, 78
Marxism, 78, 96, 125–6
Middle Ages, 3, 17, 128, 131–3
militarism, 28, 39, 54, 107
morality, 59, 63, 190
mortality, 4, 71–2
multiplicity, 15, 107, 111–12, 129, 136
myth, 23, 33–4, 61, 97–8, 189
  of Niobe, 34

natality, 71–2, 156
nature, 1, 6–7, 9, 48–9, 54, 56, 73–6, 79, 82, 107–8, 128, 131, 135, 157–9, 174–5
  telluric, 57–8
Nietzsche, Friedrich, 124, 175
nomadic, 100
nomadism, 100–2
nomads, 100–3, 108–9, 112
nomos, 102, 109, 149, 151
nonviolent, 27, 30–2, 37, 50, 176
norms, 13–14, 49–50, 52, 55, 110, 112–13, 125, 133, 138–9, 142, 149, 173, 179–80, 183, 192
  foundational, 48–50, 131
  social, 12–13, 17, 134, 142, 183, 191, 201, 203–4
number, 8, 11, 15, 23, 54–6, 61, 80–2, 84–5, 100, 103–5, 124, 151, 158, 162, 181
  numbered, 103–4
  numbering, 103–4

obedience, 79, 81, 84
object, 32, 72–3, 75–6, 82, 102, 105, 107, 109–12, 204
oikos, 158–62
omnipotence, 5, 203–4

order, 7–8, 10–11, 14, 16, 49–50, 95, 97–9, 103–4, 111–13, 130, 132–3, 140, 156, 177, 201
  legal, 10, 17, 29, 39, 49, 52
origins, 29–30, 96–8, 100, 159, 163, 178

pacifism, 54–5
Pan, David, 53
Patton, Paul, 93, 122
peace, 8, 51, 55, 63, 110–11, 130, 132–3, 158
people, 6–7, 9, 50–1, 62, 69, 79–82, 85, 101–2, 112, 140–1, 156–7, 181, 189, 193
philosophy, 47, 94, 182, 188
pirate, 56, 58
plurality, 71, 80–1, 87, 131
police, 10, 29–30, 84, 103, 107
polis, 5, 16, 73, 81, 106, 109, 154, 156–62
political
  action, 15, 69, 77, 86, 112, 166
  association, 10, 53–4
  decision, 13–14, 48, 50–5, 59, 63, 80, 155, 180
  theology, 41
politicisation, 15, 161–2
politics
  coming, 148, 166, 202
  Western, 142, 160–2
populace, 5–9, 14, 16, 48–51, 62–3, 80–1, 85, 87, 131, 135, 137, 139–41, 157, 201, 203
population, 50, 109–10, 122, 136–41, 148, 157
potentiality, 150, 164–5
  destituent, 164–6
potestas, 82, 151, 162
power, 2–3, 5–9, 14–15, 17, 34, 67–9, 77–88, 96–101, 121–3, 125–33, 135–6, 138, 140–2, 194–5, 203–4
  absolute, 2, 6, 8, 79, 194
  constituted, 49, 164–5
  constituting, 14, 51
  divine, 37–8
  omnipotent, 203–4
  phantasmic, 194–5
  political, 85, 102, 127–9, 132, 138, 184
  relations, 121, 125, 127–31, 135, 138, 140, 142
  sovereign, 16, 97, 129–30, 135–6, 140, 150, 152–4, 156, 183, 203–4
  structures, 84–5, 98, 125, 129
proletarian, 32–3, 38
psychiatry, 124, 134
pure means, 31, 70

racism, 16, 113, 121–3, 129, 134–5, 139–42, 157
radical-juridical, 11, 15–16, 21, 113, 166, 200–3
reason, 7–8, 10–11, 33–4, 54–5, 59, 75–6, 80–3, 85–6, 93, 101–3, 124–5, 150–1, 153–5, 157, 176–7
regulation, 11–13, 17, 81, 139, 174, 177, 179, 191, 204
religion, 41, 195
responsibility, 10, 14, 24, 40, 50, 179, 189–90
rights, 4, 102, 105, 124, 156, 182, 185
Rousseau, Jean-Jacques, 9–10, 80
rules, 13, 16, 55–6, 76, 79, 81, 84, 136, 149, 151, 162, 177–80, 192

Sartre, Jean-Paul, 78
Schmitt, Carl, 11, 46, 164, 200
science, 124–5
sexuality, 121, 124, 173
signification, 16, 174–7
Slomp, Gabriella, 58, 60–1
society, 2, 49–51, 67–8, 95–6, 110, 112–13, 121, 125–6, 128–9, 132–5, 157, 161–2, 187–8
sovereign, 3, 5–13, 82, 128–9, 131–2, 136, 140–1, 148–54, 156, 174–5, 183–8, 190–2, 194–6, 203
  authority, 10, 178
  decision, 17, 48–9, 53, 147, 156, 163, 175, 178, 180, 184
  figure, 8–9, 200
  violence, 1–2, 10–14, 16–17, 24, 62–4, 67–8, 122–4, 140–2, 162–4, 166, 173–6, 182–4, 190–2, 194–6, 200–4
sovereignty, 1–12, 14–17, 67–70, 112–13, 128–32, 135–8, 147–8, 150–7, 162–4, 173–5, 182–7, 191–5, 200–1, 203–4
  absolutist theory, 6, 51
  biopolitical, 16, 147, 155, 157–8, 163–4, 174, 191–2
  constitutional, 14, 51, 55, 63, 131
  juridical, 14, 87, 129, 175
  legal, 14, 24
  mytho-, 3, 5
  political, 49, 82, 99, 106, 109, 126, 128, 185
  populist theory, 80, 87
  proto-, 3, 5
space, 3–4, 36–7, 69, 73, 77, 81, 100–3, 109, 112, 148–9, 154–5, 157–8, 180, 183
  smooth, 99–103, 112
stasis, 147–8, 158–64
State, 4–8, 27–9, 32–3, 48–53, 55–7, 78–9, 93–103, 105–15, 122–3, 127, 129–32, 148–9, 181–3, 188
  apparatus, 79, 87, 95, 99–100, 102–8, 110–11, 113, 127, 165
  constitutional, 48, 50, 52, 63, 73, 130–1
  modern, 29, 139, 141
strength, 7–8, 53, 57–8, 74, 80, 82–3, 127
striation, 100–1, 103, 107–8
strike, 27, 32
  general, 28, 32–3, 38
  political, 32
subject, 6, 11, 72, 74, 102, 108–9, 125, 128–30, 136, 139, 154, 157, 182, 184, 189
system, 28, 31, 49, 95, 98, 123, 161, 190
  closed, 28, 46
  social, 97–8

territory, 4–5, 58, 60, 102
terror, 8, 57, 86, 96, 110, 162
theology, 46, 95, 181, 184–6
time, 3–4, 6, 9–10, 26, 28–30, 57–8, 103–4, 112–13, 132–3, 154, 157, 177, 179, 187–8
totalitarianism, 67–70, 77, 87–8
transcendence, 3, 5, 186–7
transcendent, 9, 16, 81, 186

undecidability, 151, 179–80
unity, 7, 9, 15, 98, 129–30, 132, 156–8, 176, 203
Urstaat, 94–9

values, 2, 13, 26, 50, 54–5, 58, 67, 70, 111, 123, 135, 142, 156, 174, 179–80
  fundamental, 50, 55, 63
violence, 14–17, 23–39, 46–52, 69–70, 72–4, 76–88, 99, 109–13, 122–3, 138, 140–2, 162–4, 173–8
  arche-, 176–8
  critique of, 23–6
  divine, 2–4, 6–8, 14, 23–4, 28, 31–41, 46–8, 81, 83, 87, 153–4, 178, 186
  law-making, 33–4, 178
  law-preserving, 29, 178
  mythic, 33–6, 38, 41, 48, 178
  mythic-legal, 39, 46
  originary, 16, 174, 176–7, 195
  physical, 99, 195
  police, 29
  use of, 25, 28, 79, 85–6, 174, 186

war, 54–61, 68, 93–94, 99–100, 106–12, 121–2, 127, 130–3, 140–3, 158–9, 177

civil, 131–2, 142, 147, 157–61
limited, 109–10
machine, 15, 93–5, 99–101, 103–16, 123, 127
religious, 55–7
total, 109–12
warfare, 48, 52, 55–7, 59, 78–9, 131, 158
work, 61, 70–1, 73–6, 93, 97, 99, 122, 128, 158, 160, 163–4, 174, 177, 185, 188

world, 3, 54, 63, 71–6, 78, 81, 86, 97, 105, 176, 181, 190
  human, 71–4
  political, 69, 72

Žižek, Slavoj, 38
zoē, 152–3, 155–7, 160, 162, 192–3
zone, 102, 155, 162, 190
  of indifference, 149, 160

EU representative:
Easy Access System Europe
Mustamäe tee 50, 10621 Tallinn, Estonia
Gpsr.requests@easproject.com

www.ingramcontent.com/pod-product-compliance
Lightning Source LLC
Chambersburg PA
CBHW070352240426
43671CB00013BA/2473